Colaiste Oideachais Mhuire Gan Smal
Luimneach

THE MEDIEVAL PROVINCE OF ARMAGH

1470 - 1545

BY

REV. AUBREY GWYNN, S.J.
Lecturer in History, University College, Dublin.

1946
W. TEMPEST, DUNDALGAN PRESS
DUNDALK

NIHIL OBSTAT:

AUGUSTINUS QUINN

Censor Theol. Deput.

IMPRIMI POTEST:

✠ JOANNES

Archiep. Armach.

Totius Hiberniae Primas.

Dundalk, October, 1946

PREFACE

This book is essentially a commentary on the three volumes now deposited in the Public Library of Armagh, which are commonly (but incorrectly) known as Octavian's register, Cromer's register and Dowdall's register. Since Octavian's register contains materials for the administration of his predecessor, John Bole or Bull, and his successor John Kite, it covers the whole period from 1460-1520. Cromer's register covers the years 1518-35. Dowdall's register is fairly complete for the last years of Cromer's rule and the first years of his own rule (1540-46); but then becomes no more than a very incomplete collection of scattered documents. I have made no attempt to carry the story further than the date of Dowdall's primatial visitation of 1546. The death of Henry VIII a few months after this visitation makes a convenient stopping-point.

Those who have patience enough to read through the mass of detailed information which I have collected will find, I hope, a trustworthy picture of diocesan life in the northern province of Armagh during the late medieval period. No generalisations are possible in so complicated a story, but a few comments may be helpful by way of introduction.

The organisation of the Irish Church throughout the Middle Ages can only be understood if we remember that the Anglo-Norman invasion of the late twelfth century brought a most promising movement of native Irish reform to an abrupt close. From the date of that invasion down to the sixteenth century Irish government, ecclesiastical as well as civil, suffered from the constant presence of an acute racial strife within the country. The English held Dublin, and (from the early fourteenth century onwards) they were also able to control Armagh from Drogheda. Metropolitan government was thus bound to be weak in the northern province, which included a large number of purely Irish dioceses. The Popes of the thirteenth and fourteenth centuries did their best to hold the balance even as between the two contending races in Ireland; but papal authority was weakened by the prolonged confusion of the Great Schism. The first half of the fifteenth century is perhaps the period of most obvious and unchecked abuse in the whole medieval era. Local Irish dynastic claims on the one hand, and the breakdown of central government in England during the Wars of the Roses on the other, combined to create a chaotic state of irregular and frequently bankrupt administration. This book takes up the story at a time when the contemporary Popes, though still hampered by the general laxity and disorders of Renaissance Rome, were once more making an effort to substitute ordered government for what had been so near chaos. The new strength of the Tudor dynasty in England was soon apparent in an increasingly active intervention of alien rule in Ireland; and the climax comes with the breach between Henry VIII and the Papacy. I have found no better title for the last section of this book, in which I discuss Irish reactions to the King's new religious policy, than "Years of Confusion."

No student of the Armagh registers can fail to acknowledge his immense debt to Dr. William Reeves, who was Keeper of the Public Library in Armagh for twenty-five years (1862-87), and who gave almost all his spare time and energy to the execution of his astonishingly careful transcripts of the medieval registers. I have based my own work on a study of the original texts; but my task has been eased by the fact that I could always use the Reeves transcripts as a trustworthy guide.

The late Father L. J. Murray, who died as parish priest of Dunleer in the summer of 1941, set himself to produce a summary English calendar of all the entries in Dowdall's and Cromer's two registers. His "Calendar of the Register of Primate George Dowdall" appeared in five instalments of the *Louth Archæological Journal* (1926-30). His

"Calendar of Cromer's Register" was begun in the issue for 1932. The first section of that volume—which is, in fact, a metropolitan court-book for the period of Primate Kite's absentee rule—was completed in five more instalments of the *Journal* (1932-36). The first instalment of the second half—Cromer's own episcopal register—appeared in the *Journal* for 1936; and two more instalments were printed in the issues of 1937 and 1938. But Father Murray was then beginning to feel the pressure of many other tasks, and his work on Cromer's register was left incomplete at the time of his sudden death in 1941. At the request of the Editor of the *Journal*, I completed this second portion of the register in the two issues for 1942 and 1943. I should never have attempted the studies which have led me to write this book, were it not for Father Murray's work, and I find it hard to estimate the measure of my indebtedness to a scholar who shortened his life by the zeal with which he threw himself into every work that might revive and maintain the ancient traditions of Armagh and Louth. His work is not always accurate, and needs to be checked from the original sources. But it has been everywhere a great help to me.

V. Rev. Thomas J. McEndoo, Dean of Armagh, is now the Keeper of the Public Library in which the original registers, with the transcripts made by Reeves, are deposited. To him, and to his Deputy Librarian, Mr. James Dean, I am much indebted for the courtesy with which they have granted me facilities for my work at all times. These facilities were all the more welcome since the precautions taken in Dublin for safeguarding the manuscripts of Trinity College made it impossible for me to consult the rough drafts of the Reeves transcripts, which have been deposited there for the use of students, until the summer of this year.

My debt to other friends and fellow-students is so great that I find it difficult to make adequate acknowledgments. To the Catholic priests of Armagh, and very specially to V. Rev. John Quinn, the present Administrator of the parish, I owe kind memories of encouragement that was much appreciated and of unfailing hospitality. I have acknowledged in my footnotes the help I have received from other friends with greater knowledge than I possess of local history and topography. I am especially indebted to Father John Brady of Dunboyne, who gave me full use of his notes on the parishes of Meath, and who has frequently called my attention to evidence that I had overlooked. Father Patrick Mulligan of Monaghan has given me a series of most valuable notes on the medieval abbey of Clones, and on other points connected with the diocese of Clogher. My immediate colleagues, Rev. Professor John Ryan, S.J., and Professor R. D. Edwards have (as always) been most generous with their advice and encouragement. I am also much indebted to Rev. John MacErlean, S.J., for the benefit of his advice on a phase of Irish history in which he has unrivalled knowledge.

To Mr. H. G. Tempest of the Dundalgan Press and his staff of printers I can only offer my personal thanks, and my admiration for the patience with which they have seen my much-corrected typescript and proofs through the press. It is pleasant to think that this book, which has grown out of my desire to complete Father Murray's work on the Armagh registers, should be published by the firm which gave Father Murray unfailing support in the Co. Louth Archæological Society. May their work continue to prosper!

AUBREY GWYNN.

University Hall, Dublin
July, 1946.

TABLE OF CONTENTS

PART IV. THE YEARS OF CONFUSION

BIBLIOGRAPHY.

A. The Armagh Registers.

There are at present eight volumes of primatial registers in the Public Library of Armagh. The late Dean H. J. Lawlor published a "Calendar of the Register of Archbishop Sweteman" (1362-80) in *Proc. R.I.A.* (1911); and a "Calendar of the Register of Primate Fleming" (1404-16) ibid. (1912). Dr. D. A. Chart published his "Register of John Swayne, Archbishop of Armagh and Primate of Ireland" (1418-39) at Belfast in 1935. No calendar has yet been printed of the three next volumes in the series: the registers of John Prene (1439-43), John Mey (1444-56) and Octavian del Palatio (1479-1512). Father Murray printed a "Calendar of the Register of Primate Dowdall" in *L.A.J.* (1926-30). His "Calendar of Cromer's Register" appeared ibid. (1932-38); and was completed by me, ibid. (1942-43).

Octavian's register is not a true episcopal register, but contains a large mass of loose documents bound together by Archbishop Ussher, without any regard to their chronological order, in the early seventeenth century. This volume contains many records of Octavian's predecessor, John Bole or Bull (1457-71); and of his immediate successor, John Kite (1513-21). I cite this volume as O.

Cromer's register falls into two distinct parts. The first half (ff. 1-111) is in fact, a metropolitan court-book of the years 1518-22. Since this court-book must have been ordered to be kept by Alexander Plunket whilst he was acting as official of the absentee Primate Kite during the years 1518-20, I have called it "Plunket's metropolitan court-book"; and I cite it in the marginal notes as P.

The second half of Cromer's register (ff. 1-93) is in fact that Primate's episcopal register from the year 1521 to December, 1535, when it ends abruptly. I cite this portion of the register as C.

The original of Dowdall's register is now missing, and we have no more than a seventeenth-century transcript, which is the last in the series of eight medieval registers. I cite this volume as D.

Students who find it more convenient to use the transcripts made by Dr. Reeves—whether in the form of the rough drafts deposited in the library of Trinity College, Dublin, or the finished copies now preserved in the Public Library of Armagh—should note that all my references are to the folio-numbers of the original registers. Since Reeves was everywhere most careful to note the folio of the original volume in his transcripts, there should be no difficulty in identifying my quotations in the Dublin or Armagh transcripts.

There are two sets of folio-numbers in Octavian's register. I follow the older series of numbers, which is given by Reeves at the beginning of each folio, beneath the more modern series of numbers.

The transcript of Dowdall's register is paginated, not foliated; but Father Murray, in his printed "Calendar," has used folio-numbers. To avoid confusion I have followed him in this system of citation. Students who wish to use the T.C.D. transcript have only to multiply the folio-numbers given in my marginal notes by two, to arrive at the correct page-number of the transcript.

Section B:

Analecta Hibernica, including the Reports of the Irish Manuscripts Commission. (Published by Irish MSS. Commission).

Annals of Connacht. Edited by A. Martin Freeman. (Dublin, 1944).

Annals of the Four Masters. Edited by John Donovan. (7 vols. 1851).

Annals of Ulster. Edited by W. M. Hennessy and B. MacCarthy. (Rolls Series). (4 vols. 1887-1901).

Archdall, Mervyn. *Monasticon Hibernicum* (1786).

Archivium Hibernicum, or Irish Historical Records. (Published by Catholic Record Society of Ireland).

Brady, Wm. Mazière. *Episcopal Succession in England, Scotland and Ireland*, 1400-1875. (3 vols. Rome, 1876-7).

Bryan, Donough. *Gerald Fitzgerald, the Great Earl of Kildare*. (1933).

Calendar of the Carew MSS. (5 vols. Vol. V contains the *Book of Howth*. 1871).

Calendar of Christ Church Deeds (24th Report of Deputy-Keeper of the Public Records of Ireland).

Calendar of Papal Letters. (12 vols.) 1893-1933. (I have been able to use the unpublished page-proofs and galley-proofs of Vol. XIII and part of Vol. XIV, which have been deposited for the use of students in the National Library of Ireland).

Costello, M. A., O.P. *De Annatis Hiberniæ*. Vol. I, Ulster. ed. Ambrose Coleman, O.P. (1912).

Curtis, Edmund. *A History of Medieval Ireland*. (1923. Second edition, 1938).

Dugdale, William. *Monasticon Anglicanum*. (8 vols. 1817-30).

Edwards, R. D. *Church and State in Tudor Ireland*. (1935).
The Irish Bishops and the Anglican Schism, 1535-47, in I.E.R. (Jan. and Feb., 1935).

Fiants of Henry VIII—Elizabeth (in Sixth to Twenty-second Reports of Deputy-Keeper of the Public Records of Ireland).

Gwynn, Aubrey (S.J.), *Canterbury and Armagh in the Fifteenth Century*, in *Studies* (Dec. 1943), pp. 495-509.
The Antiphonary of Armagh, in *L.A.J.*, vol. *XI*, I (1945), pp. 1-12.

Hogan, Edmund (S.J.) *Ibernia Ignatiana*. (1891).

Inquisitions. Inquisitionum in officio Rotulorum Cancellariæ Hiberniæ asservatarum Repertorium. Vol. ii, Ultonia. (Dublin, 1829).

Jourdan, G. V. Chapters on "The Reformation in Ireland," in *History of the Church of Ireland*, ed. W. Alison Phillips. Vol. II. (Oxford, 1934).

Leslie, James B. *Armagh Clergy and Parishes*. (Dundalk, 1911).

Letters and Papers, Foreign and Domestic, of Henry VIII. (21 vols., 1864-1938. There is a second edition of Vol. I).

Little, A. G. and E. B. FitzMaurice (O.F.M.) *Materials for the History of the Franciscan Province of Ireland*, 1230-1450. (Manchester, 1920).

Lynch, John. *De Præsulibus Hiberniæ*, ed. J. F. O'Doherty. (2 vols. Dublin, 1945).

Moran, Patrick (Cardinal). *Spicilegium Ossoriense*. (3 vols. 1874-84).

Morrin, James. *Calendar of Patent and Close Rolls : Ireland.* Vol. I : Henry VIII to Elizabeth. (Dublin, 1861).

O'Laverty, J. *History of the Dioceses of Down and Connor.* (5 vols. 1878-95).

Raynaldus, Odoricus. *Annales Ecclesiastici.* Vol. XXI. (Rome, 1676). (A continuation of Baronius).

Ronan, M. V. *The Reformation in Dublin*, 1536-58. (1926).

Rotulorum Patentium et Clausorum Cancellariae Hiberniae Calendarium. Vol. 1, (Dublin, 1828).

Shirley, E. P. *Original Letters and Papers . . . of the Church in Ireland under Edward VI, Mary and Elizabeth.* (1851).

State Papers during the Reign of Henry VIII. Vols. II and III. (1834).

Statute Rolls of the Parliament of Ireland : Edward IV. (2 vols.) (Dublin, 1914-39).

Stuart, James. *Historical Memoirs of the City of Armagh.* New edition by Ambrose Coleman, O.P. (1900).

Stubbs, William. *Registrum Sacrum Anglicanum.* (Oxford, 1897).

Studies, an Irish Quarterly Review. (Published by the Educational Company of Ireland, Ltd.)

Theiner, A. *Vetera Monumenta Hibernorum et Scotorum.* (Rome, 1864).

Ware-Harris. *The Whole Works of Sir James Ware,* edited with additions, by Walter Harris. (2 vols. 1739. Vol. I contains the translation of Ware's *De Præsulibus Hiberniæ*).

White, Newport. *Extents of Irish Monastic Possessions,* 1540-41. (1943).

Wilkins, David. *Concilia Magnæ Brittaniæ et Hiberniæ.* (4 vols. 1737).

Wilson, Philip. *Beginnings of Modern Ireland.* (1912).

LIST OF ABBREVIATIONS.

A.F.M.	Annals of Four Masters.
A.L.C.	Annals of Loch Cé.
A.U.	Annals of Ulster.
C.P.L.	Calendar of Papal Letters.
Proc.R.I.A.	*Proceedings of the Royal Irish Academy.*
D.N.B.	*Dictionary of National Biography.*
I.E.R.	*Irish Ecclesiastical Record.*
J.R.S.A.I.	*Journal of the Royal Society of Antiquaries.*
L.A.J.	*Louth Archæological Journal.*

(I have used the letters O ; P ; C ; D to indicate the various primatial registers in the marginal notes, as explained in Section A of the Bibliography).

PART I

THE LAST MEDIEVAL PRIMATES

1. PRIMATE JOHN BOLE

Since the end of the Great Schism Armagh had been ruled by a succession of English or Anglo-Irish Primates who, by a most curious coincidence, all shared a common Christian name, John. Since the Primate's Christian name commonly appeared alone at the head of the documents issued from their court, this accidental similarity has caused a good deal of confusion in the primatial registers. Five Primates of this same Christian name ruled Armagh from 1418 to 1474: John Swayne (1418-39); John Prene (1439-43); John Mey (1444-56); John Bole or Bull (1457-71); and John Foxalls (1471-4). The story of the confusion into which the diocese was thrown by the death of Primate Bole in 1471 has to be reconstructed from various contemporary documents, of which the most important is a series of sworn depositions made before a special court of judges delegate at Drogheda on July 6, 1484.[1]

John Bole had been abbot of St. Mary's, Navan, for some years before his provision to the see of Armagh. His name is spelt John Bul in an indult which was granted to him at Rome on March 29, 1457; and the form John Bull is used throughout the long narrative of the legal proceed-

[1] The text is in Octavian's register, ff. 298-9; 304-10. Most of it has been printed by Reeves in the *Journal of the Kilkenny Archæological Society*, Fourth Series, vol. III (1874-5), pp. 357-63; but Reeves did not print the opening section, which has got astray in the register.

ings of 1477-9 in Octavian's register. There is little doubt that the new Primate of Armagh must have belonged to a prominent family of London merchants named Bole or Bull, whose members were active in the city of London at this time.[1] John Bole, the abbot of St. Mary's, seems to have gone to Rome after the death of Primate John Mey in 1456. He was granted an indult of plenary remission on March 29, and was provided to the vacant see of Derry about the same date. This provision was cancelled soon afterwards, and the abbot of St. Mary's was provided to the vacant primatial see on May 2, 1457.[2] Bole was consecrated almost immediately, and was then appointed by Calixtus III as his collector of the tithes which the Pope had imposed on all the Christian world for the succour of Constantinople, which had recently been captured by the Turks.[3]

There is no need to attempt here a detailed account of Primate Bole's administration during the next thirteen years. He does not seem to have kept a formal register, though many documents of his pontificate survive to-day in Octavian's register, where they have been bound up with the great mass of Octavian's own records. Primate Bole
O.23 ; 36-7. held a provincial council at Drogheda on June 14, 1460. It was attended by the bishops of Kilmore and Ardagh, whilst the two bishops of Derry and Raphoe were declared contumacious. These two bishops (Bartholomew
O.25. O Flanagan and Lochloinn O Gallagher) made their peace with the Primate in the following August, and were absolved from their censures. The bishop and dean of Clonmacnois
O.34. were also declared disobedient and contumacious at this time. It would seem that the Primate could count on little support from his Irish suffragans. The bishop of Meath (William Sherwood) had only just been provided to his see by Pius II and was absent from this council.[4]

[1] *Calendar of Patent Rolls : Henry VI* (1446-52 ; 1452-61), Index.
[2] Costello, p. 228 ; C.P.L. XI, pp. 291 ; 298 ; 323.
[3] C.P.L. XI, p. 59.
[4] Costello, p. 106 ; C.P.L. XII, p. 91.

Prïmate Bole was not content to sit quietly at Termonfeghin and allow his Irish dean and chapter to administer
the northern portion of his diocese as they pleased. A very
curious document has survived in Octavian's register, from O.249.
which we learn that Bole went north to Armagh in the
spring of 1466. His appearance in the cathedral city was
unusual, for most of his English predecessors had left
Armagh to the jurisdiction of the Irish dean.[1] The family
of O Mellain had been for centuries the hereditary custodians
of the Bell of St. Patrick, and held lands in the immediate
neighbourhood of Armagh. Two of this family, Tuathal
(*Twoll* in the register) and John, seem to have thought that
they might teach Primate Bole a useful lesson by stealing
his horses. The sequel is told in our extant document,
which contains the public sentence of excommunication
against the two offenders—" who claim that they are
ecclesiastical and privileged persons "—together with a
sentence of local interdict on the city of Armagh and the
deanery of Orior (*Erthyr*), which may not be lifted until the
Primate's horses have been returned to him. The story
ends abruptly at this point. We do not know whether
Primate Bole recovered his horses, or whether he had in the
end to hire a nag to take him home to Drogheda.

Englishmen are not easily discouraged, and the Primate
returned to the attack in the winter of 1469-70. He was
" in his palace of Armagh " on January 30, 1470, when he O.219.
published his tuitorial letters on behalf of the dean of
Raphoe ; and there are several documents in Octavian's
register which show that Primate Bole was in Armagh O.212 ; 218 ;
during the months of January-March, 1470, and was seeking 238-9 ; 246.
to assert his authority over all his Irish suffragans. It was
probably at this time that he sought to improve the
finances of the college of the Culdees of Armagh by granting
them the fruits of the rectory at Donaghmore.[2] How far
his efforts were successful is not clear from these legal texts.

[1] See below, p. 83.

[2] Costello, p. 22 ; C.P.L. XIII, p. 320.

But the Primate had no more than a few months to live at this date. He died on February 18, 1471.[1] On March 22
O.205. the dean and chapter issued the customary letters as custodians of the spiritualities of the vacant see.

In spite of all these activities, Primate Bole was an unlucky, and perhaps a careless administrator. What occurred after his death is proof enough that he had left the finances of his diocese in great confusion. Seven years after
O.308 his death, according to a sworn statement of the archdeacon of Armagh, Henry Corkeran, the late Primate's unpaid debts were so numerous that the jewels and other ornaments of his see were still pledged as security for their payment. These debts were also the main cause of a prolonged vacancy which left the diocese of Armagh in a pitiable state of bankruptcy and general disorder.

The see was vacant for almost a year after Bole's death. Paul II had made no provision when he died on July 26, 1471. Meanwhile the dean and chapter were acting as custodians during the vacancy. Sixtus IV, who was elected on August 9, 1471, was a Friar Minor, and had been Minister General of his order for some time before his elevation to the Holy See. Soon after his election (the exact date is unknown) he provided an English Friar Minor to the see of Armagh.[2] The new Primate's name was John Foxalls, but little is known of him save that he had been a professor of theology. Foxalls was expected to pay part at least of his predecessor's debts before he could secure the release of the papal bulls which would enable him to take over the administration of his diocese. He was unable to
O.308. meet these charges, and went to London after his consecration, where he spent the next three years. The date of his death is unknown, but a petition of some Italian merchants who had advanced him a sum of 1,100 golden florins and had failed to recover the debt, speaks of John

[1] Ware-Harris I, p. 86.

[2] The bull of provision has not been found. For what follows, see the narrative in Octavian's register, ff. 304-10. The name is spelt variously: Foxalls, Foxhals, Fayheles.

Foxalls as the late archbishop of Armagh (April 27, 1475).[1]
It is probable that Foxalls had died before November 23,
1474, when the dean and chapter of Armagh petitioned O.248.
Sixtus IV for the provision of Richard Lang, bishop of
Kildare, as the new Primate.[2]

Richard Lang's canonical position at this time is one
of the many minor puzzles which bewilder the student of
medieval Irish Church history. In his sworn deposition of
July 6, 1484, John Delahide, a citizen and alderman of O.310.
Drogheda, affirmed that the Earl of Kildare, acting as the
King's Deputy, had seized all the temporalities of the see of
Armagh immediately after the death of John Bole. There
is an undated entry in Octavian's register, in which Richard, O.237.
bishop of Kildare, states that he has been appointed proctor
for John Foxalls, archbishop of Armagh, who has been
detained abroad by certain arduous affairs. Bishop Richard
then nominates Henry Fox, archdeacon of Down, and Henry
Corkeran, archdeacon of Armagh, to act as his proctors
within the diocese. The probable date of this proxy is
c. 1472-3. But Sixtus IV was not satisfied that Bishop
Richard was in fact a canonical bishop of Kildare. Reports
to the contrary had reached Rome before the end of 1473,
and a public summons to the bishop, citing him to appear in
Rome and answer the charges brought against him, was
nailed on every church door in his diocese. The bishop sent
an indignant protest to Rome, dated from Dromiskin (one O.336.
of the two manors of the archbishops of Armagh) on
January 9, 1474.

We hear no more of these legal proceedings, but the
bishop was still holding his own in Armagh in the following
autumn. For the dean and chapter of Armagh sent a O.248 v.
petition to Rome on November 23, in which they earnestly
commend Bishop Richard of Kildare to the Pope as the most
suitable candidate for the vacant primatial see. Bishop

[1] C.P.L. XIII, p. 39.

[2] In a mandate of March 15, 1482 (Oct. Reg. fo. 301) Sixtus IV states that Foxalls had failed to pay his debts for three years at the time of his death.

Richard had apparently been administering the diocese of Armagh for the past two or three years, and the dean and chapter laud his achievements and character in surprisingly glowing terms. Possibly Bishop Richard Lang was the candidate of the powerful Earl of Kildare, whose good-will meant much in the Anglo-Irish Pale of those days. But the bishop failed to win the Pope's approval, and he seems to have left Ireland soon after this petition. He was acting as suffragan to the bishop of Chichester in 1480, and to the bishop of Winchester in 1488.[1]

With the death of John Foxalls and the withdrawal of Richard Lang from Ireland, the way was open for a new provision to the see of Armagh. In their petition of November 23, 1474, the dean and chapter had complained that the diocese was without an archbishop for almost four years. Their troubles were not yet at an end. On April 27, 1475, the group of Italian merchants who had advanced the large sum of 1,100 golden florins to John Foxalls in 1471 obtained a mandate from Sixtus IV, declaring that this debt was a charge on any successor that might be provided to the see.[2] Future archbishops of Armagh were thus faced with the double charge of the still unpaid debts of Primate Bole and the unpaid debt which had been incurred by Foxalls soon after his provision to the see. Since every new provision meant some further additional fees, which had to be paid to the Roman authorities before the bulls of provision were finally released, it is plain that the problem of finding a successor to Bole and Foxalls was likely to be troublesome.

The vacancy was thus prolonged for another two years, when it was once more ended (or rather interrupted) by the provision of an Englishman named Edmund Connesburgh

[1] Stubbs, p. 206. There does not seem to be any record of the provision of Richard Lang to the see of Kildare, and the Pope may have had good reason for questioning his canonical position.

[2] C.P.L. XIII, p. 39. The names of the merchants are given as Benedict de Salutatis, Leonard de Vernaciis, Alexander de Bardys, John Salomei and Francis de Pazzis (all of Florence) and Laurence Mattio (of Rome).

or Quenisbrogh. The new archbishop-elect was consecrated in Rome by English bishops, but he was embarrassed from the first by the problem of the Armagh debts. A Roman tribunal had decreed that he was liable for payment of the 1,100 florins borrowed by John Foxalls, though he was permitted to pay this sum in two instalments within the next three years. Edmund consented to this arrangement, and was duly consecrated archbishop of Armagh; but the promise was easier than the fulfilment. He had returned to England before June 21, 1477, when Edward IV sent him over to Ireland with power to hear and determine the controversies which prevailed there.[1] Two weeks later (July 3) the King granted him restitution of the temporalities of his see, with power to recover any diocesan property that had been wrongfully seized since the death of Primate Bole.[2]

2. OCTAVIAN'S FIRST MISSION TO IRELAND

Edmund Connesburgh was thus sure of the King's favour in Ireland; but meanwhile he had lost the confidence of Sixtus IV. Apparently the new archbishop's bulls of provision had been lodged with the group of Italian bankers to whom the debts of John Foxalls were still due, as security for their payment. Connesburgh must have left Rome without satisfying these creditors of his diocese, and the Pope was not prepared to risk further complications. On May 13, 1477, he issued a rescript by which he nominated O.286v.
Octavian del Palacio, a Florentine priest and a doctor of the decretals, as "his nuncio and governor of the church of

[1] Rymer, *Fœdera* XII, p. 44-45. See also Stubbs, p. 204.
[2] *Statute Rolls (Ireland): Edward IV*, Part II, pp. 495, 547.

Armagh, in spirituals and in temporals, with power and authority to collect and levy all and singular the fruits, rents, and issues of the said church, until we either provide for the see or until Edmund shall have discharged his obligations." Armed with this plenary commission, the future archbishop of Armagh set out for Ireland as the Pope's special nuncio and commissary.

Before we continue the story it is natural to inquire into the antecedents of this new papal nuncio. His name is given as *Octavianus del Palacio* in the Pope's rescript of April 19, 1477, and in all the extant contemporary documents. The Annals of Ulster give the name as *Octavianus de Spinellis* in their obit (a. 1513). The nuncio was certainly a Florentine by birth, and the surname " del Palacio " may have been given to his branch of the family owing to their connection with the Holy See in Rome. A Florentine banking family of the name Spinelli was prominent in the international diplomacy of the early sixteenth century. The most important member of this family seems to have been Thomas Spinelli, who was Henry VIII's ambassador in Flanders in the first year of the King's reign, and later English ambassador in Spain.[1] Thomas had a brother, Leonard, who was in the Pope's diplomatic service during these same years. Other members of the family are mentioned as bankers in the private letters of Thomas, who was never slow to say a word on behalf of his kinsmen. I have not been able to find any definite link between this Thomas Spinelli and Primate Octavian—though Thomas was English ambassador in Flanders during the last three or four years of Octavian's long life. None the less, it seems to me most probable that the new Primate of All Ireland was a member of this same Florentine family ; and that Sixtus IV sent him to Ireland in 1477, hoping that his banking connections would make it easier for the new nuncio to bring some sort of order into the confused finances of the see of Armagh.

[1] See the Indexes to the early volumes of *Letters and Papers* for Thomas Spinelli and his kinsmen.

Edmund Connesburgh crossed over to Dundalk in August, 1477, and was met by the dean and chapter on September 5 in the convent of the Friars Minor. Seven years later Archdeacon Corkeran told the story of that O.308.
interview. The dean and chapter, including the archdeacon himself, came to the interview expecting to meet an archbishop who would be able to present them with his papal bulls. But Edmund could do no more than plead his poverty in excuse for his failure to redeem the bulls in Rome, and then asked them to admit him to the rule and administration of his diocese. Once he had got control of the revenues of the diocese, so he explained to them, he would be in a position to pay his debtors and thus release his bulls. All that he could show them by way of proof that he was in truth the canonical archbishop of Armagh was a testimonial letter, under the seal of one of the consecrating bishops, concerning his consecration. The dean and chapter knew their canon law and replied that they themselves would incur the censures imposed by the Decretals in such cases, if they admitted him to the administration of his diocese without his bulls. Edmund was made to understand that there could be no question of yielding on this point. He then begged them to hand over the primatial cross, which was carried by custom before every archbishop of Armagh and which had been in the custody of the dean and chapter since the death of Primate Bole. They refused and the interview ended in a deadlock.

A few weeks later the Pope's special nuncio arrived in the diocese and was able to show the dean and chapter the letter by which Sixtus IV had appointed him as governor of the see of Armagh, in spirituals and in temporals. His jurisdiction was accepted by the dean and chapter, and negotiations were then opened with the unfortunate archbishop. Edmund Connesburgh had taken up his residence in Drogheda and one of the witnesses in the inquiry of 1484
deposed that he had often seen him ride through the streets O.310.
of the city and had heard him sing mass in St. Peter's and preach to the people. But he had never used the *pallium*

during these ceremonies, and had never been preceded by the primatial cross. Such a situation could not last indefinitely. Octavian del Palacio arranged to meet the archbishop at
O.401. Killeavy near Dundalk on November 10, 1477. A formal agreement was made at this interview, by which Archbishop Edmund resigned his claims to the diocese and petitioned the Pope to provide Octavian to the vacant see in his place. Meanwhile he nominated the Pope's nuncio as his own proctor and commissary, for all the practical work of administering the diocese in his name. He had already
O.400. nominated Archdeacon Corkeran as his proctor for this purpose some weeks earlier, and Octavian lost no time in renewing the archdeacon's commission under the new arrangements.

Edmund Connesburgh left Ireland soon after this interview and he must have reported his action to Edward IV before May 20, 1478. The King was not prepared to have his own decisions set aside by a papal nuncio without further consultation; and on May 20 he renewed his former grant of the temporalities of Armagh to Edmund, "who is styled and named archbishop of Armagh" (*dictus sive nominatus archiepiscopus Armachanensis*).[1] More than a year went by in these negotiations between Armagh, London and Rome. Edmund had apparently not given up hope of securing his own final admission as archbishop of the
O.308 v. diocese; but he died in England before he had found a way out of his difficulties. Meanwhile Octavian was administering the diocese by the Pope's commission and we find him using the following elaborate title in his mandates of this
O.6. period: "Octavianus del Palacio, presbiter Florentinus, decretorum doctor, nuntius sedis apostolice et ecclesie cathedralis metropolitice et Hibernie primatialis Armachane in spiritualibus et temporalibus gubernator specialiter deputatus."

Sixtus IV had his way in the end and Octavian was provided to the see of Armagh before the end of 1479. He

[1] Rymer, *Fœdera* XII, p. 58.

seems to have been absent from Ireland in the summer of
that year, and had probably gone to England.[1] The exact
date of his consecration is not known. It was certainly
later than August 31, 1479, when Octavian was still nuncio O.6.
and governor of the see. On October 29, 1479, Octavian
held an extraordinary convocation of English and Irish O.18.
clergy of his diocese in St. Nicholas', Dundalk. If we assume
that this convocation was held immediately after Octavian's
consecration as archbishop of Armagh, we get a date
towards the end of October, 1479. A calculation from
various other entries in his register makes it certain that the
new Primate was consecrated after September 30 and before
January 31, 1480.[2] He visited the small convent of nuns at
Termonfeghin on February 12, 1480; and he held his first O.268.
provincial council in St. Peter's, Drogheda, on July 5 of the O.385.
same year.

The financial difficulties which he had inherited from
his predecessors continued to embarrass the new Primate
for some years. In his sworn statement of 1484 Archdeacon
Corkeran testified that the Primate had incurred much O.309.
ill-will from his critics owing to his failure to maintain the
accustomed state of an archbishop of Armagh. Meanwhile
his Italian creditors were pressing him hard for payment of
the 1,100 florins which Foxalls had borrowed in 1471.
Octavian had undertaken liability for this debt at his
interview with Edmund Connesburgh in 1477, and the
Florentine merchants who had lent this sum appealed for
protection to the Holy See. On July 6, 1481, the Primate
appointed Master John Folan as his personal agent and O.130.
proctor in the legal proceedings which were about to begin
in Rome. Sixtus IV upheld their claims, and commissioned O.130v.
the bishop of Meath (William Sherwood) to threaten the new
Primate with excommunication, should he fail to meet

[1] The prior of St. Leonard's, Dundalk, was acting as his commissary in August, 1479. (Reg. fo. 6).

[2] Octavian was in his sixteenth year of consecration on Sept. 30, 1495 (fo. 138); and in his second year on Jan. 31, 1481 (fo. 268*v*).

their demands.[1] This was in the autumn of 1481, and Octavian decided to appeal in person to the Holy See. His own financial position had become impossible, owing to the continued obstruction ordered by the King during the two years when Edmund Connesburgh was still contesting his right to administer the see. On January 22, 1482, he issued
O.140. a commission appointing the dean of Armagh (Thomas MacCawell) and the prior of the Culdees of Armagh (Peter O Molloy) his vicars general during his absence, which is described as due "to certain most urgent causes which concern ourselves and the state and well-being of our diocese." We hear no more of this journey to Rome until
O.301-2. March 15, 1482, when Sixtus IV issued a mandate, revoking his previous commission to the bishop of Meath and releasing Octavian from the obligation of paying the debt contracted by Foxalls eleven years previously.[2] The Primate was still liable for the debts contracted in Armagh by Primate Bole
O.308 v. (for which the jewels of the diocese were still pledged in 1484); but he had pleaded successfully in Rome that his diocese could not be fairly burdened with payment of a debt contracted by an archbishop of Armagh who had never redeemed his bulls and had never visited his diocese. This visit to Rome was thus an important landmark in the long history of these financial negotiations. Primate Octavian had at last succeeded in freeing his diocese from a very grave and wholly unwarranted embarrassment.[3]

3. PRIMATE OCTAVIAN'S RULE IN ARMAGH (1479-1513)

It is unfortunately impossible to gain any detailed information as to the ordinary administration of his diocese

[1] C.P.L. XIII, p. 261. [2] C.P.L. XIII, p. 132-4.

[3] The final legal proceedings by which the Primate was declared free of this debt in the diocesan court, were not completed until the summer of 1484.

by Primate Octavian. The large number of documents which have survived in his register throw a great deal of light on the Primate's relations with his suffragan bishops and some of them help us to understand the difficulties which were bound to arise when a foreign prelate made a serious effort to reform not only a diocese, but a whole province in fifteenth-century Ireland. But the total absence of entries recording the routine administration of the archdiocese itself can only be explained on the assumption that Octavian kept two registers: one for his ordinary administration, the other for general business arising from his relations with his suffragan bishops or with the King's government in Ireland. The former register has long since disappeared and we have thus no record at all of the Primate's collations, inductions, translations, dispensations and other ordinary routine acts of administration. There is not a single list of ordinations, for example, from the thirty-four years of his rule in Armagh. The few entries which do concern the administration of his own diocese are exceptional in character, but they help us to understand the general principles of his government.

One very significant omission must be noted at the start. In the published Annates of the diocese of Armagh, there are numerous entries for the first three-quarters of the fifteenth century.[1] Then these entries cease abruptly, with one or two exceptions to which I shall return. In the Inquisition of 1609 the jurors of Armagh made the following deposition: "that the lord archbishop of Armagh for the time being doth collate and of late times in right of the said archbishopric hath collated unto all other the parsonages and vicarages within the said county of Armagh; but in ancient times the Pope did, from time to time, collate to the said parsonages and vicarages by his bull."[2] This statement is abundantly confirmed for the years prior to 1478. Are we to assume that papal collations and provisions ceased with the coming of Primate Octavian to Armagh?

[1] Costello, pp. 1-10.
[2] Inquisitions, s.v. Armagh.

A document has survived among the papal letters of Innocent VIII which shows us Octavian in action as papal nuncio and governor of the see of Armagh in 1478. Thomas MacCawell, who had been provided to the deanery of Armagh in 1477 by Sixtus IV, died in 1486 or early in 1487.[1] Peter O Molloy had been prior of the Culdees of Armagh for eight years at this time and he was provided to the vacant deanery by Innocent VIII on March 26, 1487.[2] But a question had arisen concerning the legality of his benefice as prior of the Culdees, which had been granted to him by Octavian eight years earlier. It had been alleged against his title to the priorship that the benefice had been so long vacant in 1478 that the right of collation had lapsed to the Holy See; and the collation made by Octavian as nuncio and governor of the diocese was thus held to be invalid. A bull of Sixtus IV, dated July 20, 1478, does in fact state that the vicars of the Culdees of Armagh were then keeping possession of the revenues of the priorship contrary to the Pope's right of provision; and the Pope makes a new provision of this benefice to John O Loughran.[3] The position in Armagh was so confused in 1478 that we can well believe that Sixtus IV had acted in this matter on false information, and that he made a provision contrary to the action of his own nuncio in the diocese. Peter O Molloy had held the priorship of the Culdees for eight years before the date of his provision to the deanery of Armagh in 1487. Apart from this question of a doubtful collation, he had bound himself by oath to Octavian as governor of the diocese "not to impetrate the said priory from the Holy See by way of collation, provision, commendation, union or any other title." This oath troubled his conscience in 1487, when there was question of Innocent VIII uniting the two benefices of dean and prior for his benefit during his lifetime. The Pope released him from the obligation he had incurred

[1] Costello, p. 8.

[2] Costello, p. 9; C.P.L. XIV (unpublished galley proofs).

[3] Costello, p. 23; cf. p. 9.

by his oath in 1478, and provided him to the two vacant benefices.

An oath of this stringent character, apparently against the rights of the Holy See, is at first sight a surprising condition for any papal nuncio to impose in Armagh. But a simple explanation is suggested by the absence of papal provisions to the benefices of this diocese during the next thirty or forty years. No abuse was more disastrously common in fifteenth-century Ireland than the plague of unscrupulous "Rome-runners," who set off on their journey to Rome armed with a denunciation of some rival at home whose benefices they coveted, and prepared to use any means, fair or foul, to secure this benefice at the expense of their rival. The published volumes of the *Calendar of Papal Letters* for this period make dreary reading, owing to the monotony with which cases of this kind are recited according to a set formula and a court of judges delegate is set up to hear the case in Ireland and take action on behalf of the plaintiff, should his charges against the defendant be proved true. Octavian seems to have come to Ireland with the firm determination that this abuse must be abolished in Armagh; and it is very probable that his instructions from the Holy See in 1477 included a mandate to check an abuse that must have been a perpetual problem for papal judges of this period. The oath which he administered to Peter O Molloy in 1478 is thus a most valuable witness to one aspect of his reforming programme; and the absence of papal collations in Armagh during the thirty-four years of his rule as Primate suggests that Octavian de Spinelli was a man who knew how to enforce his will in his own diocese.

One entry in his register lets us see that the Primate had trouble with his own archdeacon some ten or twelve years after his consecration. Henry Corkeran had been O.307.
archdeacon of Armagh for more than fifteen years in the summer of 1484, when he made his sworn deposition concerning the financial distress of the diocese.[1] At that

[1] Henry Corkeran may have been of Irish birth; but his name is never written O Corcoran in the register.

time he was plainly a loyal supporter of the new Primate who had come to Armagh from Italy, and spoke out plainly against critics who complained that Octavian was not spending his money as freely as his predecessors. But Archdeacon Corkeran must have been an elderly man in
O.271 v. 1484. By the summer of 1491 the Primate was pressing him to accept an assistant in his double work as archdeacon and rector of St. Nicholas, Heynestown. The archdeacon was not prepared to admit that he needed any help in his duties. The Primate offered him William Heneman, a vicar of St. Nicholas, Dundalk, as his assistant. The archdeacon refused to accept Heneman, but made a counter-proposal. Thomas Hunt had been official of Armagh for many years and was probably a friend of the archdeacon. He was a canon of the diocese and a bachelor of canon law—and the archdeacon plainly thought that no better colleague could be desired. We have to-day no means of assessing the personal factor in this quarrel. Primate Octavian refused point-blank to accept the nomination of Thomas Hunt. If Archdeacon Corkeran would not accept William Heneman let him name another substitute—provided that he was a lawyer with the customary degrees (*in iure peritum et graduatum*).

A deadlock followed. It is not easy to see why a compromise was impossible. Students of modern history can always look at some old and faded photograph and get some hint as to the causes of a quarrel that is often no more than a conflict of two temperaments. Primate Octavian, Archdeacon Corkeran, Canon Hunt and the other dignitaries of medieval Armagh are no more than names to us. We know no more than the bare facts. The archdeacon appealed to the Holy See against the Primate's action. His
O.271 v. public protest was read in the parish church of Termonfeghin on June 24, 1491, by John White, rector of Carrick. Six or seven weeks earlier (May 1) the Primate had commissioned three Irish priests—Donald O Cullen, chancellor of Armagh, with Eugene O Neill, one of the canons of Armagh and William O Fallon, a clerk of the diocese—to

visit the Irish portion of his diocese in his name, since he himself was about to visit Rome "for the good of his own soul and on account of certain important affairs of the diocese." Archdeacon Corkeran's opposition is an obvious clue to this vague statement.

What happened in Rome during the next few months? Our records fail us. The Primate was certainly in Dublin on June 4, 1491, when he signed (*manu propria*) a petition to the King on behalf of the Great Earl, who had failed to obey a summons from Henry VII to appear before him in England.[1] He was back in Ireland for the summer of
1492, when he held a provincial council at Drogheda on O.404.
July 14; followed by an important convocation of the
English clergy at Drogheda on September 13. There are O.18.
signs that Octavian was having trouble with many of his English clergy at this time. John Folan, who had been his proctor at Rome in 1481, was provided to the see of Limerick in 1489.[2] The new bishop was unwilling to vacate the rectory of Clonmore which he had held in the
diocese of Armagh and the Primate appealed to Pope O.110.
Innocent VIII in December, 1492. At the provincial council of July, 1492, the Dominican bishop of Meath, John Payne, was summoned by the Primate to answer certain charges that had been brought against him. There
was a violent scene at this council, ending in a public protest O.187.
by the Primate against the disobedience and contumacy of his suffragan.[3]

Whilst these disputes were troubling the Primate at home, negotiations were in progress at Rome which suggest that others were striving to gain some personal profit for themselves out of the confusion in Armagh. Archdeacon Corkeran must have either resigned his archdeaconry or been deprived of it in 1491. Patrick O Heed, whose name
does not occur again, is named as archdeacon in an entry O.111.
for June 18, 1493.[4] James MacMahon, a grandson of the

[1] See below, p. 34. [2] Brady II, p. 41. [3] See below, p. 119.

[4] An Irish archdeacon of Armagh is unusual: see below p. 81-2.

coarb of Clones, had secured a provision of the archdeaconry for himself, together with Henry Corkeran's rectory of St. Nicholas, Heynestown, on February 8, 1492. Two days later another Clogher priest, Donald MacCreever, secured a provision to the priory of the Culdees in Armagh; and on May 17 yet a third Clogher priest, James O Beirne, had secured a provision to the Abbey of SS. Peter and Paul at Knock, near Louth, in the diocese of Armagh.[1] None of these provisions seems to have had permanent effect, for we can trace other names as archdeacon of Armagh and prior of the Culdees in the Primate's registers for the next few years. There seems to be little doubt that these fortunate Irish claimants were in Rome during the winter of 1491-2 and succeeded in persuading the Roman authorities that they were the most suitable candidates for the vacant benefices in Armagh. Primate Octavian had probably gone back to Ireland before James MacMahon and his friends began to pull the strings in Rome.

Whatever may be the true explanation of these complicated intrigues, the Primate found it necessary to go back to Rome once more in the summer of 1493. On June
O.110-11. 18 he nominated Thomas Hunt, his official and vicar of St. Peter's, Drogheda, to act with John Wood, prior of St. Mary's, Drogheda, as his two vicars general during his absence. On the same date the Primate commissioned Patrick O Heed, the archdeacon, and Eugene O Neill to visit the Irish portion of his diocese. Once again the Primate explains his absence as due to the need of travelling "to the Holy See and elsewhere on important and most urgent business of the diocese." The dispute with the bishop of Meath may well have been the cause of this third visit to Rome.

During the Primate's absence abroad his commissary John Wood was called upon to intervene in a dispute which
O.130. had broken out in the parish of Termonfeghin. Henry Dowdall and some of his friends had assaulted Master

[1] Costello, pp. 10-11.

Christopher Dowdall, vicar of the parish, and had robbed his house of certain papers and other properties.[1] The cause of the quarrel is unknown, but the offenders were duly excommunicated by the Primate's commissary.

It is tantalising to get such brief glimpses into the life of the diocese of Armagh during these last years of the Anglo-Irish medieval system. Primate Cromer's register gives us very much more detailed information for the years after 1523; but by that time the new Tudor dynasty was well in the saddle in England, and Henry VIII had already journeyed far on a road which was to end in a final separation of England from Rome and from all that Rome stood for in the life of Europe. Primate Octavian had to deal with Edward IV, Richard III and Henry VII. In his day Ireland was still under the unchallenged sway of the great Irish and Anglo-Irish feudal families. We get a general impression from his register that the Primate stood well with the Irish clergy of his diocese, but was in constant trouble with the more overbearing English or Anglo-Irish dignitaries of the Pale. But our evidence is far from being complete and it is safer not to risk any general estimate of Primate Octavian's rule in his own diocese.

We are on surer ground when we turn from the diocese of Armagh to the nine suffragan dioceses over which the Primate had metropolitan jurisdiction. Here Octavian's register has more to tell us, and its evidence is supplemented by a large mass of contemporary Roman documents. A detailed study of the situation as it is revealed to us in these documents will be found below.[2] On the whole, they make it plain that Primate Octavian was a very assiduous and efficient metropolitan. If he was so constantly active in his control of the suffragan dioceses of his province, we may fairly assume that he was no less active and no less efficient, in the administration of his own diocese of Armagh.

[1] The vicar is most probably to be identified as the archdeacon of Meath: see below, p. 24-5.

[2] See below, Part III.

The Primate's register contains numerous documents concerning the provincial councils which were held every three years at Drogheda during the thirty-four years of his administration. The series is not complete, but records survive from the councils of July 5, 1480; July, 1483; July 10, 1486; July 6, 1489; July 14, 1492; July 6, 1495; July 8, 1504; and July 12, 1507.[1] Since these records have survived in haphazard fashion, there is no good reason for doubting that provincial councils were also held at Drogheda in 1498, 1501 and 1510. The council of 1504 was held at Ardee, since an outbreak of the plague had made Drogheda unsafe for that season of the year. There is a badly mutilated copy of a set of provincial statutes at the end of Octavian's register. They were confirmed by the provincial council of 1483, but no record has survived of the prelates who attended this council. The bishops of Meath, Down and Connor, Derry and Clonmacnois are known to have been present at the council of 1480. Meath, Kilmore, Raphoe and Derry were present in 1486; whilst Meath, Clogher, Dromore, Derry, Raphoe, Ardagh, Kilmore and Clonmacnois are named as having been present at the sessions of the council in 1489. This is the largest number recorded at any of these councils. In 1492 Down and Connor, Ardagh, Kilmore and Clonmacnois were present: Meath was absent, but Bishop Payne was cited to appear before the council and answer some charges that the Primate had brought against him. Meath, Down and Connor, Derry and Kilmore were present in 1495. The attendance at the last two recorded councils was also small. Meath, Raphoe, Kilmore and Ardagh were present in 1504; whilst Down and Connor, Derry, Kilmore and Ardagh were present in 1507. Bishop Rokeby of Meath had been consecrated shortly before this council, and he was admonished for his failure to attend. Absence from the sessions of any particular council is, of course, often to be explained by some accidental cause. The absent bishop was usually represented at

[1] Register, fo. 385 (1480); 389 (1486); 404 (1492); 397 (1495); 414 (1504); 287 (1507). The records for 1483 and 1489 are on separate membranes, now bound in at the end of the register.

Drogheda by lawfully appointed proctors, and it is plain that Primate Octavian's authority was accepted without serious question throughout the suffragan dioceses of his province. Friction with the bishop of Meath was fairly constant and the situation in Clogher was irregular for the first twenty years of the Primate's administration.

As was perhaps inevitable, this Italian Primate who had been set the problem of ruling over dioceses that were partly Irish, partly English, was inclined to look to his native Italy for men to help him in his work. On November 12, 1479—soon after the most probable date of Octavian's own provision and consecration, Sixtus IV provided another Italian, named Giovanni de Rogeriis, to the see of Raphoe. The provision may well have been made on the report and advice of Octavian, who had been acting as papal nuncio in Armagh for the past two years. On February 14, 1483, Sixtus IV provided yet another Italian, Tiberio Ugolino, to the united sees of Down and Connor. Here again Octavian's advice may fairly be presumed, for he had been on his first visit to Rome in the autumn of 1482. Two months later (April 18, 1483) the same Pope provided a Greek, and a native of Athens, named George Braua, to the see of Dromore.

Only one of these three experiments was really successful. Tiberio Ugolino ruled Down and Connor from 1489 to 1519. The two dioceses over which he ruled were as characteristic of the division between Irish and English clergy as was Armagh itself ; and Bishop Tiberius seems to have followed the line taken by Octavian. When he died, the English hold on Down had been very much weakened, whilst the local Irish dynasty of Magennis had established an almost undisputed control over both Down and Connor. Bishop Giovanni de Rogeriis had died within two or three years of his provision to the see of Raphoe and his place was taken by an Irishman who was also a native of the diocese : Menelaus MacCarmacan. Bishop George of Dromore paid one brief visit to his new diocese in 1486-7. He then went off to England and spent the next few years in seeking for a diocese that might suit him better. Twenty years later the Primate was still looking for a bishop who would be willing to take up permanent residence in the diocese of Dromore—but this time he was backing an Irish candidate, who was a native of the diocese.

In the more purely Irish territories Primate Octavian was faced by the formidable opposition of native local dynasties that were very much more concerned with their own family interests than with ecclesiastical reform. In Ardagh, Kilmore, Clogher, Derry, Raphoe, these dynasties were all-powerful. There was little to choose between these strong dynastic families, when there was question of preferring some local candidate whom the Primate might favour. O Farrell, O Reilly, MacBrady, Maguire, MacMahon, O Donnell, O Gallagher: they were all alike in this, that they were determined, with or without a papal dispensation, to hold what they had. In more than one of these territories the undue interference of lay influence in diocesan government had led to a widespread breakdown in clerical celibacy. We shall meet with some lamentable examples of this abuse in the course of our narrative.

The most serious scandal which Primate Octavian had to face in his early years was in Kilmore, where two rival bishops, both claiming jurisdiction by papal provision, were contending for their rights. The Primate sought at first to settle this dispute by arbitration. For a time he succeeded in working out an agreement by which the two bishops consented to halve the diocese between them on a territorial basis. Then the dispute broke out afresh. The Primate ended by giving his full support to Bishop Thomas MacBrady, who seems from the first to have been the more suitable candidate and who died with the reputation of a zealous reforming bishop in 1511.

In Derry the provision of the Observantine friar, Donald O Fallon, to the see by Sixtus IV in 1485 opened the way for a new era in the history of the diocese. Derry, which had been sorely tried by incompetent and unworthy prelates during the fourteenth and fifteenth centuries, stands forth in the later years of Henry VIII's reign as the diocese in which the Irish reforming movement was strongest. In Bishop Rory O Donnell (1519-50) it had a bishop who was able and willing to give a courageous lead to the whole country. It is not clear how far Primate Octavian had any share in recommending Donald O Fallon as a suitable candidate for the vacant see in 1485 ; but he certainly gave him his full support after his election and consecration.

In Raphoe the O Gallagher interest proved too strong for any reform to shake its power during Primate Octavian's lifetime—though Bishop Menelaus MacCarmacan (1484-1513) died with the reputation of a capable and zealous prelate.

Clonmacnois and Dromore were the two dioceses in which episcopal rule was at its weakest during this period. In both dioceses poverty was the root cause of this failure and Primate Octavian was able to do little to help things out.

In Ardagh the Irish prince-bishop, William O Farrell (1479-1516) was a picturesque, though not very edifying figure throughout Octavian's rule in Armagh. The Primate had nothing to say to his provision and could do no more than stand aside and watch his irregular conduct in an unfortunate diocese.

In Clogher Octavian, as Primate, played his part in the long battle that was fought within the diocese from the death of Bishop Ross Maguire in 1483 to the death of Cathal MacManus in 1498. We know from his register that he did his best to support the Munster bishop whom Sixtus IV had provided to the see in 1484. But the Maguire interest, to which Cathal MacManus was bound by the closest family ties, was too strong for him in the end. After a series of unlucky and shortlived experiments, a bishop was found who was able to establish himself for more than ten years (1505-16) as ruler of the diocese. He was Eoghan MacCawell—and there is every reason to believe that he was as closely bound to the predominant Maguire interest as Cathal MacManus had been from 1483 to 1498.

In Meath Primate Octavian found himself faced with a bishop whose political influence in Dublin and in London was greater than his own. That had been the way, for the most part, in the history of Meath and Armagh for the past three hundred years. For Meath, viewed from the capital city of Dublin, lies well within the area which the Anglo-Norman settlers had occupied from the first phase of their attempted conquest of Ireland in the twelfth century. Geographically, and—to a large extent—racially, this English-settled central plain seemed to fit more easily into the province of Dublin than into the more purely Irish province of Armagh: just as the civil administration of Meath was finally allotted to the province of Leinster, not Ulster. But older traditions had proved too strong for the ambitious policy of the English-born archbishops of Dublin, and Meath remained part of the province of Armagh.

Meath was ruled by three English-born bishops during Primate Octavian's long career as Archbishop of Armagh. William Sherwood, a Yorkshireman, had been provided to the see as far back as 1460. He was eighty years old in 1481,
O.170 v. when he was joined with the Primate, the archbishop of Dublin and the bishops of Ferns and Kildare in a petition to the Holy See. An Italian clerk named Marcellus had found his way to Dublin, and was setting all the Anglo-Irish bishops of the Pale at logger-heads with one another. He had ended by summoning them all to Rome to answer charges that he had trumped up against them.[1] By the end of the following year Bishop Sherwood was dead and his place was taken in 1483 by John Payne, the prior provincial of the English Dominican friars. From 1483 to 1506 friction was constant between the Primate at Termonfeghin and his restless, but powerful suffragan in the neighbouring diocese of Meath.

The Primate held a visitation of the diocese of Meath
C-165. after Sherwood's death, and petitioned Edward IV for the appointment of a new archdeacon. Christopher Dowdall

[1] See also *Statute Rolls, Ireland: Edward IV*, Part II, pp. 195, 285.

was appointed on April 5, 1483, in place of John White who O.165.
had resisted Bishop Sherwood's efforts to deprive him for more than twenty years.[1] Dowdall remained archdeacon of Meath for the next thirty years.[2] His name occurs frequently in the Primate's register.

4. PRIMATE OCTAVIAN AND THE GREAT EARL OF KILDARE

Gerald, eighth earl of Kildare—commonly known as the Great Earl—succeeded his father Thomas, the seventh earl, in 1477.[3] He died in 1513. His active career is thus almost exactly contemporaneous with the rule of Primate Octavian as archbishop of Armagh. For more than thirty years the two men seem to have been constantly opposed one to the other. In 1478, when Octavian was still acting as nuncio and governor of the see of Armagh, Lord Grey crossed over from England as Deputy to Edward IV's infant son, George. Kildare had been acting as justiciar of Ireland until Grey's arrival in September, and had held a parliament at Naas in May, 1478. This parliament was prorogued and met again at Dublin Castle in July, and at Connell in Co. Kildare in September. As might be expected, the statutes of this parliament were entirely in favour of the Geraldine interest. But Lord Grey was, from the first, determined to assert his authority as Deputy. He summoned a rival parliament to meet him at Trim on November 6, and this parliament was then prorogued to meet again at Drogheda on November 19. Its statutes are obviously designed to break the power of the Geraldine

[1] C.P.L. XII, p. 465-6.

[2] Rev. John Brady, in I.E.R. (February 1945), p. 99.

[3] For his career see Donough Bryan: *Gerald FitzGerald, the Great Earl of Kildare* (Dublin, 1933); and also Miss Agnes Conway, *Henry VII's relations with Ireland and Scotland* (Cambridge, 1932).

party in Ireland. The tenth chapter, which deals with the mode of electing the justices of Ireland, contains a provision which concerns the see of Armagh.[1] Hitherto some Irish judges had held it sufficient that the justiciar should be chosen by seven members of the King's Council. The new statute provides that henceforth the justiciar must be elected by the whole Council, with whom the archbishops of Armagh and Dublin, the bishops of Meath and Kildare, and others should be associated. There was as yet no archbishop of Armagh when Grey's parliament met at Drogheda ; but the Geraldine interest sought to exclude these prelates from their legal right to take part in the election. Octavian, who was acting as papal nuncio at Drogheda when Grey's parliament passed this statute, must have been gaining his first insight into Irish affairs at this time. His first impressions were thus formed in a centre that was traditionally hostile to the earls of Kildare.

The deadlock between Lord Grey and Kildare was resolved a year later by the departure of Lord Grey and the appointment of the Great Earl as the King's Deputy in his place. For the first, but not for the last time, the King's policy was determined by the simple fact that no government was possible in Ireland with the Earl in opposition. Primate Octavian was to have personal experience of this simple fact some years later—very much to his own disappointment.

For the next seven years the Primate was kept busy with the financial problems of his diocese, and with the task of reorganising the government of his ecclesiastical province. He held three provincial councils during these years (in 1480, 1483 and 1486) ; and he must have felt himself very much more securely established as Primate of All Ireland when he got his first opportunity of intervening in the country's political life. Meanwhile the Great Earl had ruled Ireland, almost without opposition. Edward IV died in 1483, but Kildare's power increased during the brief

[1] Bryan, p. 37.

interlude of Richard III's reign (1483-85). Henry VII, founder of the new Tudor dynasty, was a newcomer on whom the Great Earl looked with suspicion from the first. But Henry was too busy for some years to interfere in Irish affairs, and Kildare retained the office of Deputy which he had held under Edward IV and Richard III.

There is no need to recount in detail the strange episode of Lambert Simnel's coronation as Edward VI in Christ Church, Dublin.[1] That ceremony took place on May 24, 1487. The archbishop of Dublin who crowned the boy was Walter FitzSimons. The bishop of Meath who preached the coronation sermon was John Payne. Octavian, as Primate of All Ireland, held aloof from these proceedings. His presence in Dublin would have raised once more the age-old question as to the Primate's right to have his cross carried before him within the province of Dublin. But there was more than this minor difficulty to keep the Primate in Drogheda. News had reached him from England that Henry VII had paraded the true earl of Warwick through the streets of London as a demonstration to loyal citizens. Archbishop Morton was Henry VII's chancellor, and he sent word post-haste to Armagh that Lambert Simnel was an impostor. The Pope himself took action on behalf of the English King; and the adherents of Kildare, including the archbishop of Dublin and the bishop of Meath, soon found themselves threatened with excommunication for their share in the Christ Church ceremony.[2]

Primate Octavian had thus every reason to be cautious. He had never belonged to the Geraldine party, and there was probably a good deal of personal rivalry between himself and the new archbishop of Dublin. Archbishop Walton, who

[1] See Bryan, pp. 99-124; and Professor Mary Hayden, "Lambert Simnel in Ireland," in *Studies* (December, 1915), pp. 622-36.

[2] News had evidently reached the King in London that Octavian was implicated in the Dublin affair, and Octavian's name is first on a list of pardons issued on May 25, 1488: *Letters and Papers of Richard III and Henry VII*, ed. J. Gairdner (Rolls Series) II, p. 370.

had begun to go blind in his old age, resigned his see in 1484.[1] The new archbishop was Walter FitzSimons—" a native and born in this land," as is expressly stated in the Dublin statute which granted Walton his petition to be allowed to resign in favour of FitzSimons. Walter FitzSimons was in fact the first Irish-born prelate to rule the see of Dublin since the far-off days of St. Laurence O Toole. He was not of Irish race, but one of his first acts was to petition the King for power to grant certain benefices to " clerks of the Irish nation and language," since there were large areas in his diocese where a knowledge of the Irish tongue was necessary for an active priest.[2]

The new archbishop of Dublin was thus linked with that section of the Anglo-Irish nobility in Leinster who were coming to be more and more Gaelicised in the late fifteenth century, whilst Primate Octavian's connections at this time were closest with the English interest in Louth.

Octavian's private letters have survived from a period of acute crisis. It is plain that the Primate was anxious to demonstrate his loyalty to the King at a time when so many of the Irish bishops of the Pale were falling away from the new Tudor dynasty. Ware quotes from a letter (now lost) which Octavian wrote to the Pope (Innocent VIII) at the height of the crisis: " The Clergy and Secular are all distracted at this present with a King and no King, some saying he is the son of Edward, Earl of Warwick, others saying he is an Impostor; but our Brother of Canterbury hath satisfied me of the truth, how his Majesty the King of England hath showed the right son of the said Earl to the publick view of all the City of London, which convinceth me that it is an error willingly to breed dissension."[3] The crisis was soon resolved by the King's victory at Stoke. When the Great Earl's brother had been killed and Lambert

[1] C.P.L. XIII, p. 190; Ware-Harris I, p. 342-3. Walton did not die until after 1489.

[2] Bryan, p. 84.

[3] Ware: *Annals of Henry VII* (English ed.), a. 1486.

Simnel was turning a spit in the King's kitchen at Greenwich, Octavian wrote a Latin letter to Archbishop Morton of Canterbury, in which he reports his own constant loyalty throughout the crisis and complains of the hostility which he has always experienced from the Great Earl and his supporters.[1]

" Venerable Father in Christ,

I begin with my due commendation, and do not conceal from Your Paternity that, with the sole exception of myself, no one openly opposed the wicked crime of the boy's coronation in Ireland ; and in this affair I have exposed myself to very great danger to my life. For the earl of Lincoln, being at the time furiously angry with me, went to the earl of Kildare in his uncontrolled wrath, and asked for permission and power to put into effect the royal prerogative (*iura regalia*) against all who had opposed this action. However, though Kildare refused to grant what Lincoln sought with such instance, I do not feel that I have yet regained the hearty good-will of Kildare and of the other nobles and princes who took part with him in this wicked action. On the contrary I am compelled to remain in constant uncertainty as to whether I have lost my property and temporals."

The Primate then refers to the mission of Sir Richard Edgecombe, who had been sent to Ireland by Henry VII in the summer of 1488, and who had negotiated the final pardon of Kildare and his associates.[2] The surviving narrative of

[1] Primate Octavian's two letters to Archbishop Morton have been printed in full by Reeves in *Journal of the Kilkenny Archæological Society*, Fourth Series, vol. III, pp. 364-6, from Octavian's register, ff. 251-2. A copy of the first letter is also in a seventeenth-century collection of " Precedents of the See of Armagh," which seems to have been compiled by Dudley Loftus, and is now in Marsh's Library, Dublin. James Gairdner printed this first letter from the MS. copy in Marsh's Library, as an appendix to his *Letters and Papers of Richard III and Henry VII* (Rolls Series, 1861, I, p. 383). The prelate to whom the letter is written is not named, but from internal evidence it is clear that Octavian wrote to Archbishop Morton, with whom he was in touch during this crisis.

[2] Bryan, pp. 124-141.

this mission is of great interest for the light it throws on the political situation in these months of tense expectancy. Primate Octavian came to Dublin in person, and did fealty to the King's representative in the Dominican convent on July 28, two days before Sir Richard's departure.[1]

Octavian's letter continues as follows :—

" Although Kildare and some other nobles and lords of Ireland recently took an oath of homage and fealty to Sir Richard Edgecombe, in the King's name, whom Our Serene Lord the King Henry recently despatched to Ireland as his commissary in this matter, none the less I see plainly that the dregs of their former enmity to me remain. For the aforesaid knight had hardly landed in England when they moved new complaints against me, as may be seen from the letters which I enclose herewith ; and they have been instigated in this (as I think) by my venerable brother John, bishop of Meath, my suffragan, who is soon to be sent to the King as the ambassador of Kildare and the lords.[2] It is right that I should explain to Your Paternity the matter of these new complaints. When the aforesaid coronation had been celebrated, the earl of Kildare held a Great Council in the name of him who had been crowned, at which the Lords Spiritual appeared in the Council, though I was absent ; and, being each in person sore wounded in their consciences, they granted that a certain subsidy should be levied from the Irish clergy for the Holy See, to obtain absolution from any sentence or censure that they might perchance have incurred by stirring these new tumults against the King. Afterwards, when our Serene Lord the King, from the bounty of his grace, had obtained a general absolution for all at his own expense for all who sought it,[3] Kildare strove to convert this subsidy to his own use and profit against the form of the grant, that he might use it to

[1] *The Voyage of Sir Richard Edgecombe into Ireland in 1488*, printed by Walter Harris in *Hibernica* (Dublin, 1770) I, p. 74.

[2] This was the Dominican, John Payne (1483-1507).

[3] This absolution was granted by Innocent VIII on May 16, 1488.

expedite his own business with the King in this affair. I protested and alleged that, once the cause had ceased, the effect must also cease, being anxious to defend my clergy to the best of my power. But he strove to do me fresh harm, claiming that I was always opposed to him and to the whole body of the people in this country (*toti corpori terræ contrarium fore*). And I know for certain that if the aforesaid earl of Kildare should obtain the rule of Ireland by the King's authority and should be able to order the chancellor at his beck and call, there is no hope of peace for me in Ireland. Those who were disloyal to Our Lord the King will rejoice, whilst I, for reward of my loyalty, shall gain shame and the injury of envious hatred. But if Our Most Serene Lord the King should deign to appoint me to the office of chancellor in Ireland, I shall be better able, with the support of so strong a pillar, to maintain the King's party here against his enemies, and to pay less heed to the Earl and the others who oppose me and my Lord. Wherefore I beseech Your Paternity most earnestly to suggest to our Lord the King what I have here set forth, and to give me security and aid by obtaining for me this office of chancellor. If Your Paternity should so counsel, I am ready to cross over to England in person; but whatever Your Paternity may judge best to be done, I beg you to send me speedy word by letter, which the bearer of this letter can bring back with him."

Soon after this first urgent appeal for help, Primate Octavian sent a second and more urgent letter to this same prelate in England. I have omitted some of its elaborate phraseology, and have substituted the first person singular for the more formal first person plural, which the Primate uses throughout this second letter, though not in his first. After the customary salutation and exordium, it reads as follows :—

"Good Father, I have already made you my petitioner and patron before our most Serene Lord the King, asking you in my former letter to obtain for me the office of chancellor in Ireland, as is set forth in my first letter.

Following it I now most earnestly beg you to give effect to what I wrote therein. I am compelled to trouble you thus, since threats are being uttered daily against me and new provocations arise each day, as I have written to you in times past. I then said that I was enclosing a letter which the earl of Kildare had directed to me, but owing to the messenger's haste this letter was then left aside. I now send it to you with this letter, and I come to you as my good protector, begging from your fatherly love all I need, in this and other such matters. I am indeed smitten with great fear, due to my loyalty to our Most Serene Lord the King, save that I depend on your help and the help of our Lord the King, and am in danger of being driven on the bitter shore of poverty through the past malice of the King's enemies. However, if there is no other way of restraining the importunity of other competitors for the chancellor's office, and especially of my brother the bishop of Meath, my suffragan, may it please your clemency, saving your fatherly correction, yourself to take this office of chancellor in Ireland and to join me with you in the said office as has been the custom in the past when chancellors of Ireland were joined with the lords of England. I should obey your wish in all things concerning the aforesaid office; and God is my witness that I seek no temporal gain from it, but that it is my wish that the necks of the faithful may not be downtrodden nor the horns of the wicked exalted.

"I send you, Father, by the bearer of these presents a palfrey that is indeed unworthy of your own use, but may be suitable for one of your servants. I beg that the messenger may be graciously admitted to the presence of our Most Serene Lord, for whose sake I have suffered much in the past, owing to my constant loyalty, and for whom, though I fear the violence and scandal, I am ready to suffer again in the future. I send another palfrey that is, I think, suitable for your Paternity, and shall soon send others to you which are not yet in good condition (*nondum sufficienter pastos*) together with other small fruits of this land: not once or twice, but, with God's help, repeatedly. Therefore, most reverend Lord, I trust that you will pay heed to what I have told you and that you will take compassion on my desolate state, turning your eyes towards the most bitter thorns by which I am daily pricked: so that, by the intervention of your pleading, kind Father, my aforesaid business may be brought to the notice of our Most Serene Lord the King by your own living word, and, if you so please, expounded to him with greater diligence. You will not, I believe—and I speak without personal boasting or vain-glory—find any man more suitable or more loyal for this office of chancellor in Ireland, in spite of all the slanders and detractions of the other lords and prelates of Ireland. Finally, I beg you, Father, not to show this letter and the other letter that I have sent you to any man, for fear that I should be stripped of all my temporal property through the tumult of some angry nobles, and should thus be compelled to lay aside my pastoral care and betake myself to other regions, or even—alas! be compelled to go into hiding."

These two letters speak for themselves. Primate Octavian was plainly convinced that the part he had played in the episode of Lambert Simnel's abortive rebellion against the King must expose him to the most serious dangers; and he is no less plainly convinced that his own suffragan, the bishop of Meath, was his most dangerous enemy. The event was to prove that his fears were unfounded. Neither Primate Octavian nor Bishop Payne was appointed to the office of chancellor in Ireland. The Great Earl's chief adviser and supporter, Lord Portlester, replaced Sir Thomas FitzGerald soon after these letters were written, and Primate Octavian was left to calculate whether his purchase of Irish palfreys for Archbishop Morton's personal use had been a waste of good money.

Two years after Sir Richard Edgecombe's visit to Ireland and the Great Earl's diplomatic victory, Henry VII summoned Kildare to appear before him in England within the next ten months. A safe-conduct and general pardon accompanied this summons, which was dated July 29, 1490.[1]

[1] Bryan, p. 145.

Kildare had his own reasons for doubting the sincerity of these offers. He was still in Ireland on June 4, 1491, when a letter was sent to the King on his behalf, signed by the archbishop of Dublin, the archbishop of Armagh (with a special note that the Primate had signed the letter *manu propria*), the bishop of Meath, five other prelates and seven of the principal lords of the Anglo-Irish Pale.[1] Octavian's presence in Dublin and personal signature were evidently matters of comment, and it is not easy to be sure of the exact grouping of parties in Ireland during these puzzling years. Soon after the date of this letter the Primate left Ireland for his second visit to Rome, and he was not back again in this country before the early summer of 1492. Meanwhile the archbishop of Dublin, Walter FitzSimons, who had hitherto been a consistent supporter of the Great Earl's policies, took Kildare's place as Deputy on June 11, 1492.

This change of office was almost certainly due to the appearance of a second pretender to the English Crown, Perkin Warbeck, in the month of November, 1491. Henry VII could not but suspect the Great Earl of complicity in this second plot. None the less, the appointment of a prelate as Deputy who had hitherto been noted for his Geraldine connections suggests that Henry knew the wisdom of acting cautiously. Archbishop FitzSimons remained in office from June, 1492 until September, 1493; but his term was marked by increasing disorders, due to the outbreak of open warfare between Kildare and Sir James Ormonde, his most dangerous and aggressive rival.[2] Shortly before the archbishop's appointment these hostilities had culminated in a scandalous riot within the sanctuary of St. Patrick's Cathedral in Dublin. The Dublin citizens were on the Great Earl's side in this quarrel, and Ormonde owed his life to the impulsive generosity of Kildare who rescued his enemy from what seemed to be certain death. But the

[1] *Letters and Papers of Richard III and Henry VII*, I, p. 377-9

[2] Bryan, pp. 157-65.

scene shifts suddenly, once Kildare ceases to be Deputy. In the following summer (July 20, 1493) we find the archbishop and citizens of Dublin at enmity with the Great Earl, who now marches on their city and threatens to capture it by assault. In the midst of this general confusion, Archbishop FitzSimons was relieved of his office as Deputy. The King chose Lord Gormanston as his successor in September, 1493.

This is the political background against which we must do our best to interpret Primate Octavian's movements in these years. He was in Ireland for the summer of 1492, when he held an important provincial council at Drogheda. This was the assembly at which Bishop Payne of Meath had his violent quarrel with the Primate, taunting him to his face as a would-be tyrant.[1] Political differences were probably involved in this quarrel, though the alignment of parties is not easy to trace. Bishop Payne seems to have broken with the Great Earl about this time; whilst the archdeacon of Meath, Christopher Dowdall, was involved in a bitter quarrel in his own native parish of Termonfeghin about this time.[2]

In June, 1493, the Primate decided to leave Ireland for a third time " on important and most urgent business of his diocese." In the document by which he empowered his O.III.
two vicars general to act during his absence he states that he is about to go abroad " to the Holy See and elsewhere." He must have left Ireland during the last few weeks of Archbishop FitzSimons' rule as Deputy, and he left the country without having first obtained the customary license. Had he reason to believe that the Deputy would refuse him the license if he asked for it? Or did he simply go on his own initiative, convinced that government in Ireland was once more on the verge of a complete breakdown? Did he in fact go to Rome, or did he spend most of his time at Henry's court in London?

[1] See below, p. 119.
[2] Bryan, pp. 168, 176; see above, p. 18-19.

All of these questions must go unanswered for lack of
O.329v. documentary proof. Four years later the officials of the Dublin exchequer were still pressing the Primate for fines due to his irregular conduct on this occasion, and Kildare seems to have borne him a grudge for the part he played in this crisis. We know that the Primate was back at Termonfeghin on May 30, 1494, for he then confirmed certain indulgences that had been published by his suffragan, the Greek bishop of Dromore. By that date Kildare had followed Gormanston to England, and negotiations were already being actively pressed forward in London which ended in the appointment of Sir Edward Poynings as Deputy in place of Gormanston, and the virtual cancellation of all that the Great Earl had been striving to accomplish for the past fifteen years.[1] What part had Primate Octavian played in these negotiations, since we are entitled to suspect that he was at the King's court for at least part of this critical period?

Sir Edward Poynings came to Ireland in the autumn of 1494. His brief tenure of office as Deputy Lieutenant is memorable for the new policy of subordinating the Anglo-Irish parliament and every detail of Anglo-Irish administration to the control of the King's Council in England. What part did Primate Octavian play in the deliberations of that period? His register gives us no guidance here, though it
O.226v. includes the text of the formal citation by which the Primate was summoned to present himself at the Deputy's first parliament, which met at Drogheda on December 1, 1494. The Great Earl was attainted at this parliament and all the acts of his government during the past six years were revoked. Henceforth no parliament was to meet in Ireland without license under the Great Seal in England, and no statutes might be passed by an Irish parliament which had not previously been approved by the King and his Council in England as well as by the King's Deputy and his Council
O.330. in Ireland. The Primate undertook to pay a double

[1] Bryan, pp. 179-85.

subsidy to meet the expenses of the Deputy's campaign against O Hanlon in the North, and proctors were named for this collection in June of the following year. We have no means of assessing the part which Octavian may have played in the formulation or execution of this new policy for the King's government in Ireland. Poynings probably came over from England with his plans worked out already in full detail, and the Primate could do no more than obey the orders he received.

Sir Edward Poynings left Ireland towards the end of 1495. His administration had not brought order to Ireland, and he left the bishop of Bangor (Henry Deane), who had been appointed chancellor in the autumn of 1494, to govern the country during his absence. The news from Ireland was so disturbing that the King turned once more in despair to the one man who could keep order in Ireland, and negotiations were opened with Kildare, who had been a prisoner in England since the spring of 1495. The formal agreement between the King and the Great Earl was dated August 6, 1496; and Kildare was back in Ireland by the middle of September.

At some date which cannot be far removed from the date of these negotiations a petition was sent to the Pope in Rome (Alexander VI) on behalf of King Henry.[1] It set forth that "in the island of Ireland, and especially in that part of the island which is covered with forest (*silvestris*), it is urgently desirable, for the guidance and good government of the metropolitan and cathedral churches of the said island and of the clergy and people of these churches, that some suitable remedy should be found." "Wherefore," the Pope's bull continues, "we have been humbly petitioned on behalf of the said king, with the greatest urgency, that we should provide some remedy for the aforesaid evils of our apostolic bounty." The Pope then empowers a group of English bishops—the archbishop of Canterbury (Morton), the bishops of Durham (Fox), Bath and Wells (King), and

[1] Wilkins, *Concilia* III, p. 644-5.

London (Savage)—collectively or individually, if it is found more convenient for one or two to act in the name of the others, " to summon a council of all the archbishops and bishops of this island, with their clergy and people, to some place which you shall judge to be apt and convenient." This council or convocation is to treat " of all things that concern the good estate and prosperous government of the churches, clergy and people of the aforesaid prelates, and to provide canonical sanctions thereupon according to the decrees of the holy fathers." They are also to name those who shall have power to proceed by way of ecclesiastical censures against all who may oppose these decrees or rebel against them, notwithstanding any constitutions or ordinances that may have emanated to the contrary from the Apostolic See or from the two Cardinals Otho and Ottoboni, formerly legates of the Holy See in England, or from any other constitutions published in provincial councils or synods.

There is not a word here about the jurisdiction of the two Primates of Ireland, whose authority is simply ignored. Indeed the whole purpose of the Pope's bull, which was issued from St. Peter's on October 28, 1496, seems to be the subordination of the entire Irish hierarchy and clergy to a convocation or council that was to be summoned by the Pope's authority and presided over by one or more of four English prelates. No record has survived of any such council, nor is it at all probable that any such council was ever held. Once the Great Earl of Kildare had returned to Ireland, ancient traditions were restored and the words of Peregrine O Clery were fulfilled: " The poets and the religious orders and the friars minor were granted their prayer and request of God, that is to permit the man to come back to Ireland who would succour and relieve them, that is Earl Garret."[1] But the petition which was sent to Rome in the King's name must have been drafted at a time when Henry's Council was seeking to negotiate a compromise with the Great Earl, and thus preserve the substance of the new system which Poynings had been commissioned

[1] Bryan, p. 209.

to introduce in 1494. Kildare was prepared to initial any agreements that gave him power in Ireland; among other promises he undertook to observe the statutes of the parliament that had met in Drogheda less than two years earlier and had revoked all his own earlier acts.[1] In such a background the Pope's bull of October 28 becomes intelligible. The King's Council had evidently devised a scheme by which the reform of the Irish Church, for which they professed such zeal, was to be entrusted to the archbishop of Canterbury and some of the King's most trusted prelates. Kildare would have made no difficulty at the time; but he must have known very well that the whole scheme was impracticable. It was bound to meet with equal resistance from Armagh and Dublin.

5. OCTAVIAN'S LAST YEARS

Primate Octavian disappears largely from public view during the last twenty years of his long pontificate. His register contains many documents that prove his continued interest in the government of his diocese and province, but there is little to indicate that he played an active part in the life of the country as a whole. In June, 1496, he was
appointed by the King to examine Malachy O Hanlon as to O.30.
his share in the war against Sir Edward Poynings and the Deputy's complicity in that episode. The Deputy was, of course, exonerated. One slight indication of the hostility which the Primate feared from the Great Earl and his faction in the Pale has been preserved in his register. On
January 12, 1497, Kildare issued a mandate from Ardee to O.329 v.
the chief baron of the exchequer in Dublin. He seems to have met the Primate at Ardee and to have come to some

[1] Bryan, pp. 204-9; Miss Conway, *Henry VII's Relations with Ireland and Scotland*, pp. 226-32.

permanent settlement with him. I give part of the mandate in its quaint English original.

". . . . And where we bene agreed & accord with the mooste Reverend fadre in Criste Octavyane Archebishipp of Ardmagh Prymate of all Irlande in all matiers concernyng our souverayn lorde the Kyng as twyching the said mooste Reverend fadre in cryste is absentie out of the land withowte sufficient licence And in all other matters moved agayns the said Archebishipp and Prymate and his vicaries generals in his absentie in the said Kinges eschekere for the which the mooste reverend fadre have made with us a fyne, We will that ye discharge (him) of all maner actions amerciaments fies & fynes."

The date of this agreement suggests that the officials of the exchequer in Dublin were still pressing the Primate for payment of certain fines and fees, claimed by them as penalty for a journey abroad which he had undertaken (probably in 1493) without the customary license for "going across the seas." The Deputy now made a final settlement of this legal claim ; and the Primate (we may be sure) was well content to pay whatever sum was demanded of him as the price of his relief.

Primate Octavian had more than sixteen years of active life in front of him when this debt was settled between himself and the Deputy whom he had so often opposed. Inevitably his register tells us less and less of his activities as old age began to limit his coming and going ; but I have not been able to find any document which gives accurate information as to his age at any period in his long life. Apart from the record of his provincial councils, which can be traced with one or two breaks down to the year 1507, most of the entries from these later years concern legal affairs which came before his court in the normal routine of diocesan and metropolitan business. From an entry of
O.113. May 29, 1509, we know that Thomas Hunt was still acting as his official at that date ; but his place was taken soon
O.370. afterwards by Michael Golding, who was also vicar of St. Peter's, Drogheda.

If the petition to Henry VIII on behalf of the desolate
diocese of Dromore is rightly dated to the year 1510, it is O.127.
proof that the Primate was still active in his efforts to
restore diocesan government in all his suffragan sees.[1] He
was also alive to the needs of his own diocese, for we find
him remitting the Dues of St. Patrick (*Questura S. Patricii*) O.412.
in favour of the dean and chapter of Armagh on January 18,
1509 "for the fabric, adornment, beauty and use of our
cathedral church of Armagh." Two indications that the
Primate was seeking to advance members of his own family
within the diocese have survived from these later years.
On March 26, 1500, the Primate collated a clerk named O.232.
John del Palacio to the rectory of Heynestown, which had
recently been vacated by William Palmer on his appointment to the rectory of Drummyn. A mutilated tombstone
still survives in the cemetery of Termonfeghin, on which
the name of John del Palacio, subdeacon and canon of
Armagh, can still be read. He died of the plague, most
probably in 1504.[2] Seven years later we hear for the first
time of another kinsman, Alexander del Palacio, who had
used his influence with the Primate to secure payment of a
pension of five marks per annum from Octavian Rownsfeld,
rector of Clonmore. Rownsfeld's appeal against this
imposition came before the Primate's court on September O.184.
11, 1511.[3]

The last entries which I have been able to trace in
Octavian's register are dated July 26, 1512. On that day O.183 ; 200.
the Primate presided over his court in the chapel of his
manor at Termonfeghin, and granted an absolution in one
matrimonial case, whilst another was forwarded to Rome for
dispensation. He died in the following June, and was
buried in a vault which he had built for himself in St.
Peter's, Drogheda.[4] It would be pleasant to think that this

[1] See below, p. 146.

[2] Reeves, in *Journal of the Kilkenny Archæological Society* (1874-5), p. 349.

[3] For Alexander's later career, see below, p. 111-2.

[4] Ware-Harris I, p. 89.

Italian Primate, who had come to Ireland from the Florence of Michael Angelo and Bramante, built his vault in the new Italian style of the Renaissance; but it has disappeared long since, and Sir James Ware—who saw it in the early seventeenth century—tells us nothing on this score.

Ware is responsible for another statement that has done some injustice to Primate Octavian's memory. Writing soon after 1600, Fynes Morison had quoted the first lines of a set of Latin verses which begin with the words: *Civitas Armachana, civitas vana.* They are less than complimentary to the city of Armagh with its ill-cooked food, its ill-clad women and its general air of poverty. Fynes Morison attributed these verses to "an Italian friar."[1] In 1658 Sir James Ware printed a second edition of his *De Hibernia et Antiquitatibus ejus*, and added to it a short chronicle of Irish history under Henry VII. In this work he cites these same verses in full, and ascribes them to Primate Octavian.[2] After the Restoration, when Ware had come back to Dublin, he published his *De Præsulibus Hiberniæ* in 1665. In his account of Primate Octavian Ware says nothing of these verses; but his editor, Walter Harris, prints them in the English translation of this work which he published in 1739, adding a note: "These Vulgar Rhimes are ascribed to this Prelate."[3] The truth would seem to be that Ware and Harris have been led astray by a popular attribution. The authorship of these satirical verses is uncertain, but there are reasons for believing them to be as old as the days of Giraldus Cambrensis and the first Anglo-Norman adventurers in Ireland.[4] No further mention of them is needed in any critical account of Primate Octavian's life.

[1] Fynes Morison: *Itinerary*, Part III, Book 3 (*sub finem*).

[2] Ware: *Rerum Hibernicarum Henrico VII regnante Annales*, ad ann. 1500.

[3] Ware-Harris I, p. 89.

[4] Mr. T. G. F. Paterson tells me that a copy of these verses written by Hugh Tirell and dated May 10, 1200, was preserved in the Kynton Papers in the Public Record Office in 1906. He believes the author of the lines to have been the same person as the Hugh Tirell who accompanied Philip of Worcester in his raid on the city in September, 1184. I have not been able to trace this reference, but the verses fit well into this background.

6. PRIMATE JOHN KITE (1513-21)

Henry VIII lost no time in securing the provision of an English clerk to the vacant see of Armagh. On October 24, 1513, Leo X provided John Kite, a Londoner by birth and one of the King's clerks.[1] At the time of his provision Kite, who had been educated at Eton and King's College, Cambridge, was rector of the church of Weye in the diocese of Winchester, prebendary in the two dioceses of Salisbury and Exeter, and sub-dean of the King's chapel at Windsor. Since he seems to have been elected fellow of King's College as early as 1480, the new archbishop of Armagh must have been over fifty years of age at the time of his provision. He was thus not one of the younger men who were rising to power in England at this time under the protection of Cardinal Wolsey, but his later career shows that Wolsey's friendship and patronage meant more to him than the Primacy of All Ireland.

John Kite must have been consecrated, presumably in England, at some unknown date during the winter of 1513-14. He first appears in Ireland on May 14, 1514, when he writes to Wolsey from Termonfeghin, reporting on the perilous state of the Pale and his own good work on the King's behalf. This letter is of considerable interest for the light it throws on Henry's Irish policy at this date. Wolsey had not yet diverted the young King's interest from home affairs to the more exciting and adventurous field of continental diplomacy, and Kite came over to Ireland in 1514 with the news that the King would shortly follow him in person. His mission, as revealed in this letter, was indeed more political than ecclesiastical. His subsequent loss of interest in Irish affairs was probably due to a growing sense that Ireland would henceforth no longer be the main field of Henry's (or rather Wolsey's) activity.

[1] The facts about Kite's career have been collected by Thompson Cooper in *D.N.B.* 30, p. 232-3. The date of the provision is given in *Letters and Papers*, vol. I (second edition, 1920), Part 2, no. 2395.

The letter begins with a sigh of regret for the pleasures that the Primate had left behind him when he crossed the sea to Ireland.[1] "Tho' I be far from your heaven, from the sight of our most gracious King and Queen (whom God preserve), from the wealth of all the joys of England": the man who penned that phrase was not likely to stay longer than might prove strictly necessary in the Anglo-Irish Pale. He announces to Wolsey ("my lord of Lincoln") his safe arrival on Passion Eve, and his first impressions of the country: "plenteous in corn, cattle, fish and fowl, but scant of wood in all the Englishry." Without the King's help he can see nothing but general decay. But he is "putting them in great fear by telling them that the King shall come shortly, which God grant above all things." The Primate adds a curious sentence, which reveals his attitude to the flock committed to his charge: "he is as much bound to reform this land as to maintain order in England, more bound to subdue them than to subdue the Jews or Saracens." The allusion would seem to be to the Crusade against the Turks, which the new Pope (Leo X) was just then striving to organise, though with small success. "Christ's faith," Kite reports to Wolsey, "and obedience to the Church is scant everywhere, for lack of the temporal sword." The revenues due to the King are now "spent against the Church." Finally, if he be not assured of the King's coming, Kite has no doubt "but that he will die of sorrow or be slain." He implores Wolsey to help in the redress of "this most plenteous country, most profitable to the possessor being once in order." Meanwhile he is most anxious to have sight of Wolsey's handwriting.

Three weeks later (June 7) the Primate wrote again to Wolsey from Termonfeghin.[2] He has not yet heard from Wolsey since he left England: "which is more pain to me than all the troubles I find in Ireland." He himself has sent

[1] A short abstract of this letter was printed in *Calendar of State Papers: Ireland* I (1860), p. 1. There is a very much fuller abstract in *Letters and Papers* I (1920), Part 2, no. 2907.

[2] *Letters and Papers* I (1920), Part 2, no. 2977.

several letters, but "the wind is not at will." He entreats Wolsey, "for the love of God and his many promises, not to leave him without letters, as a castaway, in this ill-ordered country." The Primate adds some curious details about his voyage across the Irish Sea, which had been disturbed by an attack from two Breton pirate men-of-war. His ship had been rescued by two Spanish ships manned by the citizens of Drogheda, who had come out to their assistance and had captured one of the pirates. Since then the Primate had hired a ship of Chester, with ordnance and men of war, which has kept the Irish coast safe from such marauders.

A third letter, written in Latin to O Neill about this time, has been preserved among the Carew papers.[1] In it the Primate assures O Neill that his safety depends on the King, and exhorts him to adopt a more civilised manner of life. "You should cultivate a mind worthy of your ability and character, and no longer take delight in wild and barbarous manners, being unacquainted with the comforts of life. For it is much better to live in a civilised fashion than to seek a living by arms and rapine, and to have no thought beyond pleasure and the belly." The Primate ends by beseeching O Neill to remember how dangerous it is to incur the King's enmity, whilst his favour can bring him happiness. O Neill's reply has not been preserved.

Primate Kite was still at Termonfeghin on May 3, 1515, when he published a sentence of excommunication against thé parishioners of Drogheda, who had refused to pay their share of the dues demanded of them.[2] During the autumn of that year he crossed over to England, having first
appointed the abbot of Mellifont (Thomas Hervey) and his O.136 v.
own chaplain (David Bedoo) as his vicars general for the period of his absence from the diocese. He was present at Westminster Abbey on November 18, when Wolsey formally received the Cardinal's hat which had been sent from Rome

[1] *Calendar of Carew Papers* I (1515-74), p. 15.

[2] Octavian's Register, Appendix, fo. 14v. (transcribed by Reeves, but now missing from the Register).

by Leo X. He was still in London on February 21, 1516, when he was one of the prelates who attended the christening of the Princess Mary at Greenwich.[1] Kite was in his
O.88. diocese again before April 26, when he issued his formal summons from Termonfeghin for a provincial council which met at St. Peter's, Drogheda, on June 23. Octavian's register contains several loose documents which deal with the business of this provincial council, but no record of attendance has survived. The Primate was still in Ireland on
O.87. August 12, when he presided over the first hearing of a suit by the prior of Lanthony concerning his right of nomination to a chaplaincy; but he had left for England before the case was concluded, having once more named Abbot Hervey and David Bedoo as his vicars general. Alexander Plunket, described here as "a bachelor in the decretals," is also named as the Primate's principal official in the court of Armagh.

Primate Kite had by now made up his mind that his devotion to the King's business and his own diplomatic career must take precedence over the claims of his diocese in Ireland. On September 20, 1516, he obtained a writ of protection for himself and his see during his absence from Ireland.[2] We know nothing of his movements during the following year; but he was sent with Lord Berners on a special embassy to the Emperor Charles V in February, 1518, and spent the next twelve months in Spain. He was back in London in March, 1519, and remained there for the next year. In the summer of 1520 he accompanied Henry VIII and Queen Catherine to the Field of the Cloth of Gold, and was also present at Gravelines when Henry met Charles V there in July.[3]

The increasing frequency of Kite's diplomatic missions seems to have made him aware that he could no longer retain his post as Primate of All Ireland if he was to continue his work for the King, at home and abroad. On July 12,

[1] *Letters and Papers* II, Part 1, nos. 1153; 1573.

[2] ibid. II, Part 1, p. 2375.

[3] *D.N.B.*, loc. cit.

1521, he was translated from the see of Armagh to the see of Carlisle by Leo X, being allowed to take the archiepiscopal title of Thebes *in partibus infidelium.*[1] Kite's later career need not detain us. He was one of Cardinal Wolsey's confidential advisers, and was used by him in every sort of mission during the next eight years. On July 13, 1530, he was one of the bishops who signed an outspoken letter to Clement VII, demanding the King's divorce. He renounced the Pope's supremacy on February 15, 1534; but was opposed to Cranmer's more radical programme of reform. He resided for a time at least in Carlisle, where we hear of him as "keeping noble household with great hospitality." John Kite's last years were clouded with ill health, and he died in his native city of London on June 11, 1537.

During the five years of his absentee rule (1516-21), the diocese of Armagh was administered by a succession of vicars general. Abbot Hervey and David Bedoo are named
in the entry of August 12, 1516. Their place had been taken O.87.
by Master Alexander Plunket before March 18, 1518, when
Plunket is named as sole vicar general in the first entry of a P.1.
new register or court-book of the Primate's metropolitan court. Since Plunket is now styled *magister* in these official records, it is evident that he must have been admitted to the *magisterium* shortly before this date. His influence is at once apparent in the compilation of two registers for the routine work of the diocese. One of these, which contains a record of all legal proceedings before the Primate's court, begins with the entry of March 18, 1518, and is continued without interruption to the autumn of 1522. The other, which contains the record of the vicar's work as representing the absent Primate in the routine work of administration,
contains entries for November 5 and December 13, 1518; C.3.
but does not begin to be a full record until the early months of 1520. These two volumes are now bound together as two separate parts of the volume commonly known as "Cromer's Register." This name should, properly speaking, be applied

[1] Brady I, p. 215.

only to the second part of the volume, which does in fact contain the official record of Cromer's primatial administration from the time of his provision in 1521 to the end of 1535.

The earlier section of "Cromer's Register" ends before Cromer had left England for Ireland, and is our sole surviving specimen in Ireland of a medieval court-book, It was compiled (we must presume) under the personal direction and supervision of Alexander Plunket, who was the Primate's chief official as well as his vicar general from the summer of 1518 to the summer of 1520. From that date to the autumn of 1523, when Primate Cromer first appears in person, two new names occur in each section of "Cromer's Register." Hugh Inge, who had been bishop of Meath since 1512, takes the place of Alexander Plunket as
P.54 v. the absent Primate's vicar general in 1520, and retains this office until his own translation to Dublin in 1522. Master Thomas Noter appears for a short time (August, 1520-May, 1521) as the president of the metropolitan court of Armagh, acting as commissary for the bishop of Meath; but his place was soon taken by a more important figure in the history of the diocese. Master Cormac Roth first appears as the Primate's commissary and president of his
P.71. metropolitan court in an entry dated May 16, 1521. He was to retain this post, with many others, until his death almost twenty years later.

Plunket's metropolitan court-book is a mine of information for the social history of Co. Louth in the first quarter of the sixteenth century; but it throws little light on the organisation and administration of the diocese of Armagh during this same period. The few entries which survive in Cromer's episcopal register from the last years of Primate Kite's absentee rule do not help us much. We
C.3. learn, for example, that Master Alexander Plunket presided over the annual convocation of the diocesan clergy *inter Anglos* on November 5, 1518, and made arrangements for the stricter control of the mendicant friars whose unlicensed begging had caused some confusion. It will be more convenient to discuss the evidence of these and other

entries in connection with Primate Cromer's administration of the diocese after his arrival in Ireland in 1523. Meanwhile a lucky accident has preserved for us a contemporary description of Armagh, as seen by an Italian visitor to Lough Derg in the summer of 1517.

Primate Kite left Ireland for good in the autumn of 1516. At that time the Pope was represented in England by his nuncio, Bishop Francesco Chiericati (*de Clericatis*), a native of Florence and an experienced diplomatist. The two men must have met during the winter of 1516-17, and it was probably this chance acquaintanceship which induced the Italian nuncio to visit Ireland in the following summer. A group of pilgrims to St. Patrick's Purgatory was organised at the same time, but the nuncio—who is quite clear in his narrative that he himself came as an onlooker, not as a pilgrim—has not troubled to give their names or any details as to their nationality. His narrative occurs in a letter to his friend and patron, the Princess Isabella d'Este, to whom he wrote from Middelburgh in Holland some weeks after his adventure.[1] The letter is dated August 28, 1517; and we know that Bishop Chiericati wrote to Erasmus from Antwerp ten days later.[2] The truth, which is nowhere mentioned in these two letters, is that the nuncio came back from his adventure in Ireland to find that his diplomatic career had been ruined by the sudden disgrace of his patron in Rome, Cardinal Adriano Castellesi. Leo X had decided on Chiericati's immediate recall from England by the end of June, 1517; and news of his disgrace had reached London

[1] Dr. Mahaffy published a translation from the Italian, made for him by Professor J. G. Smyly, in *Hermathena*, no. 40 (1914), pp. 10-15. I have not had access to the original text, which was printed by Bernardo Morsolin in "Francesco Chiericati, Vescovo e Diplomatico del secolo decimo-sesto," in *Atti dell' Academia Olimpica di Vicenza* (1873), pp. 121-237. Father L. Hicks, S.J. has very kindly checked the spelling of the place names for me from a copy in the British Museum: they have been very carelessly reproduced in Mahaffy's printed version.

[2] *Letters and Papers* II, Part 2, no. 3645.

some time during July.[1] Bishop Chiericati was most probably in Ireland when the Pope's letters arrived. An urgent letter to Wolsey, written most probably in August, some ten days after he had received his official recall, has survived.[2] Wolsey, who had his eye on some of Cardinal Castellesi's many benefices, proved unhelpful. Since Chiericati gives no exact dates for his journey to Ireland, we can only conjecture that he came to this country in June or July, 1517.

Having obtained King Henry's gracious permission for his journey, the nuncio and his companions spent five days on the road from London to Chester. They there took ship for Dublin, and made the crossing in a day and a night. Dublin is described as " one of the three metropolitan cities " (it is not clear which of the four metropolitan sees is here forgotten), and the capital city of Ireland. " Here is collected the Grand Council of the kingdom, and, as it is a maritime place, it is sufficiently populous." The nuncio and his friends were suitably entertained by the archbishop of Dublin (William Rokeby), and by the Deputy (Kildare). They were then given letters and attendance as far as Drogheda. " Leaving Dublin, we passed over level ground through country that is pleasing enough to the eye, overlooking the sea till we came to Drogheda, a fairly rich territory, five miles distant from the sea." Thence they pushed on to Dundalk : " once an illustrious city, but at the present day rather ruinous." Continuing their journey for twenty-four miles, they came to " another metropolitan city called Armagh, the seat of the Primate of the island, but it is very desolate, the best thing in it being an abbey of Canons Regular." Chiericati's next comment shows that he is writing from a too careless memory. " Thence we left the sea behind us, and began to penetrate into the mountains. Having journeyed twenty miles we came to a

[1] ibid., nos. 3406 ; 3504. For the fall of Cardinal Castellesi, who was involved in Cardinal Patrucci's plot against Leo X, see Pastor : *History of the Popes* (Eng. tr.), VII, p. 195-6.

[2] ibid., no. 3645.

cathedral city called Clogher, beyond which the country is full of thieves." At this point the nuncio's account of his journey becomes difficult to follow. He tells us that they entered a district which he calls *Armanac* (perhaps Fermanagh) "which is full of robbers, woods, lakes, and marshes." They went on their way to a place called Tremon "where there is an earl"—most probably Mag Uidhir.[1] "Here the rule of England ceases." Thence they went through a district called *Nomach* (most probably Omagh) which extended for six miles, and is described as "full of robbers and rascals." There they found many rivers, and Chiericati gives a lively, but not very convincing account of the oyster-pearls which were found "in heaps and handfuls" in these rivers. Finally, they came to St. Patrick's Purgatory, "situated among hills, lying in a valley, and in the middle of a lake which surrounds it for four miles."

Bishop Chiericati had no intention of risking his life in the famous Cave, so he remained patiently outside the Purgatory for ten days whilst his friends went through all the alarming and exhausting experiences of the medieval pilgrimage.[2] "However, the greater penance was mine," the nuncio writes to his friend in Italy; "for I was compelled to wait for about ten days, during which the greater part of our provisions failed us." He was shown an old book whilst he waited, in which he saw to his amazement the names of many former pilgrims, beginning with Guarino da Durazzo, "which I had believed to be a fable." Of his friends who made the pilgrimage he tells us that two had visions, whilst the others said that they had seen or felt nothing save cold, hunger and great weakness. All were consoled with the thought that "God had granted as a grace to St. Patrick that whoever should enter this Purgatory and do penance would not have to do penance in the Purgatory

[1] I suspect that Chiericati has here confused his outward and home journeys. Termon is probably Termon Maguirk; the party may have returned to Armagh through Fermanagh.

[2] Sir Shane Leslie has printed this portion of Chiericati's narrative in his *Saint Patrick's Purgatory* (London, 1932), p. 64.

of the other life." Bishop Chiericati had to be content with the thought that he had satisfied his curiosity, though he was afraid even to look into the famous Cave—" being terrified by the things that are said about it." He was content to stand three paces from the door and see what he could from that safe distance.

On their way home the party returned, as they had come, by Armagh; but from that point they took a different route. " We journeyed thence twenty-two miles to Verdelino, where there is a stately abbey of monks." The name, at first sight perplexing, is no more than a foreigner's effort to render phonetically the Latin Cistercian name for Newry (*Viride Lignum*) as pronounced locally, with a good northern accent. From Newry they continued their journey " to a city by the sea called Down, where we found a bishop from the city of Viterbo, a man of the age of a hundred and fourteen years." This is undoubtedly Bishop Tiberius Ugolino, who had been resident at Down for the past twenty-eight years, and who had still one or two more years of life before him at this date. His age, as recorded by the nuncio, is frankly incredible. Sixtus IV was not likely to provide a man of over eighty to the see of Down and Connor in 1483; nor is the story of his hospitality to Bishop Chiericati easily reconciled with the health and physical energy of a man of one hundred and fourteen years. " There the pilgrims made a halt for three days," we are told. " In this place I could not walk in the street because every one ran to kiss my dress, understanding that I was a nuncio from the Pope: so that I was almost compelled by force to stay in the house, so great was their importunity, which arose from a strong religious feeling." These demonstrations are a testimony to the influence which Bishop Tiberius was able to exercise at Downpatrick—for it is plain that he knew of the nuncio's coming, and had made ready for a suitable reception. He did more than that. " The good bishop received us most graciously, and procured for me," writes the nuncio, " much pleasure in fishing." He adds a story that is worthy of a true fisherman, be he from

Ireland or from Italy. "There for a shilling one can obtain a salmon weighing fifty pounds which in Italy would be of great value, and would be very highly esteemed." Even allowing for the fact that a shilling was then worth very much more than its present value, and that fifty pounds Italian are roughly equal to thirty-seven pounds English, salmon must have been cheap in Downpatrick four hundred years ago.

From Downpatrick the party went on to Saul, "passing through walled-in territory." On their way they saw "the tomb of a giant"—presumably a cromlech—which Chiericati describes as "made of flint, and forty-eight feet long."[1] In the village of Cavallo (apparently an Italian form of the Irish name Sabhall) they saw a stream of water which "gushed out from the mountain and fell far down into an open building." The pilgrims knelt beneath the flow of water, praying *Pater Noster* and *Ave Maria* in honour of St. Patrick. Thence they took ship, and passed through Strangford Lough to Dublin.

7. PRIMATE GEORGE CROMER

John Kite was succeeded as Primate by George Cromer, an English priest of the diocese of Chichester. The text of the papal provision is dated October 2, 1521.[2] It states that Cromer was then a royal chaplain, and that the King had supplicated on his behalf. Apart from these few facts, very little seems to be known of the new Primate. A chance reference in a private letter of 1534 suggests that Cromer

[1] O'Laverty, in his *Down and Connor*, vol. I (1878), p. 222, describes a cromlech in the parish of Saul, which measures nine feet six inches by five feet three inches. If this is the giant's tomb which Chiericati saw, we get some measure of his general accuracy. The well at "Cavallo" is presumably "Meran Well"—for which see O'Laverty, loc. cit., p. 232.

[2] Brady I, p. 216.

was a member of a Kentish family named Crowmer or Cromer, which is represented in this generation by Sir William Crowmer and John Crowmer. Both these gentlemen appear regularly as justices of the peace for Kent in the State Papers of this period; and there was probably some connection by marriage with the family of Sir Edward Wotton. John Gage, brother-in-law of Sir Edward Guildford, writes a letter on June 4, 1534, in which he names Sir Edward Wotton and John Crowmer as his cousins.[1] Three weeks later Christopher Hales, writing to Cromwell, puts in a good word for the archbishop of Armagh, who was then in ill repute at the King's court as being too closely connected with Silken Thomas and the Geraldine interest in Ireland. "Mr. John Crowmer," so Hales writes to Cromwell, "tells me that you are favourable to the bishop of Armagh. I know him well, and think he is misreported."[2] We may conclude that the new Primate came from a solidly established Kentish family.

Leo X granted the pallium to Cromer as archbishop-elect on October 25, 1521.[3] The text of the papal grant makes no mention of any transmission of the pallium to England and it is probable that Cromer had gone to Rome in person to make sure of his provision. If Archdeacon Lynch is to be trusted (and he compiled his *De Præsulibus Hiberniæ* more than a century after Cromer's death), the new Primate was consecrated somewhere in England during the month of April, 1522.[4] But a calculation based on various entries in Cromer's own episcopal register limits the *dies consecracionis* within the months of December-January, 1521-2.[5] This would give time for the new Primate to

[1] *Letters and Papers* VII, no. 789.

[2] ibid. VII, Appendix, no. 30. It is worth noting that the Irish Primate is often incorrectly styled "the bishop of Armagh" in English letters and papers of this reign.

[3] Brady, loc. cit.: the grant was made "domino Georgio Cronumer (? Crouumer) electo Armachanen."

[4] Lynch, *De Præsulibus Hiberniæ*, ed. J. F. O'Doherty (Dublin, 1944) I, p. 123.

[5] Very few of the entries in Cromer's register are dated in this way. Father Murray has unfortunately ignored this system of dating in his published summary calendar of this register.

return from Rome to England. The record of his consecration has most probably been preserved in some as yet unpublished English register.

Once Cromer had taken up his duties in Ireland (November, 1523), his register becomes our main source of information for his various activities. Earlier biographical notices are unsatisfactory, since they ignore this evidence; and there is a further source of positive error, which must here be briefly mentioned. In the late seventeenth century, when anti-Catholic feeling caused by the Titus Oates plot was at its height, Robert Ware, son and literary executor of Sir James Ware, published a series of forged letters, purporting to be letters from Archbishop George Browne of Dublin to Thomas Cromwell.[1] Primate Cromer is mentioned more than once in these spurious letters as the centre of a secret party that was working in Ireland for the cause of the Pope against the King. The notice on George Cromer which Canon Dixon contributed to the *Dictionary of National Biography* in 1888 is based in great part on these forgeries of Robert Ware.[2] Dr. R. Dudley Edwards has recently revised this notice, eliminating from it all statements that are ultimately derived from Ware's forgeries and adding some new material.[3] But Dr. Edwards did not make any use of the evidence to be found in the Primate's register, and his notice is thus itself in need of revision.

A year and a half went by before the new Primate was ready to go to Ireland. Restitution of temporalities was not granted by the King until June 20, 1523, with a clause

[1] The most recent discussion is by Dr. R. D. Edwards in *Church and State in Tudor Ireland* (1935). Canon Jourdan accepts Ware's forgeries as genuine in the chapters which he contributed to the *History of the Church of Ireland* II (ed. W. Alison Phillips, 1933). For this, and other reasons, Canon Jourdan's narrative needs to be read with caution. The two new letters which Father John Brady has recently printed in *Archivium Hibernicum* VIII (1941), pp. 236-7, belong to the series of Ware's forgeries, having been copied into one of Sir James Ware's note-books, as was Robert's custom.

[2] *D.N.B.* XIII, p. 144-5.

[3] *Bulletin of the Institute of Historical Research* XI (1934), pp. 54-55.

making the grant retrospective from the date of the archbishop's consecration some eighteen months earlier.[1] No
record has survived to account for this long delay. Cromer's
episcopal register confirms his absence from the diocese
during the first two years of his pontificate. He first appears
C.12 v. in Ireland on November 13, 1523, when he presided over a
session of his metropolitan court at St. Peter's, Drogheda.
Meanwhile there had been a change in the administration of
the diocese. Bishop Hugh Inge is last mentioned as vicar-
C.9v. general of the diocese on July 2, 1521. On that day he
presided over a synod of the Armagh clergy *inter Anglos* in
the name of the absent Primate Kite. William Rokeby,
who had been archbishop of Dublin since his translation
from Meath in 1512, died on November 21, 1521; and Inge,
who had succeeded Rokeby as bishop of Meath in 1512,
now followed him from Meath to Dublin. Bishop Inge's
C.11. place as vicar-general of Armagh was taken by Master
James White, who had been archdeacon of Armagh since
1497. Another name appears in the register at this point.
Master Cormac Roth, who had been Primate Kite's official
since May, 1521, presided over a convocation of the clergy
C.10 v. *inter Anglos* at St. Peter's, Drogheda, in November of that
year. He and Archdeacon White acted as sub-custodians
P.103 v. of the vacant see during the interval following Kite's
resignation in the summer of 1521. Henceforth Cormac Roth
appears regularly in Cromer's episcopal register as the
Primate's official, whilst Archdeacon White remained
vicar-general until the Primate's arrival in the summer or
autumn of 1523.

From the autumn of 1523 to the autumn of 1530 Cromer seems to have been normally resident in his diocese—though he may have crossed over to England for short visits more than once in those seven years. His register contains singularly little of general interest at this time. The normal business of the diocese, so far as it lay within the immediate

[1] Rymer, *Fœdera* XIII, p. 796; *Letters and Papers* III, Part 2, no. 3119.

jurisdiction of the English-speaking Primate, was continued without interruption. Synods were held regularly at St. Peter's, Drogheda, and were attended—more or less regularly—by the English clergy of the diocese (*clerus inter Anglos*). Within the limits of the English-speaking Pale the Primate exercised his powers in the transaction of routine business, collating to vacant rectories and vicarages and occasionally dealing with some matter that had come up to his court on appeal from one or other of his suffragans. But there is a noteworthy absence of any public business—
with one exception. On April 6, 1528, the Primate presided C.33.
over a convocation of the clergy *inter Anglos*, at which he warned his clergy against the tendency to rebellion shown by some of the English subjects, particularly in Louth and Meath, and asked for the appointment of a committee of the English clergy who would seek a remedy for these disturbances. At a later session of this same convocation the clergy *inter Anglos*, under the presidency of Master Cormac Roth, came to an agreement with the Primate's official as to the subsidy which the Primate claimed in the form of procurations. The Primate, on the last day of this convocation, thanked his clergy for their generous settlement.

The evidence of Cromer's register can be supplemented here by the surviving State Papers of the reign of Henry VIII. From his first arrival in the autumn of 1523 the Primate must have been a member of the King's council in Ireland, but there is little to prove that he was an active or important member. His name occurs in a letter of August 27, 1526, when Wolsey advised the King that it might be helpful to summon the Primate (here called " the bishop of Armagh ") to England for consultation.[1] Kildare, who was then Deputy, had already been summoned to England. When he heard of Wolsey's plan, the King thought that the Primate should not be summoned " as Kildare the Deputy and others are coming over, and he fears that the absence

[1] *Letters and Papers* IV, Part 2, no. 2433.

of so many might cause disorder." Two years later the Primate seems to have been somewhat more active. His signature is found to two joint letters from the council, dated May 15 and November 15, 1528. In the first of these letters the council reports to Wolsey the confusion that has been caused among the Englishry in Ireland by the capture of Lord Delvin, Kildare's vice-deputy, who had rashly entered into negotiations with O Conor Faly.[1] In the second letter their report is even more gloomy : "Owing to divisions and lack of captains, the Englishry were never weaker since the conquest, nor were the Irish ever stronger in the days of any man living."[2] Small wonder that the Primate thought fit to warn his clergy at Drogheda against the discords that were weakening the Englishry of Louth in these anxious days.

Cromer's register begins to be of more general interest during the years 1530-35. The interest is due to various causes. During these fateful years Henry VIII was finally separating the Church of England from the jurisdiction of the Pope in Rome, and the schism which he had thus successfully brought about in England was planned to affect Ireland also. During these same years, for a variety of local reasons, many of the Primate's suffragans or some of their discontented subjects appealed to the Primate's metropolitan court. Cromer's register thus begins to throw light on the whole northern province of Armagh at this crisis. Finally, for a few brief years Primate Cromer moved into the full limelight of Anglo-Irish history. He took office as chancellor in Ireland in the summer of 1532, and played an important part in the general policy of the King's Irish council during the two following years. These years also witnessed a final struggle for power between the King's party in Ireland, led by Archbishop Allen of Dublin, and the "Old English" party, led by the Geraldine Earl of Kildare. Primate Cromer, as we shall see, was drawn into

[1] *State Papers of Henry VIII* (1834), vol. II, p. 127 ; *Letters and Papers* IV, Part 2, no. 4263.

[2] *Letters and Papers* IV, Part 2, no. 4933.

this political struggle on the Geraldine side. He falls back again into relative obscurity with the overthrow of the Geraldine house in 1534-5.

John Allen or Aleyn, the able and ambitious archbishop of Dublin who was Cromer's chief rival in Ireland during these critical years, was an English clerk who had risen to power in England as a favourite of the all-powerful Cardinal Wolsey.[1] Wolsey had obtained his promotion to the see of Dublin in August, 1528. A few weeks later Allen was also named chancellor of Ireland (September 19, 1528). He held this office until July 5, 1532, when a dramatic change took place in King Henry's Irish policy.

During the years 1528-9, immediately before Wolsey's sudden fall from favour in the autumn of 1529, Archbishop Allen was seeking to exercise special jurisdiction in Ireland as the English Cardinal's vice-legate in Ireland. Archbishop Cromer was consistently opposed to Wolsey's interests and policies in Ireland. " The Primate," Allen wrote to Wolsey on June 1, 1529, " his suffragans and councillors, say that you are not legate in Ireland; and they do much harm, because the see of Armagh and the whole province, except Meath, is in Ulster, among the Irish."[2] Cromer was unquestionably correct in denying that Wolsey's legatine authority had ever been extended by the Holy See to cover this country as well as England. A struggle for power between Dublin and Armagh was thus inevitable from the first.

Cromer's register for 1532 contains a copy of two letters C.65.
dated May 23, 1528. By these letters Cardinal Wolsey, using his legatine authority, instituted and inducted by proxy Master Reginald Drummyn as vicar of St. Peter's, Drogheda, on presentation from the prior and convent of

[1] There is a good notice of Allen's early career by James Gairdner in *D.N.B.* I, p. 305-6. The name is spelt variously, but I use here the form " Allen " for convenience.

[2] The full text of Allen's letter to Wolsey has been printed in *State Papers* II, p. 102-4. But the editor of this volume has overlooked a marginal note, most probably in Allen's own hand, which I quote from Brewer's *Letters and Papers* IV, Part 3, no. 5625.

Lanthony in Gloucestershire, who were patrons of St. Peter's before the suppression of the monasteries in England. These letters have not been copied into Cromer's register in their natural place among the entries for 1528. They occur among the entries for the last months of 1532, when the Primate had just been nominated chancellor in Ireland and when Cardinal Wolsey's legatine authority was no more than a recent memory. We may fairly suspect that this entry is in some way connected with the controversy as to Wolsey's jurisdiction in Ireland. Allen had not yet been appointed archbishop of Dublin in May, 1528, when Wolsey issued these letters, making direct use of his legatine authority within the jurisdiction of the archbishop of Armagh. Archbishop Allen would have held that this appointment was good and valid ; the Primate would have denied its validity. In 1532 Cromer was in a position to make good his own claims to exclusive jurisdiction in Armagh.

Wolsey's institution of Master Reginald Drummyn as vicar of St. Peter's was probably never made effective in
C.72 v. Drogheda. On August 7, 1533, an inquisition was held by the archdeacon of Armagh as president of the Primate's metropolitan court, concerning a vacancy in the vicarage of St. Peter's. According to the findings of this inquisition, the vicarage had been vacant since the death of Master Michael Golding, the last vicar. There is not a word here about Reginald Drummyn, who had been instituted and inducted by proxy in 1528, in virtue of Wolsey's legatine authority. Are we to conclude that Reginald Drummyn had come to Drogheda as vicar of St. Peter's in 1528 ; that he had died soon afterwards ; that his place had been taken by Master Michael Golding ; and that Golding had also died before August, 1533 ?

This supposition is excluded by an earlier entry for 1519.
P.49. Master Michael Golding is here named as vicar of St. Peter's. It is thus certain that the vacancy recorded by the inquisition of 1533 had existed since Golding's death at some date earlier than May, 1528. The Primate's metropolitan

court here simply ignores the attempted institution of Reginald Drummyn by the English Cardinal as *ultra vires*, and recommends that the vacancy, which must have existed for at least five years, be finally terminated by the institution of Master William Hamling, who is now presented by the prior and convent of Lanthony as patrons of the vicarage. If my interpretation of these two puzzling entries is correct, the story of this vacancy in Drogheda is a minor episode in a much greater struggle for power between the Irish Primate and the English Cardinal.

8. PRIMATE CROMER AND HENRY VIII

Cromer's register throws new light on another aspect of this struggle for power. Cardinal Wolsey lost the King's favour in the autumn of 1529; he died, a broken man, on November 29, 1530. Cromer was in Ireland at the time of Wolsey's sudden fall, and he remained in his diocese until the following autumn. He then appointed Master Cormac C.51 V
Roth, who had just succeeded James White as archdeacon of Armagh, to rule the diocese as the Primate's vicar-general during his absence *in remotis*. Nothing is known of the reasons which kept Cromer away from his diocese for the next two years, but his episcopal register proves that Cormac Roth was administering the diocese in his name from October, 1530 to November, 1532. And we know that the Primate was in England at this time, for there is an entry of January 22, 1531, recording a gift to the King of two hobbies from "the bishop of Armacan."[1]

If we remember what was happening in England during these two critical years, we may perhaps guess at the true reason of the Primate's long absence from his diocese.

[1] *Letters and Papers* V, p. 753.

The Long Parliament, Henry VIII's chosen instrument in the accomplishment of his new religious policy, was opened on November 3, 1529. During 1530 Cranmer's new policy of forcing the royal divorce through without a dispensation from the Holy See was put into action, and the King had already begun to collect the opinions of the universities of Europe in favour of his contention. Wolsey's death in November removed the last hope of restraining the King from a decisive step, and the winter of 1530-31 was spent in bringing pressure to bear on the English bishops who had hitherto refused to contemplate the possibility of a final breach with Rome. On February 11, 1531, the clergy in convocation reluctantly recognised Henry as "Supreme Head of the Church of England," with the feeble restrictive clause "so far as the law of Christ permits" (*quantum per Christi legem licet*). Cromer was in England when that vote was obtained from the English convocation. He must have known well the nature of the threat to which the clergy had yielded,—the threat of *Præmunire,* a statute so vaguely worded and capable of such rigorous interpretation that only the bravest were prepared to face the consequences of a direct refusal to obey the King's command.

Cromer was still in England a year later when the first act was passed by parliament against the payment of annates to the Pope (January, 1532). Henry was now striking at the sources of the Pope's revenues, and he could count on the support of the commons whenever there was question of keeping money within the realm. In that same month the commons petitioned the King against the jurisdiction exercised by the clergy in their ecclesiastical courts, and against various other causes of old-standing anti-clerical grievances. Their attack was followed (May, 1532) by the abject submission of the clergy in convocation, who were now prepared to accept any legislation that might be forced on them by the Crown. In the House of Lords the bishops still resisted, but the pressure was now so strong that the King carried all before him. Sir Thomas More surrendered the seals of office on May 13. Bishop Gardiner of Winchester, who had led the bishops in the House of Lords, retired in disgrace to his see; and the aged archbishop of Canterbury (Wareham), who had failed to give the bishops the lead they were looking for from their Primate, died in the autumn of that year. At the last moment he discharged his conscience by a final dignified, but ineffectual protest against any law, past or future, that might be derogatory to the Church's powers or that might tend to diminish the prerogatives and liberties of the metropolitan and primatial see of Canterbury.

Archbishop Cromer took no immediate part in these grave actions, which did not as yet directly affect the Church in Ireland. But the statute of *Præmunire*, that had sufficed to break the resistance of the clergy in England, contained implications that might well imperil every bishop and archbishop in Ireland. Archbishop Allen of Dublin became liable to its penalties for having acted as Wolsey's vice-legate, and was heavily fined for his offence in 1531.[1] The example of the English hierarchy in this crisis was not such as to inspire heroic conduct in a prelate who had once been royal chaplain to Henry VIII. When Cromer returned to Ireland in the summer or autumn of 1532, the political situation had been suddenly altered in favour of the Geraldine interest to which he was attached. But the situation of the Church in England was now desperate, and the outlook for an English-born prelate in Ireland was far from encouraging. Henry VIII had probably summoned Cromer to London in the autumn of 1530, so that he might see with his own eyes the fate that awaited any churchman rash enough to attempt to thwart his royal will. The Primate learned a lesson in practical politics during those two years that was not easily forgotten.

When Cromer went to England in October, 1530, Sir William Skeffington had just taken office as Lord Deputy and Kildare had returned from his first imprisonment in the Tower. During the summer of 1532 the Earl made his final

[1] *Letters and Papers* V, p. 657.

bid for the King's favour and for power in Ireland. He returned from London as Deputy in August of that year, and his victory over his rivals was made more complete by a change in the office of chancellor. Archbishop Allen had been chancellor since September, 1528. On July 5, 1532, he surrendered the seals of office to Primate Cromer, who was known to be a supporter of Kildare. The Geraldine interest was thus, for the moment at least, established in power.

An anonymous and undated report on the state of Ireland, which was sent to Thomas Cromwell at some time in 1533, contains the following unflattering account of Cromer's policy as chancellor. It is, of course, the report of an enemy, who was working for the overthrow of the Geraldine interest[1]:

"The Chaunceller, that nowe is, is of great unskylfullness, and nothing soo worthy to exercyse that rowme as his predecessor; but dredith soomoche the noble men there, that he shewith him self more lyker their chapelayn or parishe preste, then the Kinges Chaunceller; and for his opyn parcialitie, in all thErle of Kildares procedinges, many folkes doo put their right in suspence, taking that eleccion, rather than to jeopardie theym to the tryall of him."

This alliance between the English-born archbishop of Armagh and the great Anglo-Irish earl of Kildare was no doubt due in part to the Primate's opposition to Archbishop Allen who represented Wolsey's legatine jurisdiction in Ireland. But Wolsey had fallen from power in October, 1529, and it is not so easy to understand why the Primate should have risked the King's displeasure in 1532 by throwing in his lot so openly with Kildare. Like many others of his day, he may have believed that Kildare was the only man capable of holding Ireland for the King. There may have been also the hope that Kildare would be able to hold in check the increasingly active anti-papal minority on the King's council.

[1] *State Papers* II, p. 148.

We need not enter here into the details of the political situation in Ireland during the two years of Cromer's chancellorship; but one long report from the King's council must be mentioned. It was entrusted to the new master of the rolls, John Aleyn, for submission to the King.[1] The report is not dated, but it is later than July 9, 1533 (when Aleyn was made master of the rolls) and before the end of that year.

The council ordered their messenger to "instructe the Kingis Highnes of the grete decaie of this lande, which is so farre fallen into myserie, and brought into soche ruyne, that noither the inglish order, tonge ne habite been used, neither the Kingis lawes obeied above 20 miles in compasse." Unless the King finds some remedy for these disorders, "the litle place (being now obediente) shalbe shortelie brought to the same case as the residewe is." There follows a well-known analysis of the various abuses that have led to this almost total collapse of English power in Ireland: "the immoderate takeing of coyne and lyverey, without order, after mennes awne sensuall appetites"; the lack of English inhabitants, who are being supplanted everywhere by Irish tenants; the lack of sufficient armed protection for English houses and lands; the liberties of the great Lords in Ireland; the "black rents and tributes" which Irishmen have imposed on the King's subjects; "the committing of the governaunce of this lande to the lordes, native of the same"; the frequent change of Deputies; neglect in keeping the King's records, and the appointment of "onlerned" clerks to the King's courts. Finally, "oon of the gretest hurtes is, that the Kinge hath lost and gyven away his manours, lordshipes, fee farmes, custumes, and other his revenues, so as he hath not now wherof to mayn-teyne a Deputie, for defence of his subjectis."

Cromer's signature is the first of thirteen signatures appended to this remarkable document; and the same thirteen names appear at the foot of the "Articles for

[1] *State Papers* II, pp. 162-6. For convenience I use the spelling "Allen" for the archbishop, and "Aleyn" for the master of the rolls.

Reformation" which were submitted for the King's consideration together with the report of the council. But it would be wrong to infer that the chancellor was himself the moving spirit in the drafting of this report, which can have been little to the liking of Kildare and his supporters in Ireland. Cromer's signature is followed at the foot of each document by the signatures of John Allen, archbishop of Dublin, and Edward Staples, bishop of Meath. These two prelates belonged to the party in the King's council that was consistently opposed to the Geraldine interest. We may guess that the council's report is one of many signs that the Deputy's influence was being undermined in Dublin at this time. The chancellor's personal share in the drafting of this strong report was probably no more than a surrender to the pressure of forces beyond his control.

The Primate's position as chancellor in Ireland was thus becoming uneasy in the latter months of 1533. His difficulties were not lessened by the fact that these same months saw the final consummation of the breach between the King of England and the Holy See. Henry was secretly married to Anne Boleyn on January 25, 1533; and Cranmer was provided to the see of Canterbury by Clement VII on February 21. The new archbishop of Canterbury pronounced the sentence of royal divorce on April 23, and Anne was crowned as Queen of England on June 1. These open acts of defiance towards the Pope's authority in England were answered by the formal sentence of excommunication against Henry, which was pronounced on July 11, 1533, though the actual penalty did not take effect until the following September. Henceforth Primate Cromer, though he had not yet been guilty of any formal act of disloyalty towards the Holy See, was in the difficult position of representing the authority of an excommunicated King in his lordship of Ireland. His difficulties were not to grow less as the year 1534 followed 1533.

C.66 v. On March 15, 1533, the Primate heard an interesting case which was brought before his metropolitan court by the Observantine Friars Minor of Armagh and Galway. The Observantine friars were noted for their loyalty to the Holy See at this period, and they were soon to be counted as the most active opponents of King Henry's religious policy in Ireland. But their position in relation to the existing Irish communities of the Conventual Friars Minor was disputed. They themselves claimed their right, by virtue of papal bulls, to be recognised as ordinary members of the two Franciscan communities of Armagh and Galway. The Conventual friars of these two houses resisted this claim, and had obtained a sentence in their favour from two Irish ecclesiastical judges. The Observantine friars disputed the jurisdiction of these judges, and appealed from their decision to the Holy See. Meanwhile, and in accordance with long-established custom, they appealed for protection to the Primate pending the hearing of the appeal in Rome. The Primate accepted their appeal and issued tuitorial letters on their behalf on March 15. The Conventual friars of Armagh and Galway were ordered to admit the Observantine friars to their houses, and " to such possession as is in accordance with their status as mendicant friars " until the Holy See should otherwise decide.

Apart from its interest as throwing light on the history of the Observantine movement in Ireland, this document raises an interesting question of general policy. During these very weeks Henry VIII was forcing through Parliament at Westminster an act forbidding appeals to Rome from the sentence of an English court. When he accepted this appeal in the spring of 1533, Primate Cromer was not defying the King's authority in Ireland, for the English Act had no force outside the kingdom of England. But he must have been painfully aware that a breach between himself and the King was inevitable, if he continued to rule his diocese according to the principles and customs that had hitherto directed his policy as Primate of All Ireland. And the news from England was not encouraging.

The Primate was active throughout his diocese during the first half of 1533, though his duties as chancellor must

have involved continual absences in Dublin. Archdeacon
Cormac Roth, who was still the Primate's trusted official,
appears frequently as acting in the Primate's name during
these months. The Primate presided in person over a
C.68 synod of the English clergy at St. Peter's, Drogheda, on
July 1, 1533. Some local abuses were then corrected, and
the usual routine business of the synod was transacted.

C.69-70. On July 4, 1533, the Primate issued tuitorial letters on behalf of Richard Comptor, the English-born abbot of Mellifont who was later to surrender his abbey to the King's officers in 1539.[1] The document throws a sadly disappointing light on the last days of a house that had once been the greatest Cistercian monastery in Ireland. Since the middle of the fourteenth century the English had succeeded in forcing a series of English-born abbots on what was the oldest Irish foundation; and the same policy had been successful in many other Irish Cistercian houses. The history of this great order in Ireland during the later Middle Ages makes sad reading for those who remember the days of St. Bernard and St. Malachy.

The year 1534 marks a turning point in Primate Cromer's career, as also in the general course of Anglo-Irish history. Kildare had been summoned to England in the autumn of 1533, there to answer complaints which had been received in London from his opponents in Ireland, chief among them being the former chancellor, Archbishop Allen. For a time Kildare was able to plead the effects of a wound he had received during the siege of Birr Castle in the summer of that year. But the King was insistent, and the Earl finally set sail for England; leaving his son, Lord Offaly—better known as Silken Thomas—as his vice-deputy in Ireland. News was soon brought back to Ireland that Kildare was a prisoner in the Tower of London. News came soon after—false news—that the Earl was dead. There followed the famous session of the King's council in Dublin at which the Lord Thomas threw down the sword of

[1] See below, p. 106.

state and renounced his allegiance to the King of England. Primate Cromer presided over that session, which was held in the chapter-house of St. Mary's Abbey, Dublin, on June 11, 1534. Stanihurst has left us a narrative of the scene, and we can well believe the substance of his story. The Primate was almost overpowered by his own emotion as he begged the young noble not to go forward with his rash project.[1] He knew well how fatally Lord Thomas was playing into the hands of his unscrupulous enemies in Dublin. If Silken Thomas led the Irish in open revolt, the Pope's authority, no less than the King's authority, must be placed in great peril.

His appeal was in vain. A few weeks of armed revolt were followed by the attempted flight of Archbishop Allen from Dublin, his failure to escape across the sea, and his murder by some of the supporters of Silken Thomas at Artane on July 27 or 28, 1534. Neither side could now afford to look back. The Primate could do no less than concur in the sentence of excommunication that was pronounced soon after the murder against all who were held to be guilty of the crime, including the Lord Thomas himself. A text of this ecclesiastical sentence has been preserved among the State Papers in London.[2] It is a copy of the document sent from Dublin to the lieutenant of the Tower in London—apparently for the purpose of showing it to Kildare who was still a prisoner in the Tower, an old and broken man. The terms of the sentence are very savage and the document reads more like a Government proclamation, drafted for the purpose of striking terror into the hearts of those who were still wavering, than an ecclesiastical sentence. It is not clear who published this censure. Cromer was still chancellor, but he is not mentioned in the document. The text itself states that the sentence has been pronounced "by the kepers of the spirituall juris-

[1] Stanihurst's narrative was included by Holinshed in his *Chronicle* (ed. 1808) VI, p. 289-92. It has been used by Stuart in his *Historical Memoirs of Armagh* (ed. Coleman), p. 137.

[2] *State Papers* II, pp. 217-9.

diccion of the Metropolitan See of Dublin, the same See being voyde." Who nominated these *custodes spiritualitatis* of the vacant primatial see? An unpublished document from the collection of old deeds of the Guild of St. Anne, Dublin, makes it probable that the dean of St. Patrick's and the prior of Christ Church were the *de jure* custodians of the spiritualities of the see during time of vacancy.[1] This formal censure was thus issued in their name, though they had probably little to do with the composition of the actual text.

Soon after the news of the murder of Archbishop Allen had reached England, the King dismissed Cromer from his office as chancellor. Lord Trimleston was named his successor on August 16, 1534.[2] But the Primate did not surrender the seals of office until the autumn of that year, as
C.80v. is proved by an entry in his register for October 14 and 15, 1534. Four of the "Old English" nobility then presented themselves before the Primate as chancellor in his manor at Termonfeghin, and sought to exonerate themselves from a penalty that had been imposed on them. They were Robert Plunket, Lord Dunsany; James Taaffe of Talonstown; Richard Hadsor of Keppok; and Walter Chever of Maston. Unfortunately the entry in Cromer's register gives no details as to the penalty from which they sought to be discharged, nor how they had incurred it. But it seems probable that these four gentlemen of the Pale had incurred the King's displeasure by some action taken during the crisis of the rebellion of Silken Thomas. The Primate had been dismissed from his post as chancellor two months before the date of these visits, but he had not yet surrendered the seal. He was probably not sorry to be able to make one last use of his legal powers to assist these four gentlemen in their hour of trouble. He himself was already a sick man, and

[1] Royal Irish Academy, Deeds of the Guild of St. Anne, no. 719 (August 17, 1511).

[2] *Letters and Papers* VII, p. 1122.

Master John Aleyn was doing most of the chancellor's work in Dublin at this time.[1]

An entry for October 1, 1534, lets us see that the Primate was anxious to reward his archdeacon, Cormac Roth, for all that he had done to assist him in the administration of his diocese during the past eleven years. By letters patent issued from his manor at Termonfeghin on that date, Cromer united the rectory of St. Nicholas, Heynestown, which was then vacant through the death of Master Charles O Kaan, to the archdeaconry of Armagh during Cormac Roth's lifetime. The grant was made "in view of the archdeacon's great merits," so as to enable him to maintain his position in the diocese in a manner suitable to his dignity. This personal favour is all the more noteworthy since the archdeacon was already a marked man in the eyes of the King's officials. Writing from Dublin on December 26, 1534, John Aleyn, master of the rolls, reported that "the official of the bishop of Armachan," like the archdeacon of Meath and the dean of Kildare, was one of the "learned counsellors" who were then supporting Silken Thomas in his hazardous adventure.[2] Primate Cromer was thus doing honour to a man whom a more cautious prelate might have been inclined to overlook in the crisis of 1534. C. 79.

Cormac Roth's own family connections are uncertain. The family of Roth was, of course, well known in the city of Kilkenny from the fourteenth century onwards; but one name occurs in the State Papers of Henry VIII's reign which suggests a personal link between the successful archdeacon of Armagh and the unfortunate Geraldine prince. When Silken Thomas had been Henry's prisoner in the Tower of London for more than a year, he wrote a letter to his "trusty and welbelovyd servant John Rothe," in which he lifts the veil for a moment and lets us see the depth of his own humiliation. "I never had eny mony syns I cam in to

[1] Aleyn's letter, requesting payment for his services when he was acting as Chancellor for the Primate "during his sickness" is in *Letters and Papers* IX, no. 147 (2).

[2] *State Papers*, II, p. 221.

pryson, but a nobull," he writes to his loyal friend; "nor I have had nothyr hosyn, dublet, nor shoys, nor shyrt, but on [one]; nor eny other garment, but a syngyll fryse gowne. I have gone wolward [clothed in wool] and barefote, and barelegyd dyverse tymes (whan ytt hath not ben very warme); and so I shuld have don styll, and now, but that pore prysoners, of ther gentylnes, hathe symtyme gevyn me old hosyn, and shoys, and old shyrtes."[1] Was John Rothe, to whom this pathetic appeal was sent in 1536, a kinsman of the archdeacon who gave Silken Thomas support and counsel in 1534? The friend to whom the imprisoned Earl wrote with such confidence from his dungeon in 1536 is most probably to be identified as "John Rowth of Ballynesragh" near the Bog of Allen, who sent messages of encouragement to the Geraldine leaders in 1539.[2] Was the archdeacon a member of this family?

From the entry which records his collation to the
C. 56. archdeaconry of Armagh in 1530, we learn that Cormac Roth was a native of the diocese of Meath. William Roth, most probably a kinsman, was vicar of Dunboyne and chaplain to the bishop of Meath in 1495; he was the official of the bishop of Meath in 1519-20, and again in 1529.[3] There is more than one townland of Ballynasrah in the neighbourhood of Clara and Rahan, within the diocese of Meath; and Father John MacErlean has called my attention to a "Graigrooth" in the parish of Cloncurry near Maynooth Castle. Beyond these few facts, we have nothing to guide us; but it would be pleasant to think that the archdeacon of Armagh was obeying an instinct of ancient loyalty when he came forward publicly as a supporter of Silken Thomas at this moment of crisis and danger.

[1] *State Papers* II, p. 402-3. [2] ibid. III, p. 140, note.
[3] Octavian's Register, fo. 339; and below, p. 128.

PART II

THE DIOCESE OF ARMAGH

I. DIOCESAN ORGANISATION

The diocese of Armagh had felt the effect of the Norman invasion within a generation of Strongbow's arrival in Ireland.[1] Almost half of its territory had been permanently occupied by the new settlers from England, and town-life had been developed in the modern county of Louth very much on the English model. From the thirteenth century onwards—and very specially from the early fourteenth century, when a long series of English or Anglo-Irish archbishops of Armagh begins some years before the death of Edward I, the diocese was recognised as being permanently divided into two almost evenly balanced parts. In the northern territory, where O Neill still ruled unchallenged, Irish customs and Irish speech prevailed, and the clergy of this area were commonly spoken of in the official records of the diocese as *clerus inter Hibernicos*. This territory corresponded with the modern county of Armagh, the south-eastern portion of the county of Tyrone, and a small portion of the county of Derry. For ecclesiastical purposes it was divided into the two deaneries of Erthyr (the modern Orior) and Tullaghog. In the southern section of the diocese, which corresponded roughly with the modern county of Louth, English customs and English speech prevailed, at least in the towns like Drogheda, Dundalk, Ardee, Louth and Carlingford. The clergy of these parishes

[1] There is no satisfactory account of the medieval diocese of Armagh. Chancellor Leslie's *Armagh Clergy and Parishes* contains much useful information, but is limited in its scope.

were known as *clerus inter Anglos*, and they were organised more or less on the model of an archdeaconry in a contemporary English diocese. The Irish name Oirghialla (Oriel or Uriel in the English documents) was often used for this territory, but it should be remembered that the former Irish kingdom of Oirghialla had been very much more extensive than the modern county of Louth.

This dual character of the diocese led inevitably to certain peculiarities in its organisation. The Primate himself was always of English speech and nationality, if not of English birth, from the death of David O Hiraghty in 1346 to the provision of the Italian Primate Octavian in 1479. With the exception of occasional visits to the cathedral city of Armagh, these English or Anglo-Irish Primates rarely went outside the territory *inter Anglos*. Their registers show that they frequently visited the neighbouring diocese of Meath in person; but Meath, like Louth, lay well within the Anglo-Irish march. They seem to have delegated their right of visitation in the dioceses *inter Hibernicos* to Irish-born commissaries, and were frequently content to nominate the bishop of the diocese as their commissary for the purpose of a formal visitation.[1] The Primate had two archiepiscopal manors within the territory *inter Anglos*. One of these was at Dromiskin, about five miles south of Dundalk. The other was at Termonfeghin, just four miles north of Drogheda. Both lay near the sea-coast, and were conveniently situated for purposes of administration. But the register of Primate Swayne (1418-39) shows that this Anglo-Irish Primate had abandoned the manor of Dromiskin, which was commonly used by his predecessors of the fourteenth century. The registers of John Prene and John Mey (1439-43; 1444-56) have not yet been calendared, but the few surviving records of Primate Bole (1457-71) suggest that this English-born Primate was more venturesome. He visited Armagh in

[1] See my article on "Canterbury and Armagh in the Fifteenth Century," in *Studies* (December, 1943), pp. 502-4.

1466, and spent several weeks there (including the Christmas feasts) in the winter of 1469-70.[1]

Primate Octavian seems to have been a rare visitor to his cathedral city; almost all his extant letters and other documents are dated from Termonfeghin. Primate Cromer, fresh from his home in Kent and from life in London, seems to have imitated his example.

For most practical purposes the parish church of St. Peter's, Drogheda, served as a pro-cathedral for the English-speaking portion of the diocese. The annual synods of the clergy *inter Anglos* were commonly held here, and the triennial provincial councils were also held at St. Peter's. Many of the Primates of the fifteenth century were buried in this church; John Colton, who died in 1404, Nicholas Fleming, John Swayne and Octavian.[2] John Prene is said to have been buried in the parish church of Termonfeghin, and it is possible that Cromer, who spent the last years of his life as an invalid in his manor, was also buried there.

The Primates had a small manse within the walls of Drogheda, where they probably lodged during the sessions of a provincial council or the like—though their manor at Termonfeghin lay so close to the town that they could easily come in and go out again within the same day. On
September 3, 1483, Octavian, with the consent of the dean O.317 v.
and chapter of Armagh who had just been present at the provincial council of that year, rented this manse, which is described as "within the gate of St. Lawrence of the town of Drogheda," to Peter John (commonly called Perote John) his servant, in reward for his past faithful services. The Primate reserved for his own personal use the principal room in the house (*camera nostra maior*), and the chapel. An orchard must have been attached to this manse, for it is named in a rental that has been copied into Dowdall's register.[3] As late as 1557 old Sir John Plunket, lord of

[1] See above, p. 3.
[2] Leslie, pp. 3-4.
[3] Printed by Fr. Murray in *L.A.J.* VI (1928), p. 223.

Bewley, was able to bear witness to the Primate's right of
D.40. ownership in this manse. As a young boy, so he testified before Dowdall's court, he and other young boys of his age used to steal apples from the neighbouring orchard "which lay to the west of the wall of the Primate's manse in Drogheda." Primate Dowdall, who was then making a valiant effort to recover properties that had been lost or dilapidated during his years of exile under Edward VI, must have blessed the old man for his kindly memory of that orchard.

The dean of Armagh ranked next to the Primate, and must have been in practice a very much greater man in the eyes of the clergy *inter Hibernicos*. So far as they can be traced in the registers the deans were always native Irishmen during the fourteenth and fifteenth centuries, and many of them bear names which show that they belonged to the principal ecclesiastical families of O Neill's land. Thomas MacCawell (whose name is spelt Machamayl in the Roman record of his provision in 1477) was dean for about ten years (1477-87).[1] He was succeeded by Peter O Molloy (O Mulmoy, etc.) who was provided to the deanery by Innocent VIII on March 26, 1487. The new dean had been prior of the Culdees of Armagh for the past eight years, and the Pope, at his petition, now united the priory to the deanery for as long as Peter should hold the two offices.[2] On his death Edmund MacCawell was provided to both deanery and priory by Julius II shortly before June 9, 1505, when the new dean bound himself for payment of the annates due for each office.[3] Edmund MacCawell remained dean of Armagh and prior of the Culdees for the next forty-five years. He died in 1550: we shall meet his name again in the story of what happened after Primate Cromer's death.[4]

[1] Costello, p. 8. Thomas was a priest of the diocese of Clogher before this date; he received a canonry in Armagh with the prebend of Clonfeacle in this same year (Costello, p. 9).

[2] C.P.L. XIV (not yet published); Costello, p. 9.

[3] Costello, p. 12.

[4] See below, p. 268-9.

Some notion of the pre-eminence of the dean's position *inter Hibernicos* during the reigns of Henry VII and Henry VIII may be formed from the sworn statements of the local jurors who were asked to testify on these points before the Inquisition of 1609. On that occasion the jurors of Armagh presented upon oath " that the dean of the cathedral church of Armagh for the time being is, in right of his deanery, parson of the several parish churches of Loghgelly, Killmore, Dromkree and Leegloyse in the said barony of O Neylan, and both parson and vicar of the two towns of Kilchrewe in Taoghey aforesaid, and parson of the Luminaries in Clancoughie, and vicar of Armagh and Clanawle."[1] It is not easy at first sight to identify some of these place-names. Loughgilly, Kilmore and Drumcree are still modern parishes. Leegloyse is a curious corruption of the Irish name *Leathbhaile-eaglais*, which is still used as an alternative name for the parish of Loughgall.[2] " Clancoughie " is obviously the old Irish monastery of Clonconchy near Lisnadill, but I can offer no explanation of the very curious benefice described in this statement as " the parsonage of the Luminaries in Clancoughie." " Clanawle " is another name for the parish of Eglish. I have not been able to identify " the two towns of Kilchrewe."

The prior of the Culdees of Armagh seems to have ranked second to the dean of Armagh in the cathedral chapter. His benefices are enumerated by the jurors of 1609 as follows: " The said prior of the said vicars choral [who had taken the place of the Culdees since the suppression of the monasteries] is, in right of his place, parson of the parish church of Creggan in the said Fiues [Fews], and parson of the parish churches of Derrynaoes, Tynon, Mounterheny and Mullaghbragh, and vicar of Leegloyse in the barony of O Neylan aforesaid." Here again Creggan, Derrynoose, Tynan and Mullaghbrack are modern parishes. We shall

[1] Inquisitions: Appendix (Armagh)—towards the end of the long sworn statement.

[2] Leslie, p. 351.

meet " Mounterheny " again when we examine the evidence as to the Primate's lands in this Irish territory.[1] The name is repeated in a later statement (*c.* 1635) of these same lands which is now preserved in Lambeth Library among the Wentworth MSS. Here the benefices of the prior are defined as follows: " The rectories of Donoughmore, Mullabrack, Cregan, Derrinous, Tynan, Mounterkenny, Clonfeacle with the vicarage of Lavallyeglish and tithes of ten villages in Kilsleve . . . were appertinent to the priory of the Colideans, or (as the Irish call them) Gallideans or God's Cockes in Armagh."[2] Two additional rectories (Donoughmore and Clonfeacle) seem to have been added to the prior's benefices between 1609 and 1635.

If the prior's benefices are added to the larger group of the dean's benefices, as occurred during the two long lifetimes of Dean Peter O Molloy and Dean Edmund MacCawell (1487-1550), it is obvious that the holder of these two dignities must have been overwhelmingly the most important prelate in the Irish portion of the diocese of Armagh. To Irish eyes he must have appeared the true representative of the ancient rights of the church of Armagh, whilst the distant English or Italian Primate at Drogheda was little more than a stranger in these northern parishes. It is thus all the more to be regretted that no record has survived of the acts of the Irish deans and their Irish colleagues in the cathedral chapter. Edmund MacCawell's name recurs from time to time in the diocesan registers, but we depend on a chance obit for knowledge of his personal character.[3] He it was, in fact, who ruled the Irish section of the diocese through the difficult period of Henry VIII's reign. Yet we can say little more of him than that he was a member of a family which had given several bishops to the diocese of Clogher, and which was always well represented in the two chapters of Armagh and Clogher during the fifteenth and sixteenth centuries.

[1] See below, p. 98-9.

[2] Printed from the Wentworth MSS. by Leslie, p. 382.

[3] See below, p. 269.

The priory of the Culdees disappears from the diocesan records after the suppression of the Irish monasteries, and Edmund MacCawell had thus no direct successor in this dignity. But the benefice survived for a time under a new title, and was then merged in the new dignity of precentor. Patrick Dorelle or Darelle is mentioned in Dowdall's register as *cantor ecclesiæ Armachanæ* on July 5, 1558. We have seen that the benefices formerly held by the prior of the Culdees were held by the "prior of the vicars choral" at the time of the Inquisition of 1609. John Symonds was admitted as precentor in 1617.[1] But by that time a new era had begun in the history of the diocese. Edmund MacCawell had in fact, no successor as prior of the Culdees.

All the known chancellors of Armagh during the fourteenth and fifteenth centuries seem to have been of Irish birth. Donald O Culean was chancellor from *c.* 1478-1491.
He was granted this benefice by Octavian *c.* 1478-9, when O.125; 326.
he was still administering the diocese as nuncio. On April 30, 1482, he succeeded in ousting Dean Thomas MacCawell from his rectory of Clonfeacle, and got confirmation from Sixtus IV of a permanent union of this rectory to the chancellorship.[2] During the absentee rule of Primate
Kite (December 27, 1520) Master Robert Tatayd (probably C.7 v.
Taaffe) was admitted as chancellor by Bishop Hugh Inge of Meath, who was then administering the diocese for the absent Primate. The name of Master Robert's successor is not known. The Inquisition of 1609 tells us that the chancellor was also vicar of Kilmore and Drumcree; and that "in right of his said dignity or place" he was also "seised of and in certain houses and parcels of land within the limits of the town and city of Armagh."

The treasurers of Armagh seem also to have been of Irish birth throughout the medieval period. James
O Fallagan was treasurer in July, 1484. Matthew MacKeon O.317.
was treasurer when he inducted Master Robert Tatayd as C.7 v.

[1] Leslie, p. 33.
[2] C.P.L. XIII, p. 795.

C.28 v. chancellor in 1520. He had died before October 28, 1527, when Primate Cromer collated Eugene MacEgyrr to the treasurership. From the Inquisition of 1609 we learn that the treasurer of Armagh was, in right of his dignity, " both parson and vicar of the parish churches of Clankarny-owtragh and Clankarny-itragh." These two churches of Upper and Lower Clankarny were situated in the area between the modern Tanderagee and Poyntzpass.[1]

The Inquisition of 1609 tells us that " there were in ancient time sixteen prebends of the said cathedral church of Armagh ; and that eight of the said prebends received their livings out of the English Pale, and the other eight of the said prebends had their livings out of the county of Tyrone." This evenly balanced proportion of eight prebends *inter Anglos* and eight prebends *inter Hibernicos* may, perhaps, have represented an ideal chapter of Armagh ; but the names of these sixteen prebends are most uncertain, and it is doubtful whether such a fully constituted chapter ever existed in fact. In his *Armagh Clergy and Parishes*, Canon Leslie suggests that the full chapter was even larger in medieval times. He adds to the sixteen prebendaries the dean, precentor, chancellor, treasurer and archdeacon, and the whole community of the Culdees of Armagh.[2] This reconstruction is certainly incorrect. There is no evidence that the Culdees, apart from their prior, were members of the chapter ; and the prior (as we have seen) held the place later held by the precentor. The other dignitaries held one or other of the prebends as their living. Chancellor Donald O Culean, for example, held the prebend of Clonfeacle ; and
C.56. Cormac Roth, as archdeacon, held the prebend of Kene. Prebends were constantly being formed and reformed by some new union of parishes, as is plain from the Roman documents of this period. In theory there may have been eight prebends of the chapter *inter Hibernicos ;* but we need

[1] See below, p. 98. Clonkarney is south and west of the village of Markethill. The parish is now known as Kilcluney.

[2] Leslie, p. 31.

not conclude that there were always eight prebendaries.

Passing from the northern Irish territory of the diocese to the territory within the English Pale, we find ourselves in a new world. Here the Primate rules the diocese in person, with the help of an archdeacon and an official—whose chief function was to preside over the ordinary sessions of the Primate's metropolitan court. The archdeacons were almost invariably men of English speech and training, if not of English birth. When Primate Octavian took over the administration of the diocese in 1477, Henry Corkeran was archdeacon and Thomas Hunt the Primate's official. A serious dispute between the Primate and his archdeacon seems to have ended in the resignation or death of Archdeacon Corkeran soon after 1491.[1] The situation during the next few years is obscure, but James White was archdeacon during Octavian's last years, and Master Michael Golding was acting as the Primate's official. Archdeacon O.370. White died *c.* 1530, and his place was taken by Master Cormac Roth—who had been acting as the Primate's official and as president of his metropolitan court since 1523.[2] Patrick Galtrym, formerly prior of St. Leonard's, Dundalk, became archdeacon on Roth's death in 1539 or 1540, whilst the future Primate, George Dowdall, took over Roth's duties as the aged Primate's official and vicar general.[3]

The last three archdeacons of Armagh before Cromer's death—James White, Cormac Roth and Patrick Galtrym— C.56-7; D.28v. were also vicars of the parish church of Termonfeghin. This church was not strictly impropriate to the archdeaconry, for the advowson of Termonfeghin was held by the prior of St. Mary's, Louth, down to the time of the dissolution of the Irish monasteries.[4] It should be noted that the Inquisition of 1609 makes no mention of any benefice held by the archdeacons of Armagh in the Irish portion of the diocese, with which alone the commissioners were concerned at the time of this Inquisition. As compared with the other

[1] See above, p. 16. [2] See above, p. 56.

[3] Leslie, p. 49: and below, p. 254. [4] Leslie, p. 421.

dignities of the chapter of Armagh, the archdeaconry was not of ancient origin. The first archdeacon whose name we know is Luke Netterville, who seems to have become archdeacon a few years before his own election as Primate in 1217.[1] Luke Netterville was the first archbishop of Armagh who was not of Irish birth ; and the archdeaconry, whatever its first beginnings may have been, seems to have been associated with foreign interests throughout its later history.

According to the Inquisition of 1609, there must have been eight prebends in the English-speaking portion of the diocese, at least in theory. Annual synods of the clergy *inter Anglos* were held in the early summer of each year, usually at St. Peter's, Drogheda ; and convocations of the same clergy were held in the autumn, usually to nominate proctors for collecting the Primate's dues. There seems to be no evidence at all that the whole chapter ever met as a single body. Synods of the clergy *inter Hibernicos* were, no doubt, summoned from time to time by the dean at Armagh, but no record of their proceedings has survived. We get one curious glimpse into the relations between these two distinct bodies within a single chapter in an answer which Primate Swayne sent to the Lord Deputy in 1427. The Primate had been cited to attend a forthcoming royal council in Dublin, with the customary proctors of his chapter. He excuses himself, owing to the traditional insistence on the Primate's right to have his cross carried before him within the province of Dublin. As was customary, he sent two English proctors to represent him in Dublin, and adds a few words of explanation to account for the absence of Irish proctors : " As for the dean and chapter of our church of Armagh, they are mere Irishmen and dwell amongst the Irish (*sunt meri Hibernici et inter Hibernicos conversantes*). They are not accustomed to attend royal

[1] Netterville had at least one Irish predecessor : see the letter of Innocent III, dated September, 1202, in Migne, *P.L.* 214, col. 1060 ; and King John's letter of the same year in *Cal. Doc. Ireland*, I, no. 168.

councils, nor is it fitting that the council's secrets should be revealed to them."[1]

Sunt meri Hibernici et inter Hibernicos conversantes: that terse phrase of an archbishop of Armagh who had himself been born in the border county of Kildare sums up a whole philosophy of life. The secrets of the King's council were most certainly not to be revealed to an Irish chapter, whose allegiance must always have been to O Neill, not to the King of England. But this fundamental dualism within the chapter of Armagh must have affected a great mass of purely ecclesiastical business as well as the political questions that concerned the council in Dublin. Joint meetings of two groups so distinct as were the clergy of Armagh *inter Hibernicos* and the clergy of Armagh *inter Anglos* would have been difficult to organise and control. In what language would the business of the chapter be transacted? Some official means of communication must have existed, by which the clergy of one portion of the diocese might be made aware of what was being done in the other portion. But the Primate himself probably knew little of what was being done by the dean and chapter in Armagh; and the dean and chapter very probably knew less and cared less as to what was being done by the Primate, his archdeacon and official and the rest of the English clergy within the English Pale. From the Primate's point of view, it was perhaps best so—provided that his customary rents and dues and tithes were being collected by his Irish official in Armagh, and forwarded to him in Drogheda. The dean and chapter were, from their point of view, content to maintain the existing order—provided that O Neill or his followers did not make life too difficult for them on the border.

The absence of any Acts Book of the dean and chapter of Armagh deprives us of information that would have been most welcome as to the organisation of grammar schools in either section of the diocese. In England, where diocesan records were kept on a more elaborate system, one of the

[1] *Swayne's Register* (ed. Chart), p. 53; Leslie, p. 31.

chancellor's main functions was to issue licenses for approved schoolmasters in the diocese. Entries recording the issue or confirmation of such licenses are frequent in the chapter-books of the medieval period. No information of this kind survives in the Armagh registers. Father Murray has made the very plausible suggestion that grammar schools were maintained in connection with the chantry foundations for which there is abundant evidence in Louth and Meath during the fifteenth century.[1] But his own very valuable study of the Ardee chantry, as to which documentary evidence is unusually plentiful, has failed to produce any direct proof of the existence of a grammar school at Ardee during this period[2]; and the foundation-charters of some of the Meath chantries, which have been preserved on the Irish Statute Rolls, make no mention of any duty that would suggest the existence of organised schools.[3] A collegiate building was erected at Ardee shortly before 1487 by the principal chaplain of that foundation, Walter Verdon; and it is clear that the various chaplains of the church were expected to reside there. Similar foundations existed at Drogheda, Dundalk, Termonfeghin and Stabannon—possibly elsewhere in the English portion of the diocese; and we may conjecture, though proof is lacking, that some of these resident chaplains were expected to act as schoolmasters for boys who sang in the chantry-choir.

The Primate's metropolitan court met regularly in Drogheda, and its president was usually the Primate's official or vicar general, or some other priest of the diocese who had obtained his doctorate in canon law. The court-book which is now bound as the first half of the volume known as "Cromer's Register" contains the proceedings of this metropolitan court during the last years of the absentee rule of Primate Kite.[4] Numerous documents from the

[1] See his note in *L.A.J.* VII (1932), p. 554.

[2] "The Ancient Chantries of Co. Louth," in *L.A.J.* IX (1939), pp. 184-208.

[3] *Statute Rolls: Edward IV*, Part I, p. 323 (Dunsany); 455 (Dunshaughlin); Part II, p. 233 (Skreen); 577 (Greenoge).

[4] See above, p. 47-8.

archives of this same metropolitan court survive as loose leaves in the volume known as "Octavian's Register," and it would be well worth while for some legal student to take these surviving records and make a special study of ecclesiastical law as it was administered in the Anglo-Irish Pale on the eve of the great religious revolution under Henry VIII. The court-book for the years 1518-22 contains no entries of law-suits between Irishmen resident in the northern or Irish portion of the diocese. This fact alone would make us suspect the existence of a separate court, subordinate to the Primate's court, for the territory *inter Hibernicos*. Actually we find one or two occasional allusions to this separate Irish court in the registers of Cromer and Dowdall.

On September 28, 1531, Cormac Roth—then acting C.60.
as the Primate's vicar general owing to Cromer's absence in England—appointed Senekyn MacDewyn the Primate's official in Armagh, with power to hear and decide matrimonial suits. Master Eugene MacGuinness is also named as Senekyn's colleague; but either of the two has power to decide a case in the absence of his colleague, or in case his colleague should fail in his duty. Primate Dowdall issued a
similar commission to Senekyn's successor, Dermot D.25.
MacDewyn, on December 19, 1543. Here the official's commission is clearly defined as extending throughout the whole deanery of Erthyr (Orior) as well as in the city of Armagh. He is given full power to consider, determine and finish all matrimonial cases in this area, and to exercise and expedite all things that are known to pertain to the duty of the Primate's official. Dermot MacDewyn, like his predecessor, Senekyn, probably had a colleague in this office. His jurisdiction was limited to the city of Armagh and the deanery of Erthyr. Presumably a second official had similar jurisdiction for the deanery of Tullaghog.

The full extent of the duties of this Irish official in Armagh will be more easily understood when we have examined the very complicated holdings and revenues of the Primate in his diocesan territory *inter Hibernicos*.

2. THE PRIMATE'S LANDS AND REVENUES

No detailed study of the Primate's lands, in his own diocese and in his various suffragan dioceses, has yet been attempted. The present sketch is no more than an outline of the subject, and is concerned mainly with those lands and revenues which happen to be mentioned in the registers of Octavian, Cromer and Dowdall.[1]

So far as English law could establish his position, a very full confirmation of the Primate's feudal rights in all the lordships and manors of his archbishopric may be found in a charter which Edward IV granted to Primate Bole at Drogheda on February 9, 1467. Parliament had met in Drogheda a few days earlier, and the Primate seems to have taken advantage of this assembly to obtain a formal confirmation of his legal rights, which was witnessed by the archbishop of Dublin (Michael Tregury), the bishop of Meath (William Sherwood), the bishop of Kildare (Richard Lang), with the Earls of Desmond and Kildare and two local knights, Sir T. Plunket and Sir R. Dowdall. The charter enumerates all the customary feudal rights of the period, and makes special mention of a weekly market at Armagh, Inishkeen, Termonfeghin and Nobber; and the grant of a pillory in Termonfeghin, Dromiskin, Nobber and Clogherhead. This charter was formally inspected and attested at Drogheda on June 1, 1558, within a few weeks of Primate Dowdall's death; and a copy has thus been preserved in Dowdall's register.[2]

[1] I have used the Inquisitions of 1609 as being the most vivid description of the Primate's position during the medieval period; but students who wish for more precise details should consult the charter of 18 James I, by which the King, having accepted the Protestant Primate's surrender of all his lands, re-granted them to him in detail: see the *Calendar of Patent Rolls* (*Ireland*) *of James I*, pp. 477-9.

[2] Father Murray has printed a very inadequate summary of this charter in *L.A.J.* VII (1929), p. 82; and has dated it wrongly to February 10, 1558.

Apart from his two manors at Dromiskin and Termonfeghin, the Primate does not seem to have been an extensive land-holder within the parishes of the English Pale. The most important source of his revenue from this portion of his diocese seems to have been the annual collection known as the "Dues of St. Patrick" (*Officium S. Patricii*). The registers contain frequent entries concerning the collectors of these dues, who were apparently nominated by the Primate in March or April of each year. The collection was made by rural deaneries and extended to the diocese of Meath as well as the diocese of Armagh. In 1533, for example, Cromer nominated Dermitius Dungan of Skreen as C.67. collector for the deaneries of Duleek, Ratoath and Skreen, with an assessment of 15 marks and "the fee of the court." William Kyraty of Trim was nominated for the deanery of Trim, with an assessment of seven marks; Peter Leyns of Knock for the deaneries of Clonard, Fore, Ardnurcher, Loughsewdy, Mullingar and "the bishopric of Clonard," with an assessment of 17 marks; John McLaghlin for the deaneries of Drogheda, Ardee and Dundalk, with an assessment of 18 marks; and Richard Ledwich of Kells for the deaneries of Kells and Slane, with an assessment of 9 marks. These deaneries are grouped differently in the entry for 1535. Here Kells and Slane are again rented to Richard Ledwich; C.85 v. and Duleek, Skreen and Ratoath to Dermitius O Donnelan, who seems to be identical with Dermitius Dungan of 1533. But the deanery of Fore is rented separately to Morianus O Huggin, whilst the deaneries of Trim, Loughsewdy and Mullingar are rented to Gelacius O Moran of Rathconnell.

Since these entries invariably describe this annual arrangement as *Locatio Officii S. Patricii*, we must presume that the collectors nominated by the Primate were allowed a commission on their collections. The nature of these collections is defined in an interesting entry for 1540, when D.9. Dowdall was acting as vicar general for the aged Primate Cromer, and was apparently reorganising this annual collection. In a special commission to Dermicius O Donnelan for the deaneries of Skreen, Duleek and Ratoath, the Primate

gives his collector power to seek, levy and receive all first-born of cattle and first-fruits of crops and fatted beasts (*martos*) and the principal quarter of each animal that has been set aside (*nominati*) for the blessed apostle and patron of Ireland. A deanery of Ardagh is included in the annual
D.16; 20; 23. entries of Dowdall's register—an addition which suggests that Dowdall was renewing some ancient claim in territory that was adjacent to the western section of Meath diocese.

These collections were obviously intended for the maintenance of the Primate as "coarb of Patrick," and probably went back to very ancient times in the history of
O.412v. the Irish Church. One entry in Octavian's register tells us that this Italian Primate waived his personal claim to the "Dues of St. Patrick" for the year 1509. The dean and chapter had represented to him that the fabric of the cathedral church was in need of repairs, and the Primate made them a grant of these dues on condition that they were solely applied to the fabric, adornment and use of this church.

The muniment room of the Armagh Diocesan Registry contains an ancient rent-roll, which dates from about 1620 A.D.[1] From this rent-roll we learn that the Protestant Primates of the early seventeenth century owned various holdings in Meath: the rectory of Athboy, the two manors of Kilmoone and Nobber, some land at Duleek and a house with an orchard at Trim.[2] A survey of *c.* 1605-7 made by the Protestant Bishop Montgomery of Derry lets us know that the Primate still claimed lands in the O Cahan country at Clooney and elsewhere in the diocese.[3] A note from a lost section of Swayne's register proves that the Primates of the early fifteenth century still claimed lands in Tuam.[4] This list of outlying holdings could probably be very much extended; but the Primate's main holdings were undoubt-

[1] Printed in *Archivium Hibernicum*, VIII (1941), pp. 99-120.

[2] Loc. cit., pp. 117-8; see also R. C. Simington, *The Civil Survey: Meath* (Dublin, 1940), p. xix.

[3] *Analecta Hibernica*, XII (1943), pp. 93, 96.

[4] *Swayne's Register* (ed. Chart), p. 206; and a sixteenth century note in Antiphonary of Armagh (T.C.D. MS. B. 1. 1.), fo.54v.

edly in the counties of Armagh and Tyrone, where ancient custom gave him valuable, though very complicated rights as "coarb of Patrick."

The Inquisition of 1609 makes it plain that the Primate's lands were scattered through all the parishes of the northern portion of his diocese; and the rent-roll of *c.* 1620 confirms the statements made at the time of the Inquisition. In the parish of Ardtrea, for example, the archbishop "was seised in fee out of the erenagh land containing twelve tullaghs (whereof the erenagh had one free from exactions); the yearly rent of four marks per annum, and a coshery for one night yearly in his visitation, and not otherwise." In Clonfeacle there was erenagh land "containing eight ballyboes, the yearly rent of four pounds eight shillings and six pence per annum, and fines for bloodshed." In Ardbo the erenagh land contained twelve tullaghs; the Primate had here a yearly rent of four marks "and one coshery yearly in his visitation, as before, and not otherwise; and that the erenagh of this land was to bear two thirds of the charge in repairing and maintaining the parish church." So the list goes on, from parish to parish and from the land of one sept to another, in all those portions of the diocese of Armagh that lay *inter Hibernicos* in the modern counties of Armagh, Derry and Tyrone.[1]

As might be expected, there was an exceptionally large concentration of the archbishop's mensal lands round the city of Armagh. Here the jurors of 1609 give us very precise indications:—

"First the said jurors do upon their oaths say and present that the town or city of Armagh, and the lands which have, time out of mind, been reputed the lands of the said town or city, are meared and bounded as followeth: viz.,the said town and lands are bounded south and by west upon the town of Lisdrombroghas in Toaghy, and west

[1] These details will be found in the Inquisition, under each of these three counties. A "ballyboe" is defined by O Curry as a homestead with land sufficient to graze twenty cows. But the exact meaning of "ballyboe" and "tullagh" seems to have varied locally.

upon Toaghy, and north-west upon Boditarren, and north upon Ballylyeye, and north-east upon Ballemickegillemor-reyietragh, and east upon the grange Ballenanmc coade, and east and by south upon Ballidromoldmore, and south-east upon Edenyseagh, and south upon Ennislaar, and south and by west upon Rowanmoyledigen."

Within these bounds, so precisely defined, lay "twenty balliboes or thereabouts, of the like measure or quantity as other balliboes are found to be in the said county." Here the Primate "was seised in his demesne, as of fee, within the meares aforesaid, in right of his archbishopric, of and in certain lands called Ferrannioynter Cellaghane, Knockya-moyell and Dromarge, containing in all two sessiaghs, every sessiagh containing one third part of a ballyboe." One of these lands (Dromarge) was the site of the Primate's palace,
C.60. which is mentioned once in Cromer's register as "the archiepiscopal palace of the Primate in the city of Armagh, commonly called Drummarge." This land and the remainder of the two sessiaghs defined as above, constituted the Primate's demesne land. The greater part of the twenty balliboes within the boundaries of the city's land was held by a group of Irish families who (as the jurors of 1609 did present upon oath) "have time out of mind possessed and inherited, according to the Irish custom, certain towns and parcels of land hereafter specified, lying within the meares and bounds aforesaid, and being parcel of the said twenty balliboes aforesaid, yielding unto the archbishop of Armagh for the time being, in right of his archbishopric, only the rent and duties ensuing." An enumeration of these various rents and duties would be too tedious and lengthy for our purpose; but the names of these Irish families who held land in the immediate neighbourhood of the city of Armagh in the early seventeenth century are worth recording here. The rent-roll of *c.* 1620 once again confirms the sworn statements of the jurors, and has the added interest of showing us the sharp contrast between the names of the Primate's tenants within the walls of the city—who were almost all Englishmen in 1620—and the names of the Irish

families who still retained their lands around the city. As set forth in the Inquisition of 1609 these families were: the sept of Pierce McGillechrany; the sept of David McOwen; the sept of the Kennyes; the sept of Neale McCoddan, Patrick McCoddan and Owen McCoddan; the sept of the Duganes; the sept of Art O Quin; the sept of Owen oge O Mellane; the sept of the Moyeres; the sept of McCawan; the sept of Salomon Coffey[1]; the sept of Patrick McGillwora; the sept of James O Casydy; the sept of Patrick McKenny; the sept of James O Fallagan; the sept of the Rathes; the sept of Art O Donill.

At the end of this long list of Irish families, with the exact details of the rent and other customary duties which each sept owed yearly to the Primate, the jurors of 1609 added the following significant statement: "And further the said jurors do upon their oaths say and present that the lord archbishop of Armagh for the time being could not at any time at his will and pleasure remove the above named septs or families, or any of them, nor any of their ancestors, out of their said possessions or freeholds aforesaid."[2]

Apart from the rents and other payments due to the Primate from his mensal and other lands, his official in Armagh was also responsible for the collection of yearly tithes throughout the northern portion of the diocese. Here again the jurors of 1609 give us valuable details. The customs for payment of these tithes varied from one district to another. In Armagh, for example, the jurors presented "that all the tithes within the said county of Armagh (with a few minor exceptions) . . . have time out of mind been taken, perceived and received by the lord archbishop of Armagh, in right of his archbishopric; the abbot of the said late abbey of SS. Peter and Paul of Armagh, in right of his said abbey; the dean of the cathedral church of Armagh, in right of his deanery; the prior and vicars choral

[1] The modern form of this name is Haughey or Hoey.

[2] For evidence that O Neill claimed lands from the Primate in this area, but was compelled more than once to admit the Primate's counter-claims, see below, p. 265-6.

of the said cathedral church of Armagh, and other ecclesiastical persons, in right of their dignities and places ; but how the same have been, or ought to be apportioned among them, the said jurors know not." They also presented " that there hath been, time out of mind, one market weekly holden in the town or city of Armagh, and that all the tolls and customs arising or growing by reason of the said market have time out of mind been taken, perceived and received, partly by the lord Primate of Armagh and other ecclesiastical persons, and partly by the freeholders of the town."

In Tyrone the jurors presented " that the manner of paying the tithes within the said county of Tyrone was and is as followeth : viz., that in the diocese of Armagh the tithes of corn, wool, fish and flax were ever paid in kine, and for every milch cow four pence, and out of every herd of swine one pork ; and that no other tithes were ever paid in the diocese, either in kine or otherwise." Much the same customs prevailed in those portions of Tyrone which lay within the dioceses of Derry and Clogher ; but the tithe for milch cows was less in Clogher than in Armagh, being only eight pence for three cows. The archbishop of Armagh, or the bishops of Clogher and Derry, were not the only recipients of these tithes. We learn from the jurors that in all places within the said county of Tyrone the erenagh, to whom a third of the tithes were paid and out of which he paid a rent to the archbishop or bishop, " had and hath as good estate in the said tithes as in his erenagh land, and could not be removed out of the same by the bishop."[1]

The English prelates and lawyers who acted as the King's commissioners for this Inquisition in 1609 were plainly puzzled by this Irish system of erenagh lands, and they questioned the local jurors of each county as to the origin and conditions of this form of land-tenure. The answers of the jurors for each county are given in full, though the jurors of Armagh do not seem to have been questioned on this point. The sworn statements of the jurors are of

[1] These statements will be found at the end of the long Inquisition on Tyrone.

interest as confirming the well-known account of erenaghs and coarbs which Sir John Davies set down about the same time, on the evidence of a learned clerk and student of the Brehon law in Fermanagh.[1]

The jurors of Tyrone replied to the questions of the English commissioners as follows:

"And the said jurors do upon their oaths find and present that the erenagh land was at first given by the temporal lords immediately to the first founders of the churches; and those founders did give the same to several septs, for paying rents and other duties to the bishops and for repairing and maintaining their parish churches, wherein they often times did bear a third part, and some times two third parts of the charge, and for keeping of hospitality; and that these septs or erenaghs have, time out of mind, inherited the said lands according to the Irish custom of tanistry, and that neither the said lord archbishop nor any other bishop, nor their predecessors, could at any time heretofore, or now can, remove the said erenaghs out of the said lands; and further they say that termon land had the same beginning as erenagh land, only they differ in that the termon land had often times more privileges, as sanctuary and the like, which was not allowed to many of the erenaghs; again the chief tenant of the termon land was called a corbe, but in common speech he is called by his surname, but the chief tenant of the erenagh land is always known and called an erenagh; and that the corbe in many places hath under him one or more erenaghs, to whom he giveth a portion of land free, or for rent or customs, and other liberties as he thought fit."

The English-born Primates of the fourteenth, fifteenth and sixteenth centuries must have been sorely puzzled to know how far they might safely push their claims to payment of all these multiple rents, tithes, fines and other

[1] Printed by C. Vallancey in his *Collectanea de Rebus Hibernicis*, vol. I (Dublin, 1770), pp. 131-74; and by H. Morley in his *Ireland under Elizabeth and James I* (London, 1890). A useful extract is given by James F. Kenney in his *Sources for the Early History of Ireland*, vol. I (New York, 1929), p. 33.

customary dues. The whole system of payment was most intimately linked with ancient Irish law and custom, and was rooted in the oldest traditions of the land. Only an Irish-born official, who was familiar from birth with Irish speech and Irish custom, could deal with the thousand and one local problems which were bound to arise from the administration of so vast and complicated an estate. We may now turn to the appointment and duties of this Irish official, whose activities are frequently noted in the Primate's registers.

3. THE PRIMATE'S IRISH OFFICIAL IN ARMAGH

Two entries in Octavian's register give us some insight into the organisation of the Primate's estate *inter Hibernicos* in the last years of the fifteenth century. The earlier is
O.317. dated July 16, 1484. It contains a note on the oath of fidelity which Menelaus MacCarmacan, the new bishop of Raphoe, took to the Primate, who was represented by Dean Thomas MacCawell as his proxy, before the high altar of the cathedral in Armagh. The oath was witnessed by a second Thomas MacCawell as abbot of the monastery of SS. Peter and Paul; Peter O Molloy, the future dean, who was then prior of the Culdees; James O Fallagan, treasurer; Patrick O Hega, canon of Armagh; Maurice O Molloy, who is described as *bajulator canonis*[1]; Odo O Conor, master of the works of the church (*magister operis ecclesie*); Philip Bargy, the Primate's chaplain; William Folan and Thomas Lang,
O.326. public notaries. The second entry is dated May 1, 1491, and records a commission which the Primate issued to Donald O Culean, chancellor of the diocese, Eugene O Neill, a canon of the diocese, and William Offelone (probably

[1] This title is unfamiliar, but is obviously connected in some way with the Book of Armagh (*Canóın Phádraig*).

identical with William Folan above). The Primate was about to leave Ireland on his second visit to Rome, and he commissioned these three to visit his diocese *inter Hibernicos* during his absence. But the following limitations were placed on their jurisdiction. They were not to interfere with the Primate's palace and the land of Triensagart on his demesne; nor were they to have jurisdiction over Eugene, the Primate's official in the city of Armagh or over Patrick McGillamurra, the Primate's chaplain and master of the fabric of his church, or over the guardian (*custos*) of the Primate's palace in Armagh.

This last entry distinguishes clearly between the three separate posts of official and master of works and guardian of the Primate's palace. Eugene, who is here stated to be the Primate's official in Armagh, seems to be Eugene O Neill, one of the three to whom the Primate issued his commission in 1491. Odo O Conor had been master of works in the cathedral church in 1484, but Patrick McGillamurra had taken his place by 1491. The official of Armagh is not mentioned in the entry of July 16, 1484. An earlier entry of January 22, 1483, tells us that David McDavyn was O.140.
official in the city of Armagh at that date, and Master O Folan the Primate's proctor for the dues of St. Patrick. This last office does not occur again in the registers, and it seems probable that the Primate's official in Armagh was responsible for collecting the Dues of St. Patrick, with all the other revenues of the Primate, in the territory *inter Hibernicos*. The duties of the master of works seem to have been concerned with the maintenance of the fabric of the cathedral in Armagh. The jurors of 1609 were questioned on this office, and presented upon oath that the master of works in Armagh held "the half town of Ballenawona" from the Primate for a yearly rent of eleven shillings and four pence. A series of obits which have been entered on some pages of the sixteenth-century Armagh Antiphonary, now among Ussher's manuscripts in the Library of Trinity College, includes the obits of John, Nicholas and John McGillamura, who held office as master of works in

Armagh before their deaths in 1556, 1574 and 1576.[1]

David McDavyn, who was the Primate's official in Armagh in 1483, belonged to a family which seems to have established a hereditary claim to this office. In 1425 Primate Swayne appointed Christin McDewyn as the assessor (*æstimator*) of his tithes, victuals and other necessaries in his city of Armagh.[2] Ten years later two of the same Primate's chaplains, Thomas O Luchran and David McDewyn, acted as the Primate's commissaries and receivers from his lands *inter Hibernicos*.[3] In 1438 David McDewyn and Philip McKewen were commissioned, jointly and severally, " to let, sell and rent, in the name of the archbishop and his church of Armagh, the archbishop's tithes in the city of Armagh . . . and also his mensal sheaves."[4] The absence of any printed calendar for the registers of Prene and Mey makes it difficult to trace the link between these members of the McDewyn sept in the fifteenth century and their successors under Octavian, Cromer and Dowdall.

C.11. On July 5, 1522, Senekyn McDewyn was acting as official in Armagh at a time when Primate Cromer had not yet appeared in his diocese. We know nothing of the official for the next nine years, but Senekyn seems to have been in fairly constant trouble with his Irish tenants
C.60. around Armagh. On September 28, 1531, when Cromer was absent in England, Master Cormac Roth—acting as the Primate's vicar general—confirmed Senekyn McDewyn as " receiver of all the temporal emoluments of the primatial see *inter Hibernicos*." The same trustworthy official was also appointed *custos* of the archiepiscopal palace in the city of Armagh, " which is commonly called Drummarge," and of all its fruits and emoluments. On the same date the vicar general issued a mandate to the Primate's Irish tenants, ordering them to obey Senekyn and again threatening with

[1] This Antiphonary is now T.C.D. MS. B.1.1. I have printed these obits in *L.A.J.*, vol. XI (1945), pp. 1-12.

[2] *Swayne's Register* (ed. Chart), p. 41.

[3] ibid., p. 159. [4] ibid., p. 177.

excommunication and interdict any who might oppose him
in the exercise of his duties. Twelve years later (December
19, 1543) Primate Dowdall appointed Dermicius McDewyn D.25.
his official for the city of Armagh and the whole deanery of
Erthyr (Orior), giving him full powers to hear all matrimonial
cases in this area. Dermicius or Dermot McDewyn seems
to have held this office for the next fifty troubled years, for
he is almost certainly to be identified with "the pore old
man of four score and seventeen years of age" whom Hugh
O Neill mentions in a letter of 1591, and whom he describes
as "the official of Armagh, well learned in civil and common
laws."[1]

The confirmation of Senekyn McDewyn in the autumn
of 1531 probably caused local jealousies and disturbances
as to which we have no clear information. Within the next
eighteen months a series of raids on the Primate's lands
began, and seems to have got steadily worse. On March 19,
1533, James McKywan, who seems to have been one of the C.66 v.
Primate's tenants, obtained monitorial letters against Henry
O Neill and others who had seized some ninety head of cattle
on the Primate's lands. Three weeks later a more serious
incident is recorded. John O Kellaghan is mentioned as C.11.
the Primate's clerk and messenger who was used by Senekyn
McDewyn in 1522 as the bearer of the official citation to a
forthcoming provincial council, issued by the Primate to his
suffragans *inter Hibernicos*. He is almost certainly to be
identified as the John O Kelleghan, clerk of Armagh, who
was murdered by Bernard O Dywin in March or April, 1533.
On April 10 the Primate granted faculties to the dean of C.67 v.
Armagh to absolve the murderer, provided that he humbly
submitted himself to Holy Church and begged for mercy.
On the same day the Primate issued a certificate that John
Kyar McEweyr, who may perhaps have been implicated in
the murder of John O Kelleghan, had done public penance
on Holy Thursday, and had been ordered to appear every

[1] Leslie, p. 33. But Senekyn, as "official of Armagh," witnessed the agreement between Conn O Neill and Primate Dowdall in December, 1555: see below, p. 266.

Sunday in the cathedral of Armagh, clothed in white as a penitent, and offer a pound of wax in honour of St. Patrick until the Primate shall have decided that his penance is complete. The absolution of Bernard and John McEweyr is postponed " until peace or a truce has been established between O Neill and his adversaries of the race of Hugh (*de stirpe Odonis*), when Bernard may be able to come to us in safety for further examination."

These entries reflect some obscure incident in the border warfare that was a permanent source of trouble to the diocese of Armagh. This warfare was intensified in the summer and autumn of 1534, when news of the Geraldine revolt in Dublin and Kildare had begun to spread throughout
C.78-9. Ireland. On September 30, 1534—two months after the murder of Archbishop Allen in Dublin—Cromer issued monitorial letters to the dean of Armagh and other dignitaries of the chapter. The Primate had received a complaint from his chaplain, whose name is given as Patrick Yheany (probably O h-Eidhnigh) and who was one of the Primate's tenants on the land of Munterheny. This district appears as an organised unit of the diocese about this time. Thomas O Ferghran is named as vicar of Munterheny on March 13, 1533, and again in a bull of Paul III for 1534-5.[1] In his monitorial letter of September 30 the Primate states that the chaplain is his tenant " on the lands of Monterheny, Dompnaghregh, Mullaghglass, Lyssbayn, Cargyn Netragh, Cargyn Yetraghe, Bayll Drumnalagh and Istertcowe." These names occur, with slight variations, in a statement made for the Inquisition of 1609, when the jurors presented " that the sept of O Hanlon and their ancestors, for the space of one hundred and fifty-three years, were and continued possessed of the six towns of land ensuing : viz., Tawnaghkeagh, Mulloghglasse, Carriginotragh, Carriginietragh, Lisboane, the half town of Kilcowe and the half town of Dromlege in the said barony of Orier ; paying in ancient fines to the lord archbishop of Armagh for the time being eight porks or some money in lieu thereof per annum."

[1] Costello, p. 24.

These precise statements enable us to identify these lands as lying within the modern barony of Lower Orior, between the towns of Tanderagee and Poyntzpass. The modern equivalents of these strangely spelt Irish names are Tannyoky, Mullaglass, Lisbane, Cargans, Ballynaleck and Lisnakea.[1] The accurate date of 153 years before the Inquisition of 1609 is curious, and suggests very strongly that the sept of O Hanlon had newly acquired this territory towards the middle of the fifteenth century. The Annals of Ulster record the death in battle of various leaders of this sept under the years 1476, 1481, 1493, 1495 and 1497, when they were evidently being hard pressed by their neighbours; and the entry in Cromer's register for 1534 shows us that they had lost their hold on this territory again before that date. The sept of O Heny were neighbours of the O Hanlons, and the Inquisition of 1609 fixes their holdings in the modern townlands of Terryhoogan, Aughlish, Monclone, Druminargal, Shaneglish and Tullymacan. They seem by this time to have pushed the sept of O Hanlon out of the holdings which were being disputed in 1534.

In his letters of September 30, 1534, the Primate complains that Eugene O Hanlon, captain of his nation, with Malachy and others of the same nation, have seized the lands of Munterheny against the will of the Primate's chaplain and tenant. The Primate orders restitution to be made, but we hear no more of the incident. In 1609 the wheel had come full circle, for another member of this same sept, Sir Ohie O Hanlon, was then holding the ancestral lands of the O Heny's as a tenant of the Protestant Primate, Henry Ussher.

During the winter of 1534-5 fresh incursions were made into the Primate's lands in the immediate neighbourhood of Armagh. Cromer was by now a sick man, confined to his

[1] I am indebted to V. Rev. M. J. McDermott, P.P. and Mr. T. G. F. Paterson for the identification of these local names.

The parish of Munterheny is now represented by Ballymore (Tanderagee). The Church of Munterheny was probably a ruin in 1609. The foundations still exist in the old churchyard of Belnabeck in Aughlish townland—one of the townlands belonging to the O Heny sept.

manor of Termonfeghin; but he issued two letters from this manor on February 16, 1535. Both of these letters deal with complaints which he had received from Senekyn
C.83. McDewyn, his official in Armagh. Conn óg O Neill, son of Conn Bacach (to whom, as captain of his nation, the Primate now appeals for the aid of the secular arm) had joined with members of the McGyrran sept in a direct attack on the Primate's palace at Armagh. Reports had reached the Primate which may well have alarmed him. The marauders had broken down the doors of the palace and had done much other damage. They had stolen horses from the stable, and had gone off with fish, victuals and other goods from the official's store. The official seems to have offered some resistance to the raiders, for we hear that Art McDonnell had "sacrilegiously inflicted divers injuries on Senekyn McDewyn, clerk, our custodian of the said manor and our officer and receiver among the Irish." The Primate now declares that Art McDonnell has *ipso facto* incurred major excommunication by his act, and pronounces a similar sentence against Conn óg O Neill and all others who unlawfully detain the Primate's property. This sentence of excommunication, with an accompanying interdict, is to be published, with all the customary and awe-inspiring solemnities of medieval canon law, in the city of Armagh and throughout the northern deaneries *inter Hibernicos.* But censures of this kind had become little more than a routine part of diocesan administration here in Ireland and in most European countries of the sixteenth century.

C.82-3. The Primate's second letter of the same date (February 16, 1535) deals with another complaint which he had received from Senekyn McDewyn, who seems to have incurred the enmity of his neighbours by the success of his own career. On July 2, 1534, the Primate had united the two rectories of Magherafelt (Teachfeakle) and Ardtrea, both lying in the modern county of Derry, for Senekyn's benefit during his lifetime. On May 6 of the same year Bernard O Loughran, who had gone to Rome to better his fortunes at the papal court, bound himself for payment of the annate due for the union of the three parishes of Ardtrea, Maghera-felt (*Thenafigad*) and Lissan, which had been erected into a canonry and simple prebend for his benefit.[1] Here was an open clash of personal interests. Bernard O Loughran had obtained his papal grant some two months before Cromer's grant of the two parishes to Senekyn McDewyn ; and he lost no time in asserting his claims.

In his letter of February 16, 1535, Cromer states that Bernard O Loughran had obtained a court of three judges delegate from the Holy See : the (unnamed) prior of Dungewin, Donatus O Cawyll (presumably MacCawell) and Bernard Magunshenan. These three judges had given sentence in favour of Senekyn's rival ; but—according to a long-standing tradition of similar litigation all over Ireland in the fifteenth century—Senekyn questioned the validity of the papal commission by which these judges had claimed power to hear the case, and appealed to the Primate for protection whilst he pursued his case in Rome. Cromer issued the customary letters tuitorial on February 16, but he must have known enough of the King's new religious policy to guess that his official's appeal to the Holy See would not go much further without encountering strong opposition from the King's officers in Dublin.

Senekyn McDewyn's post as official of the Primate *inter Hibernicos* was thus no sinecure. Even when times were peaceful, he had more than enough to do in the adminis-tration of the Primate's extensive Irish properties. When times were not peaceful—and there was little peace in Ireland during the winter of 1534-5—he risked getting a knock on the head for his pains from one or other of the Primate's restless Irish tenantry.

[1] Costello, p. 13.

4. RELIGIOUS HOUSES IN THE DIOCESE OF ARMAGH

The diocese of Armagh included an unusually large number of religious houses, some of them among the oldest and most important in all Ireland. Archdall's *Monasticon Hibernicum* gives some desultory information about these foundations, and further details have recently been made available to students in a welcome edition of the *Extents of Irish Monastic Possessions* at the time of their suppression. But there is as yet no satisfactory and critical account of Irish monastic history during the late medieval period. This short sketch gives no more than a few indications of the general position, as it is revealed in the Primates' registers and some other published sources.[1]

The oldest, and in Irish eyes the most venerable of these religious communities was the Patrician monastery of SS. Peter and Paul in Armagh. Like most of the older Irish monastic foundations it had been reformed as a monastery of Augustinian Canons in the general reform of the twelfth century. Thomas MacCawell, who seems to have been distinct from his contemporary and namesake the dean of
O.317. Armagh, was abbot of SS. Peter and Paul in the early years of Primate Octavian's pontificate. A commendatory abbot

[1] Mervyn Archdall's *Monasticon Hibernicum* was published in Dublin as far back as 1786. Dr. Moran, then Bishop of Ossory, later Cardinal Archbishop of Sydney, planned a new edition of this work, " with extensive notes " for which he engaged the collaboration of other Irish scholars ; but no more than the first volume of this new edition was published (Dublin, 1873). As in Archdall's original edition of 1786, it groups the monasteries under the modern counties, in alphabetical order. Armagh and Derry are thus included in this volume, but not those houses which were situated in the counties of Louth and Tyrone. Mr. Newport White's recent edition of the *Extents of Irish Monastic Possessions*, 1540-41 (Dublin : Irish MSS. Commission, 1943) includes the properties of the religious houses in Co. Louth, but not those in Armagh, Derry and Tyrone. Details of the suppression of the Irish monasteries will be found in Morrin's *Calendar of Patent Rolls : Ireland*, vol. I (Dublin, 1861). See also Dr. R. Dudley Edwards : *Church and State in Tudor Ireland* (London, 1935), pp. 68-73.

of this monastery is mentioned occasionally in Cromer's register as one of the chief dignitaries of the clergy *inter Hibernicos* shortly before the suppression of the monasteries, but he is not named in any of these documents. Patrick O Hagan is named as the abbot of this monastery in an Inquisition taken at the time of the general suppression in 1539-40, and he may very well be identical with the unnamed commendatory abbot of Cromer's register. The actual surrender was made by James O Donnelly as prior of the monastery in 1557.[1] The long list of monastic lands printed by Archdall from the Inquisition taken in this year (I Elizabeth) gives us some notion of the abbey's former importance in the life of the diocese. But there is little sign that the monks of this community took an active part in the religious life of their district in these last years of medieval Armagh. The Inquisition of 1609 enumerates several churches and townlands in the counties of Armagh and Tyrone which had formerly been held by the abbots of SS. Peter and Paul in Armagh. C.78-9; 82.

The community of the Culdees of Armagh was a later growth, and was most probably due to an attempt at internal reform within the larger community in the eighth or ninth centuries. The Culdees of Armagh retained their character as a distinct religious community to the time of their suppression. As has been stated already, the office of prior of the Culdees of Armagh was held by two successive deans of Armagh from 1487 to *c.* 1550.[2] The community seems to have disappeared soon after this latter date.

There were several other old Celtic foundations within the territory in the diocese *inter Hibernicos* such as Clonfeacle, Ardtrea, Errigalkeerogue, Kilmore and Killeavy. This last was a foundation of Irish nuns, dating back (according to local traditions) to St. Patrick's sister, St. Monenna. The convent seems to have survived to the eve of the suppression, for we find that Edmund Connisburgh, the archbishop of Armagh who resigned his see in favour of

[1] Archdall, pp. 26-7. [2] See above, p. 76.

Octavian in 1477, drew up the formal act of his resignation
O.401. in " the house of the accustomed residence of the abbess of Kilsleve " (*in domo solite residencie abbatisse de Kilsleve*). But the Primate's registers give us no insight into the state of religious life within the walls of these older Irish foundations, and there seems to be no other indication of their activity at this period. The King's commissioners who were entrusted with the task of suppressing the Irish monasteries in 1539-40 were not able to penetrate so far into the purely Irish territory of the diocese, and we have thus no record of their possessions or general condition in the last years of their existence. They seem to have faded out gradually in the general confusion of these transitional years.

The Cistercian monastery of Mellifont near Drogheda was the oldest Irish Cistercian foundation, and its history recalled the great names of St. Bernard and St. Malachy. In those early days the abbey had been a great centre of Irish monastic fervour, and most of the other Cistercian houses in Ireland were either daughters of Mellifont or in some way connected with the *filiatio Mellifontis*. The Irish tradition had been maintained, with increasing difficulty owing to pressure from the new English settlers, down to the middle of the fourteenth century. English monks had then got control of the monastery, whose landed possessions were still of great value at the time of the suppression.[1] Octavian's register contains several documents which deserve closer study for the light they throw on the last stages of Irish Cistercian history.

John Troy was abbot of Mellifont during most of Primate Octavian's pontificate. He was one of those prelates who took part in the coronation of Lambert Simnel in Dublin as Edward VI in 1487, and he shared in the general pardon issued by the King in 1488.[2] In 1489 Mellifont suffered severely from local raids, and Primate Octavian's provincial council passed a decree threatening all

[1] N. White : *Extents*, pp. 212-222 ; Archdall, pp. 485-9.

[2] *Letters and Papers of Richard III and Henry VII* (ed. James Gairdner : Rolls Series, 1863), vol. II, p. 370 ; Archdall, p. 485.

such marauders with severe penalties.[1] In 1490 Abbot Troy attended the parliament which the Great Earl of Kildare held that summer in Dublin, and signed the general petition which the peers of that parliament sent to Henry VII on behalf of the Great Earl.[2]

In 1493 an attempt was made to oust Troy from his position as abbot of Mellifont, and he was accused of apostacy by Thomas Hervey, one of the monks of his own community. A chapter of Irish Cistercian abbots was held at St. Mary's, Dublin, on October 1, and the assembled O.134. abbots drew up a formal statement in justification of Abbot Troy. Troy's own appeal to the chapter general of his Order, with a full refutation of the charges that had been brought against him, is dated November 11 of the same year. O.134 v. His appeal was successful, for we find him acting as *reformator* of the Cistercian order in Ireland during the next O.32 ; 137. few years. In July, 1495, the Primate had again to issue a mandate against "certain noblemen and their servants" who had molested the property and tenants of the abbey.[3] An undated report, which was written soon after 1497, gives O.121-2. a melancholy report of the general condition of these Irish Cistercian monasteries.[4] It is written by the abbot of Mellifont, and is addressed to an unnamed abbot, either of Citeaux or Clairvaux. According to Abbot Troy, there were then only two monasteries in Ireland in which the monks still wore the habit of their Order and obeyed the Cistercian rule : Mellifont and St. Mary's, Dublin. The abbot begs for protection from the accusations of monks from the other houses who are trying to drag these two monasteries down to their own level. This report is of interest as suggesting

[1] Octavian's Register, loose membrane at end of the volume.

[2] Bryan : *Great Earl of Kildare* (Dublin, 1933), p. 150 ; *Letters and Papers of Richard III and Henry VII*, vol. I, p. 379.

[3] The text of this mandate was recently found by Mr. John Ainsworth when he was examining the Moore family papers for the Irish MSS. Commission.

[4] This report mentions the death of Abbot Walter (Champfleur) of St. Mary's, Dublin, who died in 1497 : Gilbert, *Chartularies of St. Mary's Abbey, Dublin* (Rolls Series, 1884), vol. I, p. 382.

that the reform of the whole Cistercian order, which was being vigorously promoted in France at this time, was beginning to make itself felt in the Irish houses.

Abbot Troy was still *reformator* of the Irish Cistercians on July 17, 1500.[1] He was dead before September 17, 1515, when Thomas Hervey—presumably Troy's opponent in
O.136 v. 1493-4—is named as abbot of Mellifont and *reformator* of the Order in Ireland. Hervey died on March 20, 1525.[2] He had acted as one of the two vicars general for the absentee Primate Kite during the years 1515-17.

Abbot Hervey's successor was another Englishman named Richard Comptor or Coumter, who is the last of the medieval abbots of Mellifont. It was he who surrendered the monastery with all its lands to the King's officers on July 23, 1539—and on the following September 10 he was granted a pension of £40 per annum, payable from the revenues of three small parishes.[3] Abbot Comptor's name first appears in a document that has recently come to light among the papers of the family of the Earls of Drogheda. This is a certificate, dated October 8, 1527, stating that Brother Richard Coumtor, abbot of Mellifont, has been absolved from all suspensions which he had incurred for contumacy, rebellion and other crimes by two visitors appointed by the abbot of Clairvaux.[4] The names of these two visitors are given as Brother John, abbot of Bective, and Brother Lewis Thomas (*Ludovicus Thomas*), a conventual monk of the Cistercian abbey of Neath in Wales. No further indication is given as to the nature of Abbot Comptor's misdemeanours; but we may assume that his conduct immediately after his election as abbot of Mellifont had been in some way irregular.

[1] Gilbert: *Chartularies of St. Mary's Abbey, Dublin* (Rolls Series, 1884), vol. II, p. 14.

[2] Gilbert, op. cit. II, p. 220.

[3] Morrin I, pp. 56, 59.

[4] I owe my knowledge of this document to Mr. Ainsworth, who has recently found it in a box labelled "Miscellaneous old cancelled bonds and papers."

Six years later these same names recur in a document which suggests that Brother Lewis Thomas had ambitions of his own in this dispute, and that he had succeeded in dividing the community at Mellifont. Cromer's register contains the text of an appeal from Abbot Comptor, whose C.69.
position as abbot of Mellifont had been challenged by Brother Thomas of Neath. A commission of doubtful authenticity, composed of the two abbots of Tintern (Co. Wexford) and Jerpoint (Co. Kilkenny) heard the case at Baltinglass and Jerpoint, and gave sentence against Abbot Comptor. The abbot appealed from their sentence to the Holy See and meanwhile sought tuitorial letters from Primate Cromer. The Primate's letters are dated July 4, 1533. By that time Brother Thomas of Neath Abbey had been elected abbot of Mellifont by the rival faction at Jerpoint. The Primate thought it necessary to appeal for aid of the secular arm to Sir John Plunket of Bewley, Sir Oliver Plunket of Tallonstown, the mayor and sheriffs of Drogheda and other influential neighbours. His protection seems to have been sufficient to secure Abbot Comptor in his position for another few years. But his history ends ingloriously with the surrender of 1539.[1]

The Augustinian priory of St. Mary's, Louth, had once been the centre of the diocesan organisation of a see that was later reorganised as the see of Clogher.[2] It remained an important house to the end of the medieval period. Primate Octavian held an official visitation of this priory early in 1481. The last prior of this house was John Wile, who surrendered his priory with its extensive lands to the King in 1539. Its lands were granted to Sir Oliver Plunket of Tallonstown. The priory known as St. Mary's *de Urso* in Drogheda was also an Augustinian house. On its suppression in 1539 its lands were granted to the mayor of

[1] For later Catholic abbots of Mellifont, see Father Murray's notes in *L.A.J.*, VIII (1935), pp. 223-33 ; and (1936), pp. 355-7.

[2] See an article on St. Mary's, Louth, by Rev. T. Gogarty, in *L.A.J.* IV (1916), pp. 169-89 ; and the late Dean Lawlor's very able article on "The Genesis of the Diocese of Clogher" : ibid., pp. 129-59.

Drogheda. There was also a smaller Augustinian priory of St. Laurence at Drogheda, which had a similar history.[1] The abbey of Knock near Louth, another Augustinian foundation of the twelfth century, was held by the
O.268 v. MacMahon family at this time.[2] Primate Octavian visited most of these priories early in 1482 and found no serious fault in them.

Drogheda was a considerable centre of the mendicant friars since the first great expansion of these orders in Ireland during the thirteenth century. All four orders of the Franciscans, Dominicans, Carmelites and Augustinian Friars were represented within the city's walls. There was a priory of the Crouched or Crutched Friars at Ardee (St. John the Baptist's), of which the future Primate, George Dowdall, was the last prior before the suppression.[3] Another priory of these same Crutched Friars (St. Leonard's) was at Dundalk, and its last prior was Patrick Galtrym who succeeded Cormac Roth as archdeacon of Armagh in 1540. This order of Crutched Friars seems to have become largely indistinguishable from ordinary secular priests in the late medieval period; and it is probably no accident that the priors of these two houses rose to high office in the diocese after the suppression of their former priories. The Franciscans had another friary at Dundalk, whilst the Carmelites had a second friary at Ardee. We hear little on the whole of these houses during this period. In January, 1486, Primate
O.267. Octavian thought it necessary to renew the ordinary legislation of the Church's law concerning the privileges and faculties of mendicant friars in his diocese and province at a convocation of the clergy *inter Anglos*. Proctors for the
O.276v. Third Order of St. Francis were approved by Primate Octavian on May 4, 1489.

One or two entries in the "Extents of the Irish Monasteries" for 1540 give the impression of declining

[1] Archdall, pp. 453-5; N. White, *Extents*, pp. 242-3, 248.

[2] Archdall, p. 466-8; Costello, p. 11.

[3] See some comments by Father L. Murray in *L.A.J.* VII (1932), p. 554.

prosperity. There is a surprising note concerning the Dominican priory at Drogheda: "The church and a great part of the dormitory had fallen down from age before the dissolution."[1] No other note of this kind occurs in the description of the other friaries in Co. Louth. At Carlingford, for example, the Dominican house is reported as being "a strong mansion needing no expenditure on repairs, but on every side strongly fortified, and will be a very sure defence for the town in case of attack through rebellions of those living close by." The church was still standing in 1540, but had been "reserved for the accommodation of those who resort to the place in large numbers with the fleet of ships every year, to catch herrings and other fish."[2] The Franciscan house in Dundalk had been totally destroyed by order of the Deputy, Lord Grey. Their church in Drogheda was still standing in 1540, but there were then no more than the ruins of the chancel, chapels and dormitory. The same story is told of the Carmelites at Ardee and Drogheda, and of the Austin Friars at Drogheda. The houses of the Crutched Friars at Dundalk, Drogheda and Ardee seem to have been left in good condition.

The Franciscan friary of Armagh, which was situated within the grounds of the modern Primate's Palace, seems to have been of very much greater importance in the history of the Irish Friars Minor. It had been founded by the Irish Dominican Primate, Maol Padraig O Sgannail, in 1264. Numerous references occur, in the older Irish Annals and elsewhere, to its history; and in particular to its school of theology and its *lectores*.[3] During the fifteenth century the Irish Franciscan convents had been powerfully affected by the new Observantine movement within the Order, and there seems little doubt that these Observantine Friars, in Ireland as elsewhere, were the most active of all the older religious orders at the time of Henry VIII's attack on the Pope's

[1] N. White, *Extents*, p. 244. [2] ibid., p. 245-6.

[3] Annals of Ulster, a. 1264, 1266: see also FitzMaurice-Little: *Materials for the History of the Franciscan Province of Ireland*, 1230-1450 (Manchester, 1920), p. 30.

jurisdiction within his kingdom.[1] The Observantine movement was centred—so far at least as the northern province was concerned with it—in the new friary of Donegal, which had been founded by Hugh Roe O Donnell in 1474. The contemporary Annals of Ulster have some interesting entries concerning the growth of this movement in the latter half of the fifteenth century. A chapter of the Observantine Friars was held at Donegal in the summer of 1488. Niall O Neill got them a grant from Rome, by which they were permitted to take over the friary of Carrickfergus from the Conventual Friars in the summer of 1497. One of their number, Donald O Fallon, was provided to the see of Derry by Innocent VIII on May 16, 1485.[2] When the great chieftain, Hugh Roe O Donnell, died in 1505, he was buried in the friary which he had founded thirty years earlier. Menelaus MacCarmacan, the aged bishop of Raphoe who died in 1515, was also buried there; and Rory O Donnell, the bishop of Derry who led the resistance to Henry VIII's new policy for some eventful years, was buried there in 1550.[3]

Octavian's register has one curious entry about an
O.83 v Irish Friar of the Strict Observance. On July 10, 1508—
five years before his own death—he granted an indulgence to
Brother Meyler Breatnagh of the Observance, who was old
and blind and wished to end his days as an anchorite on the
C.66-7 Rock of Cashel. Cromer's register for 1533 contains the
text of a long appeal which the Observantine Friars made
to him as Primate, and to the Holy See, against the action
of their Conventual brethren who were seeking to oust them
from the two friaries of Armagh and Galway. These two
houses had been set aside for the common use of both
sections of the Order (no doubt for purposes of study), but
the Conventual Friars now claimed them as their own.

[1] See above, p. 67. [2] See below, p. 189. [3] See below, p. 191.

5. THREE ANGLO-IRISH CONVENTS

The registers of Octavian and Cromer contain a series of interesting entries which throw a good deal of light on the Anglo-Irish convents of Clonard, Odder and Termonfeghin on the eve of their suppression. Primate Octavian visited the convent of St. Mary's, Termonfeghin on February 12, O.268.
1480. Janet White appeared as prioress: the convent chapel was found to be in good order, but one of the Sisters was found guilty of disobedience and incontinence, and was ordered to do penance enclosed in her cell until the Primate should give further orders. Janet White was still prioress some thirty years later, for her name is mentioned by one of the witnesses to a troublesome lawsuit in which the convent was involved in 1520, when evidence was being taken as to the customs that had prevailed some ten years earlier.[1] This lawsuit arose from the fact that the chaplain to the convent was supported partly by the convent, partly by the vicar of Termonfeghin. In return for his maintenance, the chaplain was expected to assist the vicar and his curate in the administration of the sacraments at the parish church, and to say Mass at the convent on certain fixed days. Several witnesses who were examined in the course of the proceedings—which were lengthy, for the case was heard in all no less than twenty-one times in the Primate's metropolitan court—deposed that this custom of supporting the chaplain had existed from time immemorial. Within living memory it had been maintained by two successive vicars of Termonfeghin, Christopher Dowdall (later archdeacon of Meath) and Simon Geffrey. Geffrey died in 1507, and Primate Octavian then presented his Italian nephew, Alexander del Palatio, to the vicarage. Trouble came within a few years—possibly owing to the fact that the

[1] Father L. Murray has summarised the evidence given at this law-suit in *L.A.J.* VIII (1935), pp. 169-71. The full text is in the metropolitan court-book, now the first part of Cromer's register, ff. 49-51.

Primate's nephew was, as Father Murray has suggested, "a restless and unquiet spirit."[1] The nuns left their convent and retired to Callystown (Kaylaghton) in the neighbourhood, where—according to the Inquisition of Henry VIII's commissioners—they owned 10 messuages and 128 acres of land.[2] The chaplain who followed them to their new home was no longer expected to assist in the parochial duties at Termonfeghin, but Primate Octavian (who does not seem to have supported his nephew in this dispute) continued to supply the customary *mensa* of two days per week, which was usually a charge on the vicar of Termonfeghin. Octavian died in 1513. His nephew left Termonfeghin soon afterwards, and the vicarage remained vacant for some years. Archdeacon James White was finally presented to the vicarage in 1517, when the diocese was being administered by the absent Primate Kite's vicars general. The archdeacon refused to re-establish the old custom, which had now lapsed for some years; and the nuns, when they finally returned to Termonfeghin from Callystown, refused to bear the whole cost of their chaplain's maintenance.

The witnesses who were examined in the course of these lengthy proceedings gave evidence which allows us a welcome glimpse into the ordinary daily life of a small parish like Termonfeghin. Peter Bowdin, a priest of the diocese, deposed that he had known the convent for sixteen years, and that the chaplains had always received their *mensa* on Saturday from the vicar, and on Wednesday from the nuns. His evidence was corroborated by Richard Miler, who had known the place for forty years; by Maurice Kerbry, who had been hearing Mass at the convent for the past fifty years; and John FitzJohn, the convent's proctor, who had known the place for twenty-four years. Edward Dowdall, a gentleman of Drummyn, deposed that he remembered this custom from the days when Walter Kamocke was chaplain

[1] For Alexander, see above, p. 41.

[2] N. White, *Extents*, p. 234.

more than forty years before the date of this law-suit; and again in the time of Master William Simcock and Christopher Dowdall. From the complicated series of statements, Father Murray has been able to reconstruct a list of the names of fourteen chaplains who ministered to this convent during those forty or fifty years.[1]

When all the witnesses had been heard, a group of leading parishioners (defined in the legal record as the *sanior pars*) met in the parish church of Termonfeghin, and were recommended to submit the case to arbitration. Edmund MacCawell, the dean of Armagh—who had appeared as one of the proctors for the archdeacon in this case—was chosen as arbitrator with two gentlemen of the neighbourhood: Walter Cusack and Edward Dowdall. Their award was finally published on January 28, 1521. The costs of the litigation were to be borne equally by the vicar and the parishioners, who seem to have supported the nuns throughout these proceedings. The vicar was bound in future to support the chaplain on one day of each week, whilst the chaplain was to assist him and his curate in the administration of the sacraments. The vicar and the parishioners were to share equally in the burden of paying the two years of arrears which were due to the unfortunate chaplain. Henceforth the prioress was to support the chaplain on one day of each week, whilst he was bound to say Mass in the convent four times a year. The prioress and the parishioners were to be jointly responsible for the payment of that portion of the arrears which should have been paid by the convent for the past two years. With this reasonable decision peace seems to have returned once more to the parish and the convent—but we do not know how long the chaplain was left to enjoy the fruits of his struggle for restitution.

Almost the last entry in Cromer's register throws further light on the history of this convent within a few years of its suppression. The prioress who had taken such

[1] *L.A.J. VIII*, p. 171.

an active part in the litigation of 1520-21 was Alsona Plunket—obviously a member of some branch of the well known Meath family of that name. She had died before the autumn of 1535, and there seems to have been some doubt as to the correct procedure which should be followed in the election of her successor. The monasteries and convents of England had been suppressed at this date, and it is possible that Primate Cromer—who knew well what the King was preparing for the Irish monasteries—hesitated to make himself responsible for the election of a new prioress. On
C.92 v. October 1, 1535, Mary Cusack—who bears the name of another well known Meath family—appeared before the Primate in his manor at Termonfeghin. She was a member of the community of Canonesses of St. Augustine at Odder, near Tara, and she alleged that she had been sent to represent the abbess of Odder, who had an interest and title in the election of the new prioress of Termonfeghin. The Primate seems to have questioned this claim; and Sister Mary Cusack was sent back to Odder with a message that the abbess was to appear before the Primate, either in person or by proxy, on October 14 and exhibit such titles as she might have in this matter.

Margaret Silke was abbess of Odder at this date. She appeared in person at the Primate's manor on October 14, and again on the following day, and exhibited a bull of Pope Celestine III, dated in the year 1195, by which the Pope granted protection to the abbess and canonesses of Clonard, and also to the two houses of Odder and Termonfeghin. The text of this bull has survived and has been printed by Dugdale in his *Monasticon Anglicanum.*[1] It makes no mention of Odder and Termonfeghin, which seem to have been later foundations, dependent on the convent at Clonard which was very much older. The Primate commissioned his official, Master Cormac Roth (who was himself vicar of Termonfeghin as well as archdeacon of the diocese) to hear this case. The archdeacon appointed a new

[1] Dugdale II, p. 1043.

date (November 15) on which the abbess was to produce this bull and other muniments in her possession that might prove her contention. On November 15 the abbess again appeared C.93.
in person before the Primate's official. She seems to have satisfied him as to her legal rights—for she now presents a petition that Margaret Hubbard, one of the canonesses of St. Mary le Hogges in Dublin, should be admitted as prioress of Termonfeghin. The Primate ordered a further inquiry into the suitability of this new candidate ; and that is the last we hear of the matter in his diocesan register.

Four years later these same names recur in more tragic circumstances.[1] Margaret Hubbard surrendered the convent of Termonfeghin to the King's officers in 1539, but there is no mention of any pension offered or received. Mary Cusack, who is probably identical with the Sister who appeared before the Primate in 1535, surrendered the convent of Lismullen in Meath in 1540. Margaret Silke, who had been successful in the assertion of her rights in 1535, surrendered her abbey of Odder in 1539. We hear nothing of the old convent of St. Mary's, Clonard ; but Sir James Ware, who had access to records that have since perished, and who knew the surviving traditions of his day, tells us that this ancient abbey had fallen into such poverty in the later Middle Ages that it had become no more than a small cell of its more prosperous daughter-convent at Odder.[2] Yet even Odder was far from true security in the fifteenth century. On December 10, 1478, Edward IV directed that Elizabeth, abbess of Odder, and her convent, which depended on one ploughland for its subsistence, should be " discharged of all manner of coign or livery, subsidies and talliages and all other oppressions," provided that the nuns undertook on their part " not to receive any of the King's enemies, by day or by night."[3]

[1] Morrin I, p. 61 ; Archdall, pp. 492, 555-7, 566 ; N. White, *Extents*, pp. 234, 255, 259, 262.

[2] Archdall, p. 526-7.

[3] See Ferguson's extracts from the Memorandum Rolls of Edward IV, now in the Public Record Office, Dublin.

PART III

THE PRIMATE AND HIS SUFFRAGANS

I. MEATH

Meath—with Dublin, Louth and Kildare—was one of "the four counties" to which the Anglo-Irish Pale had been reduced by the end of the fifteenth century. The diocese of Meath is, of course, very much larger than the county of Meath. All that portion of the diocese which lies in the modern counties of Westmeath and Offaly (King's Co.) was beyond the reach of the King's officers during the reign of Henry VII and the early years of Henry VIII. But the richest part of the temporalities of the diocese lay within the Pale, and the fact that these temporalities could still be seized at the death of a bishop and held "in the King's hand" until the new bishop had done homage meant that the diocese as a whole, like the English portion of the diocese of Armagh, was within the King's control. During the fifteenth century all the bishops of Meath seem to have been English-born prelates. Meath was in fact very much closer to Dublin in its general life and policy than it was to the metropolitan see of Armagh. In its civil administration Meath has finally been absorbed in Leinster, but the diocese has always remained the most important suffragan see of the northern province of Armagh.

William Sherwood was bishop of Meath when Octavian became Primate in 1479. He had been provided to the see in 1460, and Sixtus IV addressed to him, as the principal suffragan of Armagh, a bull by which he empowered him to excommunicate the new Primate, should he fail to satisfy his financial obligations towards the Holy See.[1] The bishop was inhibited from exercising these powers by a bull of March 15, 1482, soon after Octavian's final settlement with Sixtus IV in Rome.[2] Bishop Sherwood died in Dublin before the Pope's bull had been published in Ireland (December 3, 1482).[3] Primate Octavian was henceforth left to reckon with his successor.

John Payne, who had been prior provincial of the English Dominican friars, was provided to the see of Meath by Sixtus IV on March 17, 1483.[4] It was he who published the Pope's bull at Drogheda, by which Primate Octavian was finally declared to be free from the debts contracted by his predecessors.[5]

During the first years of his rule Bishop Payne was an active supporter of the Great Earl of Kildare. He preached the sermon in Christ Church when Lambert Simnel was crowned there as Edward VI on May 24, 1487.[6] A year later he was one of the first to visit Sir Richard Edgecombe, whom Henry VII had sent across to Ireland on a personal mission. Bishop Payne preached before Sir Richard in Christ Church on July 13, when he proclaimed the bull by which Sixtus IV had excommunicated all those who took part in the rebellion, with the later absolution for those who returned to the King's allegiance and the King's pardon, which Sir Richard had brought with him from England " to every man that would do his duty unto the King's Highness."[7]

Primate Octavian had already come to recognise the bishop of Meath as his most determined enemy, and we have seen how eager he was to secure his own nomination as chancellor of the kingdom—primarily, if we are to believe

[1] C.P.L. XIII, p. 261 (Sept. 11, 1481).

[2] ibid., p. 132-4 ; Octavian's Reg., fo. 301.

[3] Ware-Harris I, p. 150.

[4] C.P.L. XIII, p. 825.

[5] See above, p. 27.

[6] Bryan, p. 107.

[7] Bryan, pp. 129-132.

his own story, so as to prevent the nomination of Bishop Payne to that office.[1] Both the Primate and the bishop were passed over in the general settlement of 1488, and the alliance between Kildare and the bishop of Meath does not seem to have lasted beyond the immediate needs of this crisis.

In the summer of 1492 Primate Octavian held his fourth provincial council at Drogheda, and Bishop Payne was summoned to answer certain charges which had been brought against him. A violent scene took place at the council, when the Primate began to press his claims to obedience from his suffragan. Bishop Payne called Octavian a tyrant more than once, and used other disrespectful terms in the presence of five of his fellow-bishops.[2] Soon after the council the Primate entered a formal protest against his suffragan's disobedience and contumacy. He complained in particular of Bishop Payne's reliance on the support of Barnaby Barnewall, one of the "Old English" settlers and justices in Meath. We hear no more of this incident, but there can have been little friendship between Armagh and Meath at this time.

A year or two later the bishop of Meath quarrelled with the Great Earl himself. Kildare had been defied by Plunket of Rathmore, and the bishop took Plunket's side in the quarrel. Plunket was defeated and slain, and the bishop was lucky to escape with his life. The *Book of Howth* tells the story with gusto: "Then the bishop of Meath bare the stroke, which upon a time the Earl watched so that he chased the bishop into a church to take succour. The Earl followed him, and commanded him to come at him. The bishop said he would not. 'No?' said the Earl. 'Then by Saint Bride I shall fetch thee out': and

[1] See above, p. 33.

[2] Octavian's Register, fo. 187v: "Vos . . . (Primatem) in presencia quinque episcoporum aperte et publice contemptibili voce vilipendendo iteratis vicibus vocastis tirannum. . . ." The Primate claimed that the bishop had incurred sentence of major excommunication by his action on this occasion.

commanded his men to follow him. The Earl went into the church with a drawn sword and came where the bishop was kneeling in the chancel, and his shorn head bare. ' By Saint Bride,' said the Earl, ' were it not that I know my prince would be offended with me, I could find it in my heart to lay my sword upon thy shaven crown.' And so he took the bishop."[1]

This incident must belong to the year 1495. A year later the bishop, who had been meanwhile released from his captivity as the Earl's prisoner, was summoned to England as one of those who had accused the Great Earl of treasonable conduct. The scene in which Kildare was confronted with his accusers and won the day by his bold manner, is familiar to all students of Irish history.[2] The Earl did not spare the " bald bishop " in his jibes, but it would be unfair to take his broad hints at the friar-bishop's loose conduct as more than an unexpected, though successful broadside from an enemy. Kildare was sent back to rule all Ireland in the King's name, and Bishop Payne must have spent the last years of his life in some anxiety. He died on March 6, 1507, and was buried in the Dominican convent of Dublin.[3]

Payne's immediate successor was another Englishman, William Rokeby—whose brother Sir Richard Rokeby was for a time treasurer of Ireland. The new bishop of Meath had been appointed chancellor of the kingdom in 1498, having previously held various benefices in his native Yorkshire ; but we know little of his early career. He had been provided to the see of Meath by Julius II some time before October 15, 1507, when the Pope authorised him to

[1] *Book of Howth :* cited by Donough Bryan, *Great Earl*, p. 189. Bryan (note 130) seems to hesitate as to whether this story refers to Bishop Sherwood or Bishop Payne. But the " shaven crown " of the bishop, like the " bald bishop " of the following story, indicates the Dominican friar-bishop whose tonsured head was a sore temptation to the angry Earl.

[2] Ware-Harris I, p. 152 ; Bryan, p. 201-3.

[3] Ware-Harris I, p. 152 (on the authority of George Cogley, a former registrar of the diocese of Meath).

hold certain benefices in addition to his new bishopric.[1] The same Pope translated him to the see of Dublin on January 28, 1512. As archbishop of Dublin he was also chancellor of the kingdom from 1515 to his death in 1521.[2]

Hugh Inge, another Englishman, was provided to the see of Meath by Julius II on January 12, 1512—the day on which Rokeby was translated to the see of Dublin.[3] He had been in the King's service for some ten years and owed this Irish provision to Wolsey's influence.[4] Bishop Inge administered the diocese of Armagh as vicar general to the absent Primate Kite during the year 1520-21.[5] On November 29, 1521, he was translated to Dublin in succession to Archbishop Rokeby by Leo X.[6] As bishop of Meath he held a diocesan synod at Trim, and caused all the ancient rolls of proxies and synodals of the diocese to be examined, compared and copied out anew.[7] His interest in Meath did not end with his translation to Dublin in 1521, for it was he who sent Cardinal Wolsey so unfavourable a report on his successor in that diocese as to cause his resignation in 1528.

Richard Wilson, Bishop Inge's immediate successor, was a Yorkshireman like Archbishop Rokeby. He had been prior of the Augustinian monastery of Drax in Yorkshire in 1507, and was acting as suffragan bishop to the archbishop of York (Cardinal Wolsey) in 1515.[8] He was provided to the see of Meath on February 27, 1523.[9] The new bishop seems to have paid one brief visit to his diocese soon after that date. In a report which Archbishop Inge sent to Wolsey on February 23, 1528, the former bishop of Meath complains that " the diocese of Meath, which is large in

[1] Costello, p. 107.

[2] Ware-Harris I, p. 153 ; *D.N.B.* 49, 154.

[3] Costello, p. 107. [4] *D.N.B.* 28, 431. [5] See above, p. 48.

[6] Brady I, p. 326.

[7] There is a copy of these rolls (made by Reeves) in T.C.D. MS. 1060 (Abbot's catalogue). Father John Brady is preparing this text for publication.

[8] Ware-Harris I, p. 154 ; not in Stubbs. [9] Costello, p. 107.

cure and most of value in this country for an honourable man to continue in, is far in ruin, both spiritually and temporally, by the absence of the bishop there."[1] Archbishop Inge adds that "it is said here the bishop will not return." This brief phrase is the only proof we have that Bishop Wilson was ever in this country.

In his report to Wolsey, Archbishop Inge advised that another prelate should be sent over from England to take Wilson's place: "If Your Grace thinks so convenient, some good man—being towards the same—might be provided unto the said bishopric, which should be to the great comfort manifoldly of all that diocese." These words were written early in 1528. They had their effect, though Inge himself was dead within the next six months. Wilson was induced to resign his see, on the understanding that half the revenues of the diocese should be appropriated to him as a pension for life.[2] The date of his resignation and the date of his death are uncertain, but his resignation had taken effect before September 3, 1529, when Clement VII provided yet another Englishman to the vacant see of Meath.

Archbishop Hugh Inge died "of the English sweat" on August 3, 1528. His sudden death opened the way for the simultaneous provision of two prelates to the dioceses of Dublin and Meath, both of whom played a very active part in the first phase of the King's new religious policy in Ireland. On September 3, 1529, Clement VII provided John Allen to the see of Dublin, and Edward Staples to the see of Meath.[3] There had been a long delay in filling these two important Irish bishoprics, which was probably due to the Pope's grave illness at this time. When news of Inge's death reached England in August, John Allen, who was one of Cardinal Wolsey's most trusted agents, appears immediately as the new archbishop-elect. Allen had been set aside for diplomatic work on the continent during

[1] *State Papers* I, p. 127.
[2] Costello, p. 108; Brady I, p. 234-5.
[3] Brady I, p. 234; 326.

the autumn; but these arrangements were promptly cancelled, and he was sent to Dublin in November.[1] The winds were less favourable than the Cardinal's good will, and Allen was kept waiting at Chester for more than two months. He reached Dublin early in February, but did not secure the Pope's bulls for his provision until the following September.[2]

Meanwhile Bishop Richard Wilson had been persuaded to resign his see, and Wolsey was thus able to secure the simultaneous appointment of two men whom he had been using as his agents in England for some years past. Both men were graduates of Cambridge, who had been incorporated in the university of Oxford in 1525: Staples as master of arts, and Allen as doctor of law.[3] Wolsey was planning his new college at Oxford just then, and Staples was one of the first canons of Christ Church. Allen, who was already far advanced on the road to promotion since his first contacts with Wolsey in 1522, had been the Cardinal's principal agent in the suppression of the smaller English monasteries during the years 1524 and 1525, with a view to acquiring funds for the endowment of the new college. The simultaneous appointment of these two men to two important Irish sees may thus be set down to the influence of Wolsey, who was still at the height of his power in 1528; though his fall was imminent in September, 1529.

John Allen was consecrated archbishop of Dublin in Christ Church on the second Sunday of Lent (March 13, 1530).[4] The new bishop of Meath may have accompanied

[1] *Letters and Papers* IV, Part 2, nos. 4647, 4757-8, 4942. Ronan (*Reformation in Dublin*, pp. xvi- xviii) gives a useful summary of Allen's early career. See also James Gairdner, in *D.N.B.* I, 305-6; but the date of Allen's provision and consecration are there given a year before the true dates.

[2] Brady (loc. cit.) gives extracts from Roman documents which prove that September 3, 1529, was the date of the provision; and September 10 the date of the mandate for conferring the pall.

[3] Wood: *Fasti Oxonienses*, ed. Bliss, (1815), p. 72.

[4] The true date is given in the White Book of Christ Church, fo. 16v: see Lawlor's *Calendar of Liber Niger and Liber Albus of Christ Church, Dublin* (Proc. R.I.A., 1907), p. 14. Ware gives the date as March 13, 1528 (English style); but the second Sunday of Lent fell on March 13 in 1530, not in 1529.

him to Ireland, but he seems to have stayed in England for some time longer. On March 13, 1530, Primate Cromer—
C.45. acting as *custos spiritualitatis* of the diocese of Meath, owing to the bishop's absence without license—presented a chaplain in the diocese. If the bishop's obligation of residence is calculated from the date of his provision, six months had barely elapsed by March 13, and the Primate had lost no time in convicting Staples of failure for non-residence. But it is probable that Cromer's register here refers to the prolonged absence of Bishop Wilson, and takes no account of the provision of Staples who had not yet been consecrated as bishop of Meath.

The new bishop must have been hampered financially by the provision that Bishop Wilson, who had resigned the see in 1528 or 1529, should retain half the revenues of the diocese for his personal support. The Pope, who had approved this settlement, sought to mitigate its consequences by dispensing Bishop Staples to retain all the benefices which he held at the date of his provision—of which the most important was his position as master of St. Bartholomew's hospital in London.[1] How long these financial arrangements remained in force is unknown, since there is no statement as to the date of Bishop Wilson's death.

In his bull of provision, Clement VII states that " Henry, the illustrious king of England who is also lord of Ireland in things temporal " had made humble supplication to him by his letters on behalf of Staples.[2] The future was to show that the King—acting no doubt on Wolsey's advice—had made no mistake in his choice of a bishop for Meath, from his own point of view. From first to last Edward Staples was and remained the King's bishop, not the Pope's.

Bishop Staples was in his diocese on February 14, 1531, when he inducted an Irish clerk whose name is given as Onerus O Coffye as prior of St. Peter's monastery near Trim.

[1] A. F. Pollard in *D.N.B.*, 54, 93. [2] Costello, p. 108.

On August 12 of the same year he collated Turlough O Kerrolan to the rectory of Knock; and on November 8 he collated Dermot McInclery to the vicarage of Ballyloghcrew, on the presentation of Oliver Plunket.[1] The Exchequer Inquisition which is our authority for these three items adds that the new rector of Knock and the vicar of Ballyloghcrew were admitted by the bishop acting through Master Alexander Plunket, who was then acting as commissary for an absentee archdeacon of Meath. It follows that Staples had paid a short visit to his diocese in the spring of 1531, but had left it again (perhaps for Dublin) in the summer of that year.

These three appointments are all contrary to the Irish statutes which forbade the presentation of Irish clerks to benefices within the Pale. But they are in harmony with many other indications that these statutes had fallen into desuetude under Henry VII and in the early years of Henry VIII. Staples was himself an Englishman, and devoted to the King's interests. We may take it that the increasing strength of the Irish revival left him with no other choice but to accept the presentation of Irish clerks, even in so strong a centre of Anglo-Irish traditions as Trim.

Bishop Staples made a very much more important appointment in the following year. Meath was divided into two archdeaconries: Meath and Kells. At some date not later than January, 1520, when Hugh Inge was bishop of Meath, Henry VIII secured the archdeaconry of Meath for his favourite physician, Dr. John Chambre.[2] Chambre was a priest in holy orders, though his duties as royal physician seem to have been his sole real charge. To reward him for his attendance on the King he had been granted a number of important benefices at this period, being canon of Lincoln with the prebend of Leighton Buzzard; archdeacon of

[1] I am indebted to Father John Brady for these details, which are taken from an Exchequer Inquisition dated "Tuesday following the translation of St. Thomas martyr, 23 Henry VIII" (July 11, 1531) in the Record Office, Dublin.

[2] *Letters and Papers* III, Part 1, 601.

Bedford; treasurer of Wells; precentor of Exeter; canon of Windsor; and warden of Merton College, Oxford.[1] Bishop Inge granted the royal favourite his license to be absent from the archdeaconry of Meath, during pleasure, as from January, 1520. On August 17, 1526, we find
C.24. Alexander Plunket described in Cromer's register as "general administrator of the archdeaconry of Meath"; and he is called "commissary of the archdeacon of Meath" in the Exchequer Inquisition of 1531. Chambre was still holding the archdeaconry of Meath as late as 1540-42. Presumably Alexander Plunket was administering the archdeaconry in his name for most of this long period.

The archdeaconry of Kells was held by another Englishman whose name is given as John Tryguram in an Inquisition of 1521.[2] He is there styled "rector of Nobber"; but the rectory of Nobber was at this period impropriate to the archdeaconry of Kells, and Tryguram must consequently have been archdeacon as well as rector. Seven years later "Master Tigram" is mentioned in a letter which an English chaplain named John Welldon sent to Thomas Cromwell, then Cardinal Wolsey's faithful agent and right-hand man of affairs. In this letter Welldon says that he has heard a rumour that Master Tigram is about to resign his benefice, and asks Cromwell to get Wolsey "to write to the bishop of Meath (Wilson) that on the voidance of the archdeaconry of Kenlis, which Mr. Tigram is likely to resign for a pension, His Grace will be ordinary *ratione sue legationis*, and that it may be given to the writer."[3] We have here an exact parallel to the situation at St. Peter's, Drogheda, about the same time. There Wolsey was seeking to assert his legatine powers in Ireland by the institution of Reginald Drummyn as vicar of St. Peter's.[4] Here Wolsey is being asked to use those same powers to collate an English

[1] Norman Moore in *D.N.B.* 10. 31, citing Le Neve's *Fasti*.

[2] *Eighth Report of Record Commissioners, Ireland* (1820): Supplement, p. 563.

[3] *Letters and Papers* IV, Part 2, no. 5131.

[4] See above, p. 59-61.

clerk to a rich benefice in Meath. We do not know whether Tryguram did actually resign his benefice in 1528; but the archdeaconry of Kells had fallen vacant before February 13, 1532, when Bishop Staples collated Master Charles Reynolds to the archdeaconry and the rectory of Nobber.[1]

The new archdeacon was soon to become prominent as one of the most active and loyal supporters of Silken Thomas in his challenge to the King's authority in Ireland. His name, in its Anglicised form, is deceptive—for it suggests Anglo-Irish origins. Reynolds is no more than the customary English version of the Irish Mac Raghnaill, the name of a princely family in the modern county of Leitrim. An inquisition of 1543 names the archdeacon as an Irishman (*Hibernicus*) and gives his family name as McGranyl.[2] He is invariably styled "Master Charles Reynolds" in Cromer's register, and it is known that he supplicated for the degree of B.C.L. at Oxford on July 17, 1528.[3] No record survives of his admission to the *magisterium*; but this ceremony must have taken place before 1534, when his name first occurs in Primate Cromer's register. His political sympathies were soon to be apparent to all, and must have been known to the bishop when he collated him to the archdeaconry in 1532. We can only conjecture that no other more suitable candidate could be found for an archdeaconry which adjoined the ancestral lands of MacRaghnaill in Leitrim and Westmeath.

These names make it possible to gain a clearer idea of the actual situation in Meath during the absentee rule of Bishop Wilson, and during the first years of the rule of Bishop Staples. Even under Bishop Inge the diocese had been ruled by two vicars general, Walter Cusack and Alexander Plunket, since the bishop himself was administering the diocese of Armagh for the absent Primate Kite.

[1] I take this date from an unpublished Exchequer Inquisition of 1543 (35 Henry VIII), of which a modern copy survives in the Record Office, Dublin. Reynolds is here inaccurately styled "archdeacon of Nobber."

[2] See last note. [3] Foster: *Alumni Oxonienses*, p. 1247.

William Roth was the bishop's official at this period.[1]
C.40. Alexander Plunket and William Roth are named as the two commissaries of the bishop of Meath on August 16, 1529—a few weeks before the provision of Edward Staples. Presumably these two had been the effective administrators of the diocese for the past three or four years. Primate
C.77 v. Cromer was acting as *custos spiritualitatis* of Meath in September of that same year, " owing to the absence of the bishop without license of the Holy See or our special license." This last entry belongs to the autumn of 1534, when all Leinster had been thrown into confusion by the revolt of Silken Thomas in the summer of that year, and Sir James Ware tells us that Bishop Staples sought safety in England for a time at the height of the crisis.[2] But it seems probable that men like Alexander Plunket, William Roth and Charles Reynolds were the true rulers of the diocese during these years of confusion and absentee government.

In the summer of 1536 or 1537 (28 Henry VIII) Bishop Staples presented Bishop Cornelius O Cahan, whose claims to the see of Raphoe were then being successfully challenged by rival Irish candidates, to the vicarage of Athlumney in Meath.[3] The bishop of Raphoe is here described as an Irishman, of an Irish princely family (*Hibernicus, videlicet de lez Ocahanes*), and his presentation to the vicarage by Bishop Staples is admitted to be against the King's statute (*contra formam statuti*). Two years later Bishop Staples is found presenting three other Irishmen to vacant benefices in Meath (November, 30 Henry VIII).

Staples was probably resident in Dublin during his first years in Ireland, though he took an active part in the repression of the Geraldine revolt in Meath once the tide

[1] These names occur in Plunket's metropolitan court-book (ff. 23-25, 45, 47, 54, 75).

[2] Ware-Harris I, p. 154.

[3] Exchequer Inquisitions (Dublin), vol. III, 23, in the Dublin Record Office: for Bishop Cornelius, see below, p. 201-2. He obtained license to be absent from his vicarage for life, on October 25, 3 Edward VI (*Fiants Edw. VI*, 386).

had begun to turn. He signed a report of the Irish Council to the King in the second half of 1533, and he was with the Deputy's army which marched into Meath from Dublin in the winter of 1534-5.[1] From 1535 onwards his name occurs constantly in the reports of the Dublin Council, and also in many of the private letters sent over to England from Ireland by Cromwell's agents. There is nothing to suggest that Staples was himself an adherent of the new Protestant gospel that was being preached with such vigour in London at this time, but he was undoubtedly a King's bishop who set loyalty to the Crown above loyalty to the Holy See in Rome.[2] English influence in Leinster was strong enough to maintain him as bishop of Meath, unchallenged by any rival, throughout the last years of Henry VIII, and he had no difficulty in accommodating his doctrine to the new policies which gained control in England under Edward VI. On June 29, 1554, he was deprived of his see by Queen Mary as being one of the married bishops of the new dispensation.[3]

The archdeacon of Kells took a very different line in these years of crisis. Six months after the murder of Archbishop Allen in Dublin we hear that Silken Thomas had sent " the official of Meath " abroad, to act as his personal representative at the courts of Spain and Rome.[4] This is our only indication that the archdeacon of Kells was also the bishop's official for two or three years (1532-34). Soon after this date an anonymous report to Cromwell states that " the traitor " (Silken Thomas) " hath sent the dean of Meath to the Emperor and to Rome a sevennight before Christmas."[5] The Act of Attainder of May, 1535, includes, among other prominent supporters of the Geraldine party, " Chale MacGrannel, *alias* Charles Reynolds, late arch-

[1] *State Papers* II, p. 233; *Letters and Papers* III, Part I, no. 1586.

[2] Edwards, *Church and State*, pp. 30-33.

[3] Morrin I, p. 337; Edwards, op. cit., p. 162-3.

[4] *State Papers* II, p. 221; see also *Letters and Papers* VII, no. 1574.

[5] *Letters and Papers* VIII, p. 176. The title " dean of Meath " is an obvious error.

deacon of Kellis."[1] An entry among the Roman documents of this year gives us our last glimpse of the archdeacon at the Roman court. On July 1, 1535, "Carolus Raynoldus, clerk of the diocese of Meath and archdeacon of the same church of Meath," binds himself for payment of the annate due for the rectory of Loughsewdy, which had been granted to Richard Walsh.[2] This latter is "Parson Walsh," who is named as an active supporter of the Geraldine cause in 1534, and who was also included in the Act of Attainder of May, 1535. We hear no more of Charles Reynolds after the summer of 1535. By English law he was adjudged to have forfeited his archdeaconry, and he seems to have died abroad soon after his mission to Spain and Rome.

Charles Reynolds had a younger contemporary, who may have been his near kinsman and whose name occurs more than once in the ecclesiastical records of these same years. On September 2, 1534, when Bishop Staples seems to have been a refugee in England, Primate Cromer—acting as *custos* of Meath in the bishop's absence—collated Master Thady Reynolds to the vicarage of St. Peter's, Clonard.[3] On November 15, 1540, Paul III provided Thady *Ranaldi* (Reynolds), who is described as doctor of civil and canon law, rector of Clonard and Clongill and vicar of Galtrim, to the see of Kildare.[4] But Thady Reynolds was less constant in his loyalty to the Pope's cause than Charles. He surrendered his papal bulls to Henry VIII, and the King's ministers in Ireland recognised Reynolds as suffragan of the schismatic Archbishop George Browne of Dublin.[5] But they did not recognise him as bishop of Kildare, since the King had already nominated William Meagh to that see. The precise status of Bishop Thady Reynolds during the

[1] *State Papers* II, p. 315, note 3; *Letters and Papers* VII, p. 525.

[2] Costello, p. 82.

[3] This collation was made at a time when Cormac Roth and Charles Reynolds were acting in close co-operation: see above, p. 71.

[4] Brady I, p. 351; *Archivium Hibernicum* II (1913): Supplement, p. 72.

[5] *Fiants:* Henry VIII, pp. 187; 276.

next few years is one of the many minor puzzles of this very complicated period.[1]

Apart from these personal problems, Cromer's register contains an entry for the year 1533 which raises a curious problem concerning the survival of a "bishopric of Clonard" as an alternative title to the bishopric of Meath. The "Dues of St. Patrick" were collected regularly throughout all this period, in Meath as in Armagh.[2] The collectors were laymen, nominated by the Primate for this office; and the collection was organised in the various rural deaneries of the diocese. But the list of collectors appointed for the year 1533 mentions "the deanery of Clonard" as distinct C.67.
from "the bishopric of Clonard." The older title of "bishop of Clonard," which had been common for most of the twelfth century, had fallen into desuetude since the time of Meath's first Anglo-Norman bishop, Simon Rochfort (1192-1224).[3] I am unable to offer any solution to the puzzle which is presented by this official entry in the Primate's register.

2. DOWN AND CONNOR

To understand the history of these two dioceses in the fifteenth century we must recall an important change of population caused by the reviving power of the O Neill in Tyrone and the neighbouring lands. Since the days of John de Courcy and his Anglo-Norman fellow-adventurers, there had been a remarkably strong colony of English settlers in that part of the modern Co. Down which corresponds with the diocese of Down. It was based on the fertile land

[1] See below, p. 263. [2] See above, p. 87-8.

[3] Simon Rochfort, with the permission of the papal legate who was then visiting Ireland in the name of Innocent III, transferred his see from Clonard to Trim in 1202: *C.P.L.* V, p. 75 (where this transfer is confirmed by Boniface IX in 1397).

lying in the two baronies of Upper and Lower Lecale, and also on the long, irregular promontory known as The Ards which lies eastward of Strangford Lough, separating that great stretch of inland water from the sea. In the thirteenth century the Anglo-Norman settlers had been strong enough to dominate the northern territory of Co. Antrim, and had thus got control of the diocese of Connor ; but they had lost their grip on this territory in the fourteenth century. One outlying " Old English " family of Mandeville still held its own in the lordship of " The Route " near Coleraine—taking Irish speech and Irish customs, and being known to its neighbours as the MacQuillans of the Route.[1] During the fifteenth century the Scottish-Irish family of MacDonnell gained control of the lordship in the Glens of Antrim, which had hitherto been held by the Norman family of Bisset ; whilst an adventurous sept of the great O Neill family of Tyrone (Clann Aodha Buidhe) fought its way across the river Bann into the western portion of what is now Co. Down, and won a name for themselves in Anglo-Irish tradition as the men of Clandeboy. English influence was now confined to the two baronies of Lecale, and the isolated peninsula of the Ards, where the family of Savage claimed a hereditary right to the position of seneschal of the earldom of Ulster.

The two dioceses of Down and Connor had been united under the rule of one bishop since the middle of the fifteenth century.[2] The see of Down had a Benedictine chapter, on the English model, since the time of John de Courcy and the first Anglo-Norman adventurers in Ireland. Its bishops had, since then, always been Englishmen ; and it was an English Benedictine prelate, John Cely or Sely, who planned the union of the two dioceses during his pontificate (1413-41). As compared with Down, the diocese of Connor was less affected by the Norman conquest. Its bishops had been once more native Irishmen since the early fifteenth century.

[1] E. Curtis : *History of Medieval Ireland* (2nd edition, 1938), pp. 238-40.

[2] O'Laverty : *Diocese of Down and Connor*, vol. IV (1895) ; and Costello, pp. 120-27.

John Fossard, an Englishman, was provided to the see of Connor by Eugene IV in 1432. In 1439 he and John Sely of Down made a mutual agreement by which both bishops pledged themselves that the two dioceses should be permanently united after the death or resignation of either prelate.[1] The union should thus have taken effect in 1441, when Bishop Sely was deprived by the Pope owing to charges of personal misconduct. But local resistance to the union was stubborn, and the union was not an accomplished fact until after the provision of Thomas Knight, another English Benedictine monk, to the united sees in 1453.

One last effort to maintain the separate existence of a diocese of Connor was made in 1459, when Pius II provided an English Dominican friar, Simon Elvington, to that see.[2] The new bishop probably never meant to reside in his new diocese. He acted as suffragan to the bishop of Exeter in 1463, and as suffragan to Sarum at intervals during the years 1459-81.[3] To add to the confusion, Nicholas V had provided another English Dominican friar, Richard Wolsey, to the see of Down in 1451, within the lifetime of the then reigning bishop of Down, Thomas Pollard. Bishop Wolsey acted as suffragan to the bishop of Lichfield in 1452, and to the bishop of Worcester from 1465 to 1479.[4] The career of these two English friars illustrates an abuse that was only too common in fifteenth-century Ireland. Vagrant English friars, in search of some title to episcopal status, had themselves provided to Irish sees which were either vacant or assumed to be vacant. They then earned their livelihood as "suffragans" or absentee assistant-bishops in some English diocese. The loose control exercised by English bishops and archbishops in Ireland, many of whom were themselves absentees, facilitated this shameless traffic in Irish dioceses.

[1] Costello, p. 121.
[2] Costello, p. 142; O'Laverty V, p. 278-9; C.P.L. XII, p. 12.
[3] Stubbs, p. 205.
[4] Costello, p. 122-4; C.P.L. XI, p. 234-5; Stubbs, p. 204.

A very curious document has survived in the archives of Westminster Abbey, which throws unexpected light on the plight of the English colony in Down during these years of confusion.[1] It is a petition, written in English and addressed to an English King; but the King's name is not mentioned in the document, and the petition is undated. It is certainly later than the union of the two sees of Down and Connor, since the first seal attached to the original roll is the seal of "the bishop of Down and Connor." Some of the other seals formerly attached to the roll have since disappeared, but the titles of those whose seals were affixed to the petition have been preserved. They were the bishop of Down and Connor, the prior of Down, the archdeacon of Down, the abbot of Bangor, the abbot of Saul, the abbot of Inch, the abbot of Grey Abbey (*de Jugo Dei*), the master of the Knights of St. John the Baptist, the city of Downpatrick, George Russell, baron, the town of Ardglass and the town of Kilclief. All these place-names lie within the two baronies of Lecale or the peninsula of the Ards. Inch and Saul lie near Downpatrick in Lecale; the two towns of Ardglass and Kilclief lie within the barony of Lower Lecale; Russell was one of the leading families of the English settlement; whilst Bangor and Grey Abbey lie within the territory of the Ards.

The petition is addressed to the King (probably Edward IV) in the name of "all the faithful and true liege people of the earldom of Ulster, which some time was named the third most royal earldom in Christianity, and now in default of lordship and people (is) with your enemies daily destroyed and under tribute constitute and thraldom." The petitioners complain of "the importable wars upon your said liege people daily continued, both by sea and land by sea, with Bretons and with Scots of the Outer Isles which both with Irishmen enemies of the land confedered: that is

[1] The full text is printed by O'Laverty: *Diocese of Down and Connor* V, p. 342. In the first edition of his *History of Medieval Ireland* (p. 322) Curtis suggested 1410 as the probable date; but he corrected this error in his second edition (p. 282). The date suggested by O'Laverty (*c.* 1490) seems to me somewhat too late, though it is not impossible.

to say with O Neill Bwy, Okane, McGwylyn, Henry Oneylle, Con Oneylle, McGyunusse, McCartan, and the Offlynnes; which within short time finally and utterly will destroy your said earldom and people, without that it be by your most gracious highness provided to send unto them a certain of people to inhabit and to defend your said ground." But the chief hope of the colonists lies in "your faithful servant and true liege man, Janico Savage,[1] your seneschal of Ulster, which hath kept and defended your said country with great adventure, daily in dread he and his men; with great care hunger thirst, watching bloodshed and manslaughter against your said enemies mortal; and even many great slaughters and discomfits in the which his friends that was to him most succour both slain and passed unrewarded as yet." The petitioners end with an urgent appeal for help, before it is too late. No names are given; but the names of the Irish chieftains suggest that this petition was sent to Edward IV by Thomas Knight, bishop of Down and Connor; Thomas Barkely, prior of Down; and Henry Fox, archdeacon of Down.[2]

Thomas Knight, who had been provided to the two sees in 1453, succeeded in establishing himself as their canonical bishop. He was consecrated by Primate Mey at Termonfeghin on May 31, 1456—almost three years after the date of his provision (August 24, 1453).[3] Throughout his pontificate he found it necessary to supplement his revenue by holding an English living *in commendam*. He was vicar of East Ham in 1459, and rector of St. Botolph's, Bishopsgate, in 1461, by dispensation of the Holy See.[4] Apart from the petition which I have quoted, very little is known of his administration.

On July 10, 1469, Paul II provided an Irish Augustinian canon, Thadeus O Morrissey (Omurgissa) to the sees of Down

[1] I believe that this Jenico Savage should be identified with the Savage who was slain by Conn O Neill in 1468 (A.U.)

[2] Reeves, *Down and Connor*, p. 176-7. For Henry Fox, see C.P.L. XIII, p. 313 and Octavian's Reg. fo. 153-5.

[3] Ware-Harris I, p. 203; Costello, p. 122.

[4] Stubbs, p. 205; C.P.L. XII, p. 192-3.

and Connor.[1] He had been prior of St. Catherine's in Waterford, and was at first dispensed to hold his former priory with his new see. He was consecrated in Rome on September 10, 1469, and made his profession of obedience to Primate Bole at Termonfeghin on November 29, 1470.[2] Owing to local opposition in Waterford, he had to surrender his former priory, and was then permitted to hold the priory of St. Mary, Kells, *in commendam*.[3] Down and Connor were evidently not counted as wealthy dioceses in the fifteenth century. Bishop Thadeus was present at the
O.385. first provincial council which Primate Octavian held at Drogheda in 1480 ; but died soon after that date.

The next bishop of Down and Connor was an Italian named Tiberius Ugolino. He was parish priest in the diocese of Nepi near Rome when he was provided to the two Irish sees by Sixtus IV on February 14, 1483.[4] Primate Octavian's success in reducing the confused state of Armagh finances to some sort of order in 1481-2 may very well have suggested to the Pope that another Italian administrator might do no harm in Ireland. But it was easier to make the appointment in Rome than to secure acceptance in Ireland ; and there were probably financial problems to settle. Tiberius had not yet succeeded in obtaining the release of his bulls when Sixtus IV died on August 12, 1484. The provision was renewed by Innocent VIII on September 12 of that year ; but an entry in the papal registers proves that Tiberius was not consecrated as bishop of Down and Connor until March 12, 1489.[5] This long delay is confirmed by Octavian's primatial register. No bishop of Down and Connor is named as having attended the provincial councils of 1483, 1486 and 1489. Bishop Tiberius appears for the first time at the council which was held at Drogheda on
O.402 ; 397 July 14, 1492, and he was again present at the council of

[1] C.P.L. XII, p. xxiv ; Costello, p. 124.

[2] Ware-Harris I, p. 204.

[3] Costello, p. 125-6 ; C.P.L. XII, p. 330 ; XIII, pp. 616, 639, 651.

[4] Costello, p. 126.

[5] Costello, loc. cit. ; C.P.L. XIV, p. 109.

1495. No record survives of the councils for 1498 and 1501. Tiberius was absent from the council of 1504, but he attended the last of Primate Octavian's councils on July 12, 1507. He was still resident in Downpatrick in 1517 when he showed hospitality to the Pope's nuncio in England, Bishop Chiericati.[1] If this distinguished visitor is to be trusted, Bishop Tiberius was then 114 years old; but the fact seems barely credible. Sixtus IV would hardly have provided a man of over eighty years to this distant see. O.287.

Sir James Ware tells us that this Italian bishop of Down and Connor "very much beautified his cathedral."[2] Dowdall's register contains a transcript of an earlier grant by which Bishop Tiberius had provided for the union of various small religious foundations in his diocese with a view to strengthening its building fund. The grant was dated from Carrickfergus on February 20, 1513; and the bishop states that he makes the grant "at the just and laudable petition of Master Gelasius Magennis (*Magnaisse*), commendatory of the cathedral of Down."[3] The older religious foundations which were incorporated in the cathedral by this grant were the former monastery of Cistercian nuns, then "lying in ruins"; the monastery of St. John the Baptist, the monastery of St. Thomas martyr, the "monastery of the Irish," with the rectory of Ardglass, the two prebends of Ross and Ballykilbeg, and the chapel of St. Mary Magdalen. With the exception of the "monastery of the Irish," which is said to have been founded by St. Malachy when he was bishop of Down, these other monastic foundations bring us back to the days of John de Courcy, who had planned to make Downpatrick a worthy ecclesiastical centre for "the third most royal earldom in Christianity."[4] D.32.

Gelasius Magennis, who is here named as "commendatory of the cathedral of Down," appears as prior of Downpatrick a few years later. He must have been

[1] See above, p. 52. [2] Ware-Harris I, p. 204.
[3] O'Laverty V, p. 282; see also *L.A.J.* VI (1927), p. 149.
[4] O'Laverty (V, p. 282) cites the full text.

marked out by the Irish party in the diocese as successor to Bishop Tiberius. But English influence was still strong enough to hold Downpatrick. Tiberius was dead before April 16, 1519, when Alexander Plunket, acting as vicar general for the absent Primate Kite, appointed Gelasius Magennis, prior of Down, as *custos spiritualitatis* of Down and Connor during the vacancy.[1] Just twelve months later Leo X, acting on the advice of Henry VIII, ended the vacancy by a disastrous provision.

Robert Blyth was abbot of the Benedictine monastery of Thorney in Cambridgeshire when the Pope provided him to the sees of Down and Connor on April 16, 1520.[2] He may have crossed over to Ireland for a brief visit in 1520 or 1521; but the Primate was then himself an absentee in England, and the new bishop of Down and Connor may have found it more convenient to make his profession of obedience to John Kite without crossing the Irish Sea. Blyth continued to reside in England for the rest of his life. His name appears on the English official records as the last abbot of Thorney, who surrendered his abbey to the King in 1540 and received in return an unusually substantial pension of £200.[3] Bishop Blyth had conformed to the King's new religious doctrines long before that date, and he was deprived of his Irish sees by Paul III in 1539.[4] For some time after the suppression of Thorney Abbey Blyth acted as suffragan to the schismatic bishop of Ely, and he seems to have died about 1547.[5] So far as our extant records bear witness, there is no proof that he ever visited Ireland. The dioceses of Down and Connor owe him small gratitude.

Cromer's register gives us some insight into the situation here in Ireland during the rule of this absentee bishop. In
C.13-14. 1524 the Primate, acting instead of the bishop, collated two clerks to rectories in Down and Connor. Early in 1526

[1] O'Laverty V, p. 283; Reeves, *Down and Connor*, p. 160. This entry is not in Plunket's Register.

[2] Costello, p. 127.

[3] Dugdale, *Monasticon* IV, p. 171.

[4] See below, p. 240.

[5] Stubbs, p. 205.

Gelasius Magennis, the Irish prior of Downpatrick, was murdered.[1] He is described in the Annals of Ulster as "a man of great lordship in church and state, and a man who was very rich." He was plainly the leader of the Irish party in the diocese. The Four Masters tell us that he was prior of Down and Saul, and abbot of the Cistercian monastery of Newry, at the time of his death.[2] The Primate appointed Brother John Swerds, of the Downpatrick community, to C.19. the vacant priory of Down, and the new prior took the customary oath of obedience to the Primate at Termonfeghin on June 19, 1526. His appointment was challenged by Conosius Magennis, evidently a kinsman of the dead prior, but it was confirmed by the Primate in the following C.21. August. About the same time the Primate collated another Irishman, Maurice O Heyle, to the vacant rectory of C.18 v. Rathsyne in Connor (Rashee, Co. Antrim) owing to the absence of the bishop from his diocese.

Bishop Blyth seems to have resented these interventions in the administration of his diocese, and he set about appointing his own administrators in 1526 and 1527. His first choice was the Franciscan bishop of Clonmacnois, Quintin O Higgin, who was unable at this time to maintain himself in his own diocese. Blyth was not satisfied with the bishop's rule, and issued a new commission on June 26, 1527, C.27. by which he empowered Bernard McCowra, the abbot of Woodburne in Connor, and Donald McKenny, rector of Carrickfergus, to act jointly as his vicars general. Primate Cromer was not prepared to accept these arrangements. On August 12, 1527, he issued a mandate in which he C.28. declared that Bishop Blyth, "who claims to be bishop of Down and Connor," had lost his right to exercise jurisdiction within the two dioceses owing to his prolonged absence "without license of the Supreme Pontiff or of the Lord Primate." The Primate annulled both the commissions of Blyth and reserved the exercise of jurisdiction in Down

[1] He was murdered by a rival party of his own sept : A.U. a. 1526.

[2] His son, Art og, was slain in 1537 : A.U.

and Connor to himself by virtue of an ancient decree of the province of Armagh which had been recently renewed at the provincial council of July, 1525.

C.26. On November 5, 1527, the Primate gave final sentence
against Conosius Magennis, who was claiming the priory of
Downpatrick against Cromer's nominee, John Swerds. He
was excommunicated by the Primate for having forged a
papal bull and for grave public scandal. On April 2, 1528,
the Primate heard the plea of Bishop Quintin O Higgin at
C.31. Termonfeghin. He now issued a new commission by which
he empowered Bishop Quintin and the archdeacon of Down,
Eugene Magennis, to act as his sub-custodians of the two
dioceses. But Bishop Quintin seems to have proved himself
an incorrigibly careless administrator. On February 28,
C.32 v. 1529, the Primate sat in his chapel at Termonfeghin, and
heard various complaints against Bishop Quintin: for his
prolonged absence from the diocese of Clonmacnois, and for
his failure to execute the terms of the Primate's recent
commission. The unlucky friar-bishop succeeded in clearing
himself from some of the charges brought against him, but
he was ordered to supply an account of the procurations and
other revenues which he had received whilst administering
the dioceses of Down and Connor. His commission as subcustodian was withdrawn, and Eugene Magennis was thus
left as the Primate's sole representative in the two dioceses.
C.51. The archdeacon's powers were further increased on October
9, 1530, when the Primate appointed him as full *custos
spiritualitatis* of both dioceses.

Eugene Magennis was a member of the ruling sept in Iveagh and could count on the support of his kinsmen. Paul III confirmed the Primate's policy some years later, when he provided the archdeacon to the two sees which had been left vacant by the deprivation of Bishop Blyth on June 16, 1539.[1] As bishop of Down and Connor Eugene Magennis compromised the Pope's cause by surrendering his

[1] Costello, p. 127.

bulls to Henry VIII in 1541.[1] We shall meet his name again in the history of these later years.

3. DROMORE

Very little is known of the diocese of Dromore during the whole of the fifteenth century. The diocese corresponds roughly with the two baronies of Upper and Lower Iveagh in Co. Down, and the ruling Irish sept was Magennis (Mac Aonghusa). The native Irish Annals tell us nothing of the bishops who ruled the see during this period. The evidence of the Roman archives is fragmentary and confusing ; but enough has survived to prove that Dromore was ruled by a succession of absentee English prelates for most of the century.

Sometimes more than one English adventurer claimed the title of " bishop of Dromore " simultaneously. One of these absentee bishops in the early fifteenth century was an English Benedictine named John Chourles, who acted as suffragan to Archbishop Chichele in Canterbury from 1420 to his death in 1433 : he seems to have been resident in London throughout that period.[2] During the last two or three years of his life two other rival English friars claimed to have secured a papal provision to the see of Dromore. One was an Augustinian friar named Thomas Radcliff, who was provided to the see in 1429, and ended his days as suffragan of Durham. The other was a Carmelite friar named David Chirbury, who was provided in 1431, and ended his days as suffragan of St. David's, in Wales.[3]

[1] See below, p. 253.

[2] For John Chourles, see E. F. Jacob : *The Register of Archbishop Chichele*, vol. I (1943), p. lxvii.

[3] Costello, p. 299. Brady's list (I, p. 297-8) is inaccurate and misleading.

The records for the middle of the century are particularly confusing, and no sure list of episcopal succession can be made out. On April 17, 1456, Nicholas V licensed an Irishman named Donatus Ohendua in the Roman archives (probably O h-Anluain or O Hanlon) to be consecrated by any bishop of his choice.[1] Donatus had been provided to the see more than twelve months before that date, but had failed to have himself consecrated within the legal period. From the terms of the petition submitted by this bishop-elect, it seems clear that he had secured administration of the temporalities of the see and possession of the church. But no more is heard of him after 1456, and the bad practice of providing absentee Englishmen was resumed. Richard Messing, an English Carmelite friar, was provided to the see by Calixtus III on July 29, 1457.[2] The see is then stated to be void by the death of Bishop Nicholas—apparently an earlier Franciscan friar-bishop named Nicholas Wartre, who had been provided to Dromore by Martin V in 1419 and who acted as suffragan to the archbishops of York from 1420 to 1445.[3] Since Bishop Nicholas used the title " bishop of Dromore " during all these years, we must conclude that during the years 1431-33 there were no less than four Englishmen using this title, though not one of them was resident in Ireland. John Chourles was in London, Nicholas Wartre in York, Thomas Radcliff in Durham and David Chirbury in St. David's.

Meanwhile another Carmelite friar named Thomas Scrope, who had been provided to the see of Dromore by Eugene IV in 1450, was still living and acting as suffragan to Norwich from 1450 to 1477. He did not die until 1499, and his memory was thus still recent when John Bale, the future English antiquarian and bishop of Ossory, entered the Carmelite convent of Norwich in 1507.[4] The provision of

[1] Costello, p. 300. [2] Costello, loc. cit. ; Stubbs, p. 206.

[3] Costello, p. 299 ; Stubbs, p. 205.

[4] Stubbs, p. 205-6 : citing an obit in Harl. MS. 211. Costello omits this name, which is given by Ware (I, p. 261-2) ; but Ware has confused Radcliff with Scrope.

Thomas Scrope is ignored in the bull by which Calixtus III provided Richard Messing to the see of Dromore in 1457. But the two men continued to use the title whilst they were serving as suffragans in York and Norwich. Messing was dead before June 15, 1463, when Pius II provided an Augustinian friar named William Egremond to the see of Dromore.[1] Egremond lived to 1501, and acted as suffragan in York during all that time.

When Primate Octavian began to take in hand the reorganisation of his province after his own consecration in 1479, Dromore had been without a resident bishop for as far back as the longest memory could carry; and there were then two absentee English friar-bishops (Scrope and Egremond) who were using the title "bishop of Dromore" in England. No diocese in Ireland had suffered more severely from the breakdown of ordinary metropolitan government in Armagh, and the new Primate was to find greater difficulty here than in any other diocese.

On April 14, 1480—a few months after Primate Octavian's consecration in Drogheda—Sixtus IV provided a Breton priest named Yvo Guillen, formerly a canon of St. Malo, to the see of Dromore; and on the same day dispensed the bishop-elect so that he might hold his former benefices with his new diocese.[2] There seems to be no explanation of this most unexpected provision, and the Pope makes it plain in his bull that the Holy See was at a loss to define the precise situation in the diocese of Dromore. The see is stated to be void by the death of Donatus or Donaldus (presumably Donatus O h-Anluain, who had been nominated in 1456), and the new provision is stated to be valid "even though the see might be void by the death of Eneas or of Robert Kirke or any other."[3] The only possible explanation of this remarkable clause is that the

[1] Costello, p. 300.

[2] C.P.L. XIII, pp. 83, 105-6.

[3] I have not been able to trace any provision of Eneas or Robert Kirke. There seems to be some confusion here with one of the Scottish sees.

Roman authorities who were responsible for keeping the lists of episcopal provisions had, as might easily happen, lost count of all the contradictory provisions of the past fifty years, and had, perhaps, confused the diocese of Dromore with some other diocese. There is nothing to connect Primate Octavian with this provision, which must be counted as the last in a long series of ineffectual, and apparently irresponsible appointments.

Primate Octavian was in Rome during the spring of 1482, and it is probable that he took advantage of his visit to report on the deplorable state of many of the dioceses in his province, including the diocese of Dromore. Chance favoured whatever plans may have been made at this time. Bishop Yvo Guillen was dead before April 18, 1483, when Sixtus IV provided George Braua, a canon of All Hallows, Dublin, to the see of Dromore.[1] Sir James Ware states that the new bishop was a Greek by birth and a native of Athens.[2] I have not been able to find any confirmation of this latter fact, but Bishop George's Greek origins are proved by an entry in the Annals of Connacht for 1530—when the bishop, who had been translated to Elphin in 1499, died in his diocese: " The bishop of Elphin died, that is the Greek bishop; and this death was not a stumbling-block to humanity" (*et ni hoilbeim don daonacht ant ecc-sin*).[3] Bishop George seems to have proved himself an ungenerous patron, to judge by this comment of the anonymous compiler of these Annals. His name is often spelt as *Brana* or *Brann*, but the form *Braua* is clearly legible in the contemporary Roman documents.[4] If the bishop was an Athenian by birth, his name does not suggest that he was of pure Greek origin; and we have no clue as to his personal history before the year 1483, when the Pope's bull of provision states that he was a canon of All Hallows. He was not the only foreigner who sought his fortune in Ireland

[1] C.P.L. XIII, p. 826; Brady I, p. xxv.

[2] Ware-Harris I, p. 263; *Rot. Pat. Claus. Hib.* 270b.

[3] *Annals of Connacht*, ed. Freeman (Dublin, 1944), p. 674.

[4] C.P.L. XIII, p. 826.

at this period. Sixtus IV seems to have favoured these foreigners when there was question of filling vacant Irish sees. Bishop George was consecrated in Rome on May 4, 1483.[1] At the time of his provision he had not even received the order of subdiaconate, but the three major orders were conferred on him within the next two weeks.

George Braua was not present at the provincial council which Primate Octavian held at Drogheda on July 10, 1486, but he is mentioned in an entry of the Primate's register for O.288. August 6, 1487. The Primate then issued a joint commission to two prelates who were to hold a visitation of Dromore in his name. One was the new bishop of Dromore; the other was Donald O Fallon, the new bishop-elect of Derry.[2] No report of this visitation has been preserved. The bishop of Dromore was at Drogheda on July 6, 1489, when Primate Octavian held his fourth provincial council there. As minister general of certain indulgences in Ireland, he had issued some indulgences which were O.147. confirmed by the Primate on May 30, 1494; but his name does not appear among the prelates who were present at the two provincial councils of 1492 and 1495. In 1497 Bishop George was working as suffragan to the bishops of Worcester and London—probably in connection with some negotiations in England concerning his future prospects.[3] On April 15, 1499, Alexander VI translated him from the see of Dromore to Elphin, which had become vacant by the resignation of Bishop Nicholas O Flanagan.[4] There is thus little evidence that this Greek prelate spent much of his time as resident bishop of Dromore. A mandate of Innocent VIII, dated May 6, 1492, is addressed to the archdeacon of Dromore and two canons of Dromore, and mentions the official of Dromore as administering the diocese.[5] Bishop George can hardly have been resident at this date.

From 1499 to 1511 Dromore was without any bishop at all, though Bishop Egremont was still using the title of

[1] Costello, p. 300; Brady I, p. 298.
[2] See below, p. 189. [3] Stubbs, p. 206. [4] Brady II, p. 197.
[5] C.P.L. XIV (unpublished galley-proofs).

bishop of Dromore in York until his death in 1501.
O.127. Octavian's register contains the full text of a most interesting petition which the Primate sent to some English King (almost certainly the youthful Henry VIII), at a time when the diocese of Dromore had been without a resident bishop for twenty years. Since Leo X gave the see a new bishop in 1511, it is probable that the petition was not sent by the Primate before 1510; and we may fairly conclude that Bishop George Braua had abandoned his diocese about the year 1490. Primate Octavian's letter to Henry VIII is in English, and is worth quoting in full, with its curious spelling, for the light it throws on the most unfortunate of all the Primate's suffragan dioceses.

"Humbely youre hyghnes besecheth yr. contynuell oratour Octavyane Archebysship of Ardmagh Prymate of all yr. land of Irland that where the bysspryk of Dromorens. withyn yr. saide land of Irland beynge in my prouynce of Ardmagh emonges wilde Irysh men which frutes rents and prouentus aswell spiritual as temporell extende not aboue the summe of xl. marces of the cowyn of this yor. land of Irland which is leasse in the thyrde parte than the coyne sterlyng for thexilitie and pouertie of the same is voide and desolate and almoste extincted this xxti wynter laste paste or moore in somych that none will sue the said byshipryk ne abide there yppon. it wolde please your mooste affluente grace to commende by your letres vnto our mooste holy fader the poape and to your procurator in rome one Arthure Magind bachelere of the holy canon lawe natyve of the dyocyse of Dromore. whom with grete instaunce I have caused to sue the said bysshipryk att this tyme in relefe of the sowles of the pouer people of the forsaide diocise and of my charge and cure pastorale to be promoted to the said bysshipryk and that for the love of God and in way cf charyte whom I commende to your mooste noble magestie."

The Primate's candidate for the vacant see in these last years of his rule was Arthur Magind (Art Mac Fhinn), who is here described as "bachelor of the holy canon law and a native of the diocese of Dromore." The family of Maginn

is mentioned frequently in the contemporary records of the diocese, and it is, of course, distinct from the ruling family of Magennis (Mac Aonghusa). Art Maginn had taken his doctorate or *magisterium* before the year 1520, when he is P.49-50.
named as one of the lawyers who appeared for the vicar of Termonfeghin in his suit against the convent of nuns. He was then a canon of Armagh, and is most probably to be identified as Master Arthur who was archdeacon of Dromore C.20.
in 1526. Primate Octavian had thus chosen a very representative priest of the diocese as his candidate for the vacant see. But the Primate's influence was not sufficient to secure his recommendation by the young King, who was already beginning to seek for every opportunity of increasing his personal authority over the Irish dioceses.

On May 11, 1511, Julius II provided an Irish Augustinian Friar named Thady O Reilly to the see of Dromore.[1] In the following January the new bishop sent a petition to the Pope which gives us some insight into the difficulties of his position. No man, he says, had been found willing for the past twenty years to preside over this bankrupt diocese; and he himself had only yielded to "the prayers of a certain temporal lord."[2] This temporal lord is not named in the petition; he may, perhaps, have been the Great Earl of Kildare, who was Lord Deputy at this time. Julius II had compassion on the bishop in his poverty and dispensed him to hold *in commendam* the Cistercian abbey of Assaroe near Donegal together with his bishopric. Seven years later the diocese of Ross fell vacant, and Leo X provided Bishop Thady to this see on December 23, 1519—uniting the two dioceses of Ross and Dromore, together with the abbey of Assaroe, during the bishop's lifetime.[3] It is not easy to see where Bishop Thady can have resided during the next few years, if he wished to fulfil his pastoral duties. But he

[1] Brady I, p. 299; *Letters and Papers* I, Part 1, no. 747. Brady's entry states that the new bishop was a Friar Minor.

[2] Costello, p. 284: ". . . . intuitu et ad preces certi domini temporalis."

[3] Brady II, p. 109.

seems to have been unable to cope with his many financial troubles and became involved in excommunication—most probably for failure to pay his debts to the Holy See. The register of Bishop Richard FitzJames of London (1506-22) contains an entry which tells us that this bishop of Dromore had celebrated holy orders in London whilst under the ban of excommunication.[1]

Bishop Thady O Reilly had died before June 6, 1526, when his successor was provided in Ross.[2] Dromore was left vacant for the next ten years. Primate Cromer, as can be seen from his register, acted as *custos spiritualitatis* of
C.20. Dromore during the second half of 1526. On June 28 of that year he united two rectories of the diocese to the archdeaconry for the lifetime of Master Art Maginn, owing to the poverty of his archdeaconry. On October 10, 1528,
C.36 v. the Primate was still acting as *custos* of Dromore, with the support of the archdeacon. On November 24, 1529, the
C.43. Primate—still acting as *custos* of Dromore—issued a formal commission appointing Master Art Maginn, archdeacon, as his official to hear all cases in the court of the diocese. In March, 1530, Clement VII issued three bulls concerning some minor benefices in the diocese of Dromore.[3] These bulls mention the archdeacon, and two canons of Dromore. One was Cormac O Shiel, the other being Eugene McGuinness—who is almost certainly to be identified as the archdeacon of Down. The Primate was still acting as
C.81-2. *custos* of Dromore in the autumn of 1534.

On May 29, 1536, when the King of England had brought matters to a head by forcing his new claims to be Supreme Head of the Church in Ireland, Paul III provided an Irish Dominican friar named Quintin Cogley (O Quigley) to this see, which had been vacant since the death of Bishop Thady O Reilly in 1526.[4] The new bishop probably never saw his diocese, for he was dead before June 16, 1539, when the Pope provided Roger Macciadh, vicar of Killaie in the

[1] No date is given for this entry, but it was probably earlier than his provision to the see of Ross. (Stubbs, p. 206).

[2] Brady II, p. 109. [3] Costello, p. 297. [4] Brady I, p. 299.

diocese, to the vacant see. This bishop-elect must have resigned his claims to the see soon after his provision, for Paul III finally ended the long vacancy by providing Art Maguissa (Magennis) on April 16, 1540.[1]

4. CLONMACNOIS

The diocese of Clonmacnois had once been very much more extensive than its present boundaries would suggest.[2] In the general settlement of Irish dioceses in the early twelfth century the kingdom of Meath was divided into two great dioceses: East Meath centring on Clonard, and West Meath centring on Clonmacnois. But the expansion of Anglo-Norman power through Meath and into the present county of Westmeath made it inevitable that Anglo-Norman bishops like Simon Rochfort and his successors should seek to include as much as possible of the former Irish kingdom in their diocese. By the end of the thirteenth century the former royal family of O Maelechlainn had been driven further and further west, towards the Shannon; and they were finally compelled to settle in that small corner of the present counties of Westmeath and King's Co. (Offaly) which corresponds with the modern diocese of Clonmacnois.[3]

Eugenius IV provided an Irish Friar Minor named John O Daly to the see on September 18, 1444.[4] His activities can be traced in the papal records down to the year 1463.[5] Bishop John attended Primate Octavian's first provincial council at Drogheda in 1480 and had died O.385.

[1] Brady I, p. 300.

[2] For the early history of the diocese of Clonmacnois, see the two valuable articles by the late J. P. Dalton in *Ardagh and Clonmacnois Journal*, vol. I (1927-9).

[3] See Fr. Paul Walsh's article on "The Ua Maelechlainn Kings of Meath," in *I.E.R.* (February, 1941).

[4] Costello, p. 154; C.P.L. IX, p. 432.

[5] C.P.L. X, p. 541; XI, p. 480-1; XII, p. 51.

shortly before March 26, 1487.[1] Yet we find Nicholas V granting a dispensation to an otherwise unknown Thomas, as bishop of Clonmacnois, on October 27, 1449.[2] This Bishop Thomas had pleaded that his see was too poor to support him and that he had no suitable episcopal residence, though himself of noble family. We can only conjecture that the diocese was disputed for some years between two rival bishops, both of whom seem to have been Irishmen. Bishop Thomas disappears from view after the date of this dispensation, but we find Calixtus III providing an English monk named William, who had been prior of the Augustinian monastery of Brinkburn near Durham, to the see of Clonmacnois on July 21, 1458. The see is here stated to be vacant by the death of a Bishop Robert, who is otherwise unknown.[3]

One very interesting papal document gives us some insight into the financial state of the diocese at this time.[4] Early in 1459 Bishop John O Daly, supported by the dean of his diocese and four canons, presented a petition to Pius II. They declared that the bishop, dean and chapter of the diocese (which then included an archdeacon and sacrist) had instituted a separate college of four priest-canons, who should be bound to the duty of residence and of singing masses and other divine offices, by day and by night. One of the rectories in the diocese (Loughloe) had been appropriated to the support of these four resident canons, since the fruits of the diocesan prebends were not sufficient to maintain the whole body of canons of the chapter. We are told that the non-resident canons, not having sufficient income to provide them with proper food and clothing, wandered about hither and thither, to the grave detriment of the diocese and the neglect of their liturgical duties.

[1] Costello, p. 155.

[2] Costello, p. 154; C.P.L. X, p. 53.

[3] Costello, p. 154-5; C.P.L. XI, p. 359-60. Stubbs does not include these two bishops (William and Robert) in his list of Irish suffragans.

[4] C.P.L. XII, p. 51.

Apart from the light which this petition throws on the finances of the diocese, it is of interest as a witness to the strong monastic traditions of the cathedral-church of Clonmacnois. Ancient tradition evidently required the canons to sing the divine office by day and night; and the breakdown of these traditional services had caused grave scandal to the faithful. The Pope confirmed the institution of this separate and smaller college of resident canons, and their claim to the rectory which had been counter-claimed by the Cistercian abbey of Granard.

Another papal document of the year 1476 lets us see only too plainly how great was the confusion in the chapter of Clonmacnois.[1] The deanery was vacant in this year, and Sixtus IV provided Eugenius Macholayn to that dignity. The bull in which this provision is made allows for the possibility that the vacancy may have been caused either by the death of Odo Omolloyn or the death of Toroleius Ymoleacylyn or the death of Odo Ymoleon or the resignation of any one of these three, or the resignation of Cucagrus Yegullen, who is described as a priest either of the diocese of Clonmacnois or the diocese of Meath. The Roman scribe who drafted this document was plainly at his wits' end to make every possible allowance for some unforeseen counter-claim. What the actual position was in Clonmacnois at this time, was no concern of his. He was faced with the immediate necessity of doing the best he could for Eugenius Macholayn, and he must have sighed to himself as he struggled manfully with all these difficult Irish patronymics.

On March 26, 1487, Innocent VIII provided Walter Blake, canon of Tuam and also of Enachdun, to the vacant see of Clonmacnois.[2] Four years earlier Sixtus IV had provided this same Walter Blake to the archbishopric of Tuam, which was then falsely stated to be vacant by the death of Archbishop Donatus. Walter must have been a young man in 1483, since the Pope dispensed him *super*

[1] C.P.L. XIII, p. 521. [2] Costello, p. 155.

defectu ætatis when making this provision. But the archbishop of Tuam did not die until 1484, and the provision of August 8, 1483, was thus invalid. Blake failed to secure a renewal of his provision to Tuam after the archbishop's death, but he had already been consecrated and was thus left a bishop without a see (*episcopus in universali ecclesia*). The death of Bishop John O Daly opened the way for a new provision and Blake became bishop of Clonmacnois early in 1487. Octavian's register shows us that Blake attended the
O.404 ; 397. two provincial councils of 1489 and 1492, but he was absent from the council of 1495. No record survives for the councils of 1498 and 1501 ; but he was absent again from
O.414 ; 287. the councils of 1504 and 1507. There is thus little evidence that he was in fact a resident bishop. The Annals of Connacht tell us that he died in 1508.

Bishop Blake was succeeded by Thomas O Mullally, of whom little is known.[1] Meanwhile the see of Tuam had been held for a brief period by the famous Franciscan archbishop Maurice O Fihilly, who died on May 25, 1513. Leo X translated Thomas O Mullally from Clonmacnois to Tuam on June 19, 1514, and Clonmacnois was left vacant for the next two or three years. On June 18, 1515, Henry VIII petitioned the Pope on behalf of a Franciscan friar named Quintin O Higgins, and Leo X ordered an inquiry to be held into the state of the diocese.[2] Cardinal Giulio de' Medici presented his report on November 10, 1516. A papal notary had examined eye-witnesses, who testified that the cathedral of Clonmacnois was without a roof and in ruinous condition ; that there was only one set of poor vestments, a cross of brass, a bell-tower with two bells and a sacristy. The revenues of the see were valued at 33 ducats yearly and were paid in kind from the crop of wheat and barley. Bad though these conditions were, we shall see that they were better than the conditions reported about the same time from the neighbouring diocese of Ardagh.

[1] The bull of provision by which Bishop Thomas was appointed does not seem to be extant.

[2] Costello, p. 155-6.

Leo X provided Quintin O Higgins to this half-desolate see soon after the date of this report.[1] His name does not occur in Primate Cromer's register until 1527, when we find him administering the dioceses of Down and Connor for the absentee English bishop, Robert Blyth.[2] In the deposition which he made before the Primate's court in February, C.32 v.
1529, Bishop Quintin pleaded that he was unable to reside in his own diocese "owing to danger to his life." Local opposition to his appointment must thus have been strong and the Pope's provision was without real effect. Bishop Quintin retained his title as bishop of Clonmacnois until his death *c.* 1539, but Clonmacnois seems to have had no resident bishop during all that time. For some years at least, the see was administered by Bishop Rory O Malone, who had been provided to the see of Ardagh in 1517, but was unable to establish himself as resident bishop in that diocese.[3] Bishop Rory had been a canon of Clonmacnois before his promotion to the see of Ardagh, and he was a member of a family which had given Clonmacnois many bishops and abbots during the twelfth and thirteenth centuries. He seems to have been able to count on sufficient local support to make his administration possible, and this personal link between the two dioceses of Ardagh and Clonmacnois is a curious anticipation of the union that was later effected between the two sees. A papal mandate of Adrian VI, dated September 5, 1522, lets us see that the family of O Malone was firmly established in the diocese at this time.[4]

An undated entry for Cromer's register, most probably C.80.
from the autumn of 1534, illustrates the close link between the two dioceses. The Primate, acting as custos of Clonmacnois, appointed the archdeacons of Armagh and Kells as his subcustodians, with full powers to visit the diocese and also "for extraordinary reasons" the diocese of Ardagh.

[1] The bull of his provision has not been found.

[2] See above, p. 139. [3] See below, p. 157. [4] Costello, p. 153.

Our records are scanty and imperfect, but it seems probable that Clonmacnois had been without an effective resident bishop since the death of the Franciscan Bishop, John O Daly, in the year 1486 or 1487. Dromore is the only other northern diocese in which there was so complete a breakdown in episcopal government; and the root cause of trouble in both dioceses seems to have been the lack of adequate revenues for the support of the bishop and his diocesan chapter.

5. ARDAGH

The diocese of Ardagh is frequently called the diocese of Conmaicne in the native Irish Annals, but that name is misleading since the diocese only includes what is properly eastern Conmaicne. It corresponds roughly with the territory of Annaly (Anghaile) in Co. Longford, over which the O Farrell family were lords, and also the territory of Muintir Eolais in Co. Leitrim over which the family of Reynolds (Mac Raghnaill) ruled.[1] During the fourteenth and fifteenth centuries most of the bishops of Ardagh had belonged to the family of O Farrell, or to the sept of MacBrady.

Towards the middle of the fifteenth century the ruling sept of O Farrell was divided into rival factions, each struggling for power. The episcopal succession was largely determined by the alternating success and failure of these dynastic rivalries.[2] Bishop John O Farrell, who had been provided to the see by Paul II on July 28, 1469, was dead before August 4, 1479, when Sixtus IV provided William O Farrell as his successor.[3] The new bishop was son of

[1] See in general J. Monahan: *Records relating to the dioceses of Ardagh and Clonmacnois* (Dublin, 1886).

[2] Most Rev. Dr. MacNamee: "The Diocese of Ardagh in the Sixteenth Century" in *Ardagh and Clonmacnois Antiquarian Society*, No. 6 (1937), pp. 5-30.

[3] Costello, p. 186; C.P.L. XII, p. 680; XIII, p. 99.

Donnchad, son of William—who had died as lord of Annaly in 1445. He was consecrated in Rome on June 11, 1482—almost three years after the date of his provision.

The Annals of Ulster throw some light on the confused strife of the next few years. Rughraidhe, son of Cathal, was recognised as lord of Annaly until 1488, when Conmac, son of Sean, son of Domhnall, was made O Farrell in his place. Conmac died in 1494 and was survived by his former rival, Rughraidhe, son of Cathal, who died in 1496 and is then given the title O Farrell in his obit. This Rughraidhe's claims had been challenged by a second Rughraidhe—son of Irial, a chieftain whose death is not recorded in the Annals of Ulster, but who had been deposed and blinded (so the Four Masters tell us) in 1473.

At this stage in the struggle for power Bishop William of Ardagh, who was himself a grandson of a lord of Annaly, intervened decisively. On the death of Rughraidhe, son of Cathal, he took Rughraidhe, son of Irial, as his prisoner, and had himself proclaimed O Farrell within this same year (1496). The bishop's bold bid for power did not go unchallenged. Cetach, son of Tomas, son of Cathal, son of Tomas, "was proclaimed another O Farrell after that." Open warfare was the result, and the bishop won the day in a battle fought early in 1497. Cetach was killed in this battle together with his son Laisech and many of his followers.

For the next twenty years Bishop William was able to hold his own as lord of Annaly. He is given the title O Farrell by the Four Masters in their account of the battle of Cnoc-tuagh (1504).[1] Bishop William had just attended Primate Octavian's provincial council at Drogheda in July of that year. In the following month he answered the summons of the Great Earl of Kildare as lord of Annaly and appeared on the battle-field with the other chieftains of O.414.
Leath Chuinn. Octavian's register tells us that this warlike

[1] An Anglo-Irish narrative of this battle occurs in the sixteenth-century *Book of Howth:* it describes O Neill's indignation at the presence of English bishops in the Deputy's council of war. (*Calendar of Carew MSS.*, vol. V, p. 181).

bishop attended the provincial councils of 1489, 1492, 1504 and 1507. He was absent from the councils of 1480, 1486 and 1495. No record of attendance has survived for the councils of 1483, 1498 and 1501. These entries are of special value, since they help to disprove Ware's statement that Thomas O Congalan had succeeded to the see of Ardagh some years before the death of Bishop William in 1516.[1] Thomas O Congalan was really bishop of Achonry and there is no doubt at all that Bishop William O Farrell ruled the see of Ardagh from 1479 to 1516.[2]

The Annals of Connacht tell us that Bishop William died in 1516 and they give him the significant title " bishop of Annaly." We hardly need contemporary evidence to assure us that this unusual situation was challenged by the bishop's enemies. A year after Bishop William's death Henry VIII petitioned Leo X on behalf of Rory O Malone as his candidate for the see of Ardagh. In his petition the King sets forth the present state of the diocese, as it had been reported to him by credible eye-witnesses: " Two other witnesses have deposed that the city of Ardagh lies in a mountainous region, in the midst of woods. There are in it no more than four timber huts and few dwell in them by reason of the continual enmities and quarrels which they have with their neighbours, especially in the time of the said Bishop William. For he wished to exercise temporal lordship there and some of his neighbours, resenting this claim, completely destroyed what remained of the city, which was never very habitable, together with the cathedral. The walls of the cathedral have to-day almost disappeared; there is only one altar and that under the open sky. Mass is celebrated there by one priest only, and seldom. The church has no sacristy, no bell-tower, no bell and scarcely vestments and vessels enough for the celebration of one mass. These are kept in a chest in the church."[3]

[1] Ware-Harris I, p. 254.

[2] See the comments by Most Rev. Dr. MacNamee, loc. cit., p. 8.

[3] Theiner, p. 521.

The King's petition is dated July 26, 1517. Leo X provided Rory O Malone, who is described as a canon of Tuam and of Clonmacnois, at a consistory held on November 14, 1517.[1] The new bishop held his see—in title at least—until his death in 1540. Cromer's register makes it plain that he was unable to exercise effective jurisdiction within his diocese. No entry concerning Ardagh occurs in the
register for 1523-29. On March 4, 1530, the Primate collated C.44 v.
a clerk to the vicarage of Shrule. On February 14, 1531,
the Primate heard a case which arose from a dispute between C.53.
the bishop of Ardagh and the abbot of St. Mary's, Dublin; he gave judgment in favour of the abbot. On March 10,
1531, the Primate collated Nicholas Nugent, of the diocese C.57-8.
of Meath, to the archdeaconry of Ardagh. No mention is made of the bishop's rights in this most important appointment, though the aid of the secular arm is invoked against any who may oppose the new archdeacon. On April 20,
1532, when the Primate was absent in England, Cormac C.62.
Roth, acting as his vicar general, collated Thady O Farrell to the vacant vicarage of Kilglass. A year later the Primate
himself collated John O Farrell to the vicarage of Mostrim. C.70 v.

The diocese of Ardagh must have been in a state of great confusion during all these years. The Four Masters record the bishop's death in 1540 and add that he had been administrator (*fer ionaid*) of the bishop of Clonmacnois as well as bishop of Ardagh. It thus seems probable that Bishop Rory O Malone, who had come to Ardagh from Clonmacnois, spent the last years of his life in his native diocese, where Bishop Quintin O Higgins had proved unequal to the task assigned to him.

6. KILMORE

The diocese of Kilmore corresponds with the Irish kingdom of Breifne and is divided into two main sections:

[1] Costello, p. 186.

East Breifne (Co. Cavan) in which the lordship was held by the family of O Reilly, and West Breifne (Co. Leitrim) in which the lordship was held by the family of O Rourke.[1] During the fifteenth century the see of Kilmore was held, almost exclusively, by bishops of the family of O Reilly and the two rival septs of MacBrady and Magauran.

Sixtus IV provided Cormac Magauran, a former prior of the Augustinian monastery at Drumlane, to the see of Kilmore on November 4, 1476.[2] An entry in a fifteenth century Irish manuscript (now Egerton MS. 1781) tells us that this bishop-elect was the son of a previous Bishop Magauran[3]—sad proof that the law of celibacy was not always observed in these years of distress and confusion. This fact seems to have been concealed from the Roman authorities when Sixtus IV made his provision in 1476. The Pope made a new provision on October 20, 1480, in favour of Thomas MacBrady, the archdeacon of Kilmore.[4] The result of these two provisions was a prolonged schism which troubled the whole diocese for the next thirty years.

A very curious witness to the confusion caused by this schism has survived in a scribal note written by Diarmaid Bacach Mac Parrthalain on November 22, 1487, in the Magauran territory of Tullyhaw. With the true scribe's wish to make an impressive and exact note of the date on which he had completed his task, Diarmaid Bacach names various chieftains who had been slain in this year and adds the note : " and at that time there were two bishops in the bishopric of Kilmore—that is to say, Cormac, son of the bishop Magauran and Tomas, son of Andrew MacBrady,

[1] See in general Philip O'Connell : *The Diocese of Kilmore* (Dublin, 1937), pp. 364-78.

[2] Costello, p. 257 ; C.P.L. XIII, p. 154.

[3] R. Flower : *Catalogue of the Irish MSS. in the British Museum* II, p. 538-9 ; see below, p. 159, note 1.

[4] Costello, p. 257. See also C.P.L. XIII, p. 277, for proceedings against Cormac Magauran.

and each man of them saying that he was the bishop."[1]
The schism had been in progress for three or four years when
Primate Octavian held his first provincial council at O.385.
Drogheda in July, 1480. Neither of the two rivals was
present at this council. More than two years later
(November 25, 1482) the Primate succeeded in arranging O.276.
that the two rivals should meet at Inismor in Loch Gowna
and come to terms. Cormac Magauran now undertook to
renounce all his emoluments from the two rural deaneries
of Drumlane and Dartry (Rossinver) in return for certain
payments from MacBrady.[2] Cormac is described in this
document as prior of Drumlane and he does not seem to have
won any recognition from the Primate or his rival as bishop
of any part of the diocese. He undertakes not to seek any
further apostolic letters against Bishop MacBrady and to
abide by the pledges given on his behalf by any nobles or
poets (*quorumcunque nobilium seu poetarum*).

This agreement was soon denounced by Cormac, who
was determined to assert his rights as bishop of Kilmore.
Seven years later, during his fourth provincial council at
Drogheda, the Primate made yet another effort to end the
schism in the diocese. On this occasion two of the bishops
present at the council—Bishop John Payne of Meath and O.386 v.
Bishop William O Farrell of Ardagh—were delegated to
settle the dispute. They met and co-opted the new bishop
of Clogher, Edmund de Courci, as a third arbitrator; but
the text of the entry in the Primate's register is mutilated at
this point and we do not know what terms were proposed to
the two rival candidates. Some working agreement must
have been reached, for we find the two rivals jointly present
at the provincial councils of 1492 and 1495 and affixing their O.397; 404.
signatures—each as bishop of Kilmore.[3] This curious

[1] Egerton MS. 1781, fo. 128: " 7 isin aimsir cetna dobí dá espoc a n-espoicdech Cille Móire .i. Cormac mac in espuic Megsamhradhain 7 Tomas mac Ainntriu Megbradaigh 7 gach fer dibh gá rádha gurub é fein is espoc ann."

[2] For Darty *alias* Rossinver, see O'Connell, p. 206-7.

[3] See also *Calendar of Christ Church Deeds*, no. 362.

arrangement could hardly have been possible without some territorial compromise and it is highly probable that Cormac Magauran was recognised as bishop of the two northern deaneries of Rossinver and Drumlane, whilst Thomas MacBrady made good his claim as bishop of the territory ruled by O Reilly. No record of attendance has survived for the two provincial councils of 1498 and 1501, but Cormac
O.414; 287. Magauran was absent from the councils of 1504 and 1507, though Bishop Thomas MacBrady was present at both of them.

These entries in Octavian's register are our only clue to the date of a definitive sentence which was given in favour of Bishop MacBrady by the Primate and the two bishops of Meath and Ardagh acting as judges delegate for the Holy See. The dispute must have been settled at some date after July, 1495—that is to say, at least fifteen years after the provision of MacBrady in 1480. But there is no doubt that Bishop MacBrady won final recognition of his claims from all parties. In their long obit, which records MacBrady's death in 1511, the Four Masters say that he was "the only dignitary whom the English and the Irish obeyed, a paragon of wisdom and piety, a luminous lamp that enlightened the laity and clergy by instruction and preaching." He died at Dromahair, whither he had gone to consecrate a church, and the Four Masters add that he had ordained priests and persons in every degree, and had consecrated many churches and cemeteries. He was in his sixty-seventh year at the time of his death and he was buried in the Franciscan monastery at Cavan, which had been handed over to the Brethren of the Strict Observance in 1502.[1] Yet even this zealous bishop seems to have failed in celibacy as a young man. His son, Thomas, who became a Franciscan, died in 1490, whilst his daughter died in 1515.[2]

One other entry in Octavian's register throws light on the activities of some clerks from the diocese of Kilmore,

[1] O'Connell, op. cit., p. 311. The O Reilly chieftains were usually buried in this monastery at Cavan.

[2] A.U. a. 1490, 1515.

though it is not probable that they were acting with the support of Bishop MacBrady. At the Primate's last provincial council of July, 1507, the abbot of Kells com- O.287.
plained that " some who assert themselves to be clerks of the diocese of Kilmore " had seized lands which belonged of right to the abbey of Kells and were seeking to incorporate them into the diocese of Kilmore—paying only such rent to the abbot of Kells as suited their own convenience. No names are given, but Kells lies near to the border of the modern county of Cavan and these clerks from Kilmore must have belonged to that portion of the diocese in which Bishop MacBrady's influence had always been strongest. The Primate, with the support of the assembled bishops (including Bishop MacBrady himself) issued a mandate in favour of the abbot of Kells and promised him protection.

Bishop MacBrady died either in February or August, 1511. His rival, Cormac Magauran, followed him to the grave shortly before Christmas of 1512.[1] Before his death Julius II had provided Dermot O Reilly to the vacant see and had simultaneously confirmed the previous sentence against the thirty years old claim of Cormac Magauran.[2] Little is known of the new bishop. Sir James Ware tells us that " he was a man of learning, and, being a lover of peace and tranquility, as the times were tumultuous in Ulster, he withdrew to Swords in the county of Dublin where for a long time he officiated as vicar."[3] He acted as arbitrator in a dispute between Hugh Inge, archbishop of Dublin, and the dean and chapter of Kildare in 1523.[4]

That a bishop of the family of O Reilly should have been unable to maintain himself in the diocese of Kilmore throws a vivid light on the disorders which troubled the diocese for so long a period. Cromer's register contains an entry for C.25.
the year which suggests that Bishop O Reilly was also commendatory abbot of Kells ; but the entry is obscure.

[1] A.F.M., a. 1511-12.
[2] Costello, p. 258.
[3] Ware-Harris I, p. 229.
[4] Ware-Harris I, p. 389.

Bishop O Reilly must have died in the summer of 1529,
for the Primate nominated Edmund Nugent, prior of the
Augustinian monastery at Tristernagh, to act as his sub-
C.41-2. custodian during the vacancy on September 10, 1529.
Nugent was a member of one of the principal Anglo-Norman
families in Westmeath and his appointment in a diocese
which had been controlled for so long by local Irish dynasties
is most significant. The prior of Tristernagh continued to
act as the Primate's subcustodian until June 22, 1530—
when Clement VII provided him to the vacant see.[1] This
provision is a clear indication that the King's authority was
increasing in the midlands and the new bishop was soon to
show himself a very tractable King's bishop. Two appeals
from his action as bishop of Kilmore came before the
C.52 v; 73. Primate's court in 1531 and 1533; but they are of no special
interest. On November 30, 1539, Nugent—who had
evidently been allowed to retain his priory together with his
bishopric—surrendered Tristernagh to the King's officers.[2]
On November 5, 1540, Paul III provided a new bishop,
John MacBrady, to the see of Kilmore.[3] But Nugent was
not so easily dislodged and he died as bishop of Kilmore
some ten years later.

7. CLOGHER

The diocese of Clogher corresponds roughly with the two counties of Fermanagh and Monaghan and the southern portion of Co. Tyrone. It lacks unity of character, if compared with the ancient system of Irish kingdoms. In Fermanagh the family of Maguire had been predominant since the early fourteenth century. In Monaghan the sept

[1] Costello, p. 258. [2] Morrin I, p. 57. [3] Brady I, p. 279.

of MacMahon was predominant, with their chief centre of influence round the ancient monastic site of Clones. During the fifteenth century the Maguire sept had gained control of almost all the ecclesiastical benefices in Fermanagh, including the bishopric at Clogher. But the dignity of coarb of Tighernach or Clones was still held by the MacMahon family. The Annals of Ulster were compiled in Fermanagh during the second half of the fifteenth century by Cathal MacManus, who died in 1480, and his son, Cathal óg MacManus, who was vicar general of the deanery of Loch Erne from 1483 to 1498. The MacManus family were intermarried with the ruling Maguire sept, and shared its interests.[1] Under the year 1486 Cathal óg sadly notes the wealth of the coarb of Clones: "Philip, son of the coarb MacMahon, namely, son of James, son of Rughraidhe, son of Ardghal MacMahon, who was canon choral in Clogher and coarb of Tigernach in Clones and parson in Dartraighe, and who had, for the greater part, all the fourths of the bishop of Oriel and the farming of the priors of Louth and Farney, died on the feast of St. John, Apostle and Evangelist." The vicar general plainly felt the loss of all these revenues from his own point of view.

Bishop Ross Maguire (Rosa Mag Uidhir), who was a younger son of Tomas óg and thus belonging to the elder branch of the ruling sept in Fermanagh, ruled the diocese of Clogher from 1448 to the date of his death (1483). His predecessor, Bishop Pierce Maguire, who belonged to the junior branch of the same family, had resigned his see in favour of Bishop Ross in 1448 and had died in 1450.[2] The Annals of Ulster make it plain that Bishop Ross was indifferent to the obligations of his priestly state. He was the father of several sons, whose descendants—most probably laymen—claimed an inherited title to the parsonage of Achad-Urcha in the diocese.[3] For reasons that are not clearly stated in our extant documents—and which

[1] See C.P.L. xi 321 for Cathal's interest in the tithes of Clones.

[2] Annals of Ulster, a. 1448, 1450; Costello, p. 54.

[3] Inquisitions of 1609, s.v. Fermanagh.

may have been connected with the domestic feuds of the Maguire family at this period—Bishop Ross resigned his see shortly before November 20, 1475. On that date Sixtus IV provided an English Benedictine monk named Florence Woolley to the see of Clogher.[1] News of the bishop's resignation seems to have been either false or premature. Ross Maguire was still bishop of Clogher when he died in 1483. Florence Woolley is found as suffragan to the bishop of Norwich during the years 1478-85; he died at Ipswich in 1500.[2]

There follows an interesting and dramatic struggle between the vicar general of the deanery of Loch Erne, who is no other than Cathal óg Mac Maghnusa, compiler of the Annals of Ulster, and a series of unsuccessful candidates who were each in turn provided by the Pope to the see of Clogher, but failed to get possession. The first of these unsuccessful candidates is named in a bull of Sixtus IV as "Nillanus." He had been provided to the see and had died at the Roman court before his bulls were expedited, before June 14, 1484.[3] There is no direct mention of this bishop-elect in the Annals of Ulster, but Cathal MacManus records the death of Niall, son of the coarb MacMahon, in that year—and adds that he died "coming from Rome in the summer." There can be little doubt that this Niall is identical with "Nillanus" of the Pope's provision. The threat to the Maguire power in the diocese is obvious. No sooner had Bishop Ross Maguire died, than the Pope had nominated the son of his principal rival, James MacMahon the coarb of Clones, as his successor. The news of Niall's death on his journey home from Rome must have eased the situation for those who stood for the Maguire interest in the diocese.

Sixtus IV had been a Franciscan before his elevation to the Holy See. He now chose an Irish Friar Minor to take the place of Niall MacMahon (June 14, 1484). The new bishop-elect of Clogher was from Munster and knew nothing

[1] Costello, p. 55; C.P.L. XIII, p. 472.

[2] Stubbs, p. 204.

[3] Costello, p. 55.

of the diocese to which he was being sent. His name is given as John Edmund Cursi in the bull of his provision and we are told that he was "of noble race."[1] Luck was against him from the first. Sixtus IV died before the bulls were expedited (August 12). The bishop-elect had to wait in Rome until the new Pope (Innocent VIII) had been elected on August 29. On September 12 Innocent renewed the provision made by his predecessor and ordered that the provision should date as from June 14, 1484.

Meanwhile Primate Octavian, acting as *custos spirituali-*
tatis of the vacant diocese, had begun to take action in
Clogher. On May 12, 1484—about a year after Bishop O.76.
Ross's death—he granted formal recognition to Philip
Maguire as archdeacon of Clogher, thus cancelling an act of
the late bishop who had deprived Philip of his archdeaconry
without due attention to canonical requirements. On the
same date he nominated Philip as his commissary to visit
the diocese of Clogher and ordered all the clergy of Clogher,
"and especially John Maguire and Thomas Maguire, canons
of the diocese," to accept the archdeacon's jurisdiction.
This mandate reads like a challenge to the powerful vested
interests which had controlled the diocese for so long under
the late bishop's rule.[2] No reader of the Annals of Ulster
can fail to note the conservatism with which Cathal
MacManus records all the fortunes of Fermanagh under the
rule of the Maguire dynasty. We may take it as certain that
he stood stoutly for the Maguire interest in the diocese.
His own attitude towards the prevailing abuses of his day
is plain enough from many entries in his Annals. There is
never an adverse comment in any of the entries which record
a failure in clerical celibacy; and there can be no doubt as
to his own choice were he asked to decide between the
interests of Maguire and MacManus on the one hand, and the

[1] Costello, loc. cit.

[2] John Maguire cannot be identified with certainty. Thomas Maguire, prior of Devenish, was granted a canonry by Sixtus IV, with the prebend of Devenish, on September 3, 1479: C.P.L. XIII, p. 700. He is described by Sixtus IV in the official grant as being "the son of a priest, but of a race of princes."

cause of ecclesiastical reform on the other. That cause was not likely to win favour in his eyes when it was championed by an Italian Primate in Armagh and a Friar Minor from Munster as bishop of Clogher.

The new bishop-elect of Clogher lost no time in journeying to Ireland. He was most probably consecrated in Rome before his departure, but there is no record of this ceremony. What happened when he came to his diocese is briefly narrated by the vicar general in an entry for the year 1485: "A Friar Minor from the Courcy country in Munster, namely Edward Courcy (and he was a doctor of divinity) went to take possession of the bishopric of Clogher this year, but his letters from Rome did not come to him this time." We can only conjecture that Cathal MacManus found some pretext for questioning the validity of the new bishop's bulls, and sent him home *re infecta*.

We hear no more of Edmund Courcy until the summer of 1488. No doubt, he had gone back to Rome to urge his cause at the Pope's court. His name does not appear among
O.389. the bishops who attended Primate Octavian's provincial council at Drogheda on July 10, 1486. The year 1487 was filled with the disturbances arising from the coronation of Lambert Simnel as Edward VI in Dublin.[1] Dublin is far from Fermanagh, and we might expect that Cathal MacManus would have little interest in these strange doings. But he makes two long entries about the English pretender. In the first he records the coming of "a great Saxon fleet to Ireland this year to meet the son of the Duke of York" (Lambert Simnel), and adds that "there lived not of the race of the blood royal that time but that son of the Duke and he was proclaimed king on the Sunday of the Holy Ghost in the town of Ath-cliath." In the second entry he records the defeat of the Yorkist and Geraldine forces in the battle of Stoke (June 20). These two entries may perhaps reflect Irish sympathies in this struggle for power in England, but Cathal MacManus had a personal reason for

[1] See above, p. 27.

taking the Geraldine side in this narrative. The new bishop of Clogher had taken the King's side. After some months of complicated negotiations with the Earl of Kildare, Henry VII sent Sir Richard Edgecombe as his ambassador to deal with the Geraldine leaders in Ireland. Sir Richard was delayed by contrary winds on his voyage from Waterford to Dublin and was compelled to take refuge on Lambay Island (July 3, 1488). Thence he "sent a man unto the land to go to Dublin to inquire for the bishop of Cloocornan, or Thomas Dartas, or Richard, the King's porter, to the intent that they or one of them should show the coming of the said Sir Richard and to have knowledge from them of the disposition of the country."[1] This contemporary narrative makes it plain that the bishop of Clogher (for that is the see so mysteriously disguised as *Cloocornan*) was in Dublin at the time and was acting as go-between in the interest of the Tudor King's ambassador. The bishop's name occurs again within the next few days, when Sir Richard had taken up residence in the Dominican convent of Dublin, "abiding the coming of the Earl of Kildare." On July 9 "the bishop of Clocornen and the treasurer of Ireland came and spake with the said Sir Richard in his lodgings." If "the Friar Minor from the Courcy country in Munster" was on the King's side in this crisis, it was, perhaps, inevitable that Cathal MacManus—who was ruling his people and writing his annals in Fermanagh—should be all for the Geraldine cause.

Edmund de Courcy was appointed papal nuncio and collector in Ireland by Innocent VIII on July 19, 1488.[2] He was thus sure of the Pope's favour as well as the King's favour in the summer of that year. On July 6, 1489, he attended the Primate's provincial council at Drogheda and was recognised there as the lawful bishop of Clogher. He was, as we have seen, one of three bishops who were appointed by the council to arbitrate in the disputed

[1] The contemporary *Voyage of Sir Richard Edgecombe into Ireland in the year* 1488, quoted by Donough Bryan, op. cit., pp. 128-9.

[2] C.P.L. XIV, p. 58.

succession of Kilmore.[1] The Primate's attitude during the
previous five years (1484-9) is not clear. The claims of
Bishop Edmund must have been brought before his notice
in 1485, but he may have abstained from a final decision at
this early stage in the dispute. The bishop-elect of Clogher
was not at Drogheda for the provincial council of 1486.
O.285v. A dispute between two priests of the diocese concerning the
rectory of Donaghmoyne was heard by the Primate during
the sessions of that council; and the Primate settled the
dispute in favour of Donatus MacMahon, as against John
O.333 v. O Flanagan, in a personal visitation of the diocese which
he seems to have held soon after July, 1486. We can only
conclude that his visitation had confirmed him in his
judgment that the diocese needed a bishop who should not
be too closely allied with the predominant Maguire interest.

Cathal MacManus could easily have told us all that we want to know about the situation in Clogher during these years. He was ruling a large portion of the diocese as vicar general for fifteen years before his death in 1498, and he was compiling the Annals of Ulster during these same years. Yet he shows an unexpected reticence in his few entries concerning this matter which affected himself and the diocese so closely. His Annals contain no mention of the two councils which Primate Octavian held at Drogheda in 1480 and 1483; and he has nothing to say about the councils of 1489, 1492 and 1495. But he has a remarkable entry about the council of 1486, and it is tempting to guess that he must himself have attended this council as representing Fermanagh: "A general chapter in Drogheda by the archbishop of Armagh, namely, the Italian Octavian, and the bishops and clergy of northern Ireland on the fifth of the Ides of July. Domhnall O Fallon, a Friar Minor of the Observance and the preacher that did most service to Irishmen since Patrick was in Ireland, was endeavouring to release his letters for the bishopric of Derry at that chapter, which had been granted to him from Rome." No mention is made of

[1] See above, p. 159.

that other Friar Minor from Munster, who was also endeavouring to release his letters from Rome at this very time. And there is no entry in Cathal's Annals as to the provincial council of 1489, at which Bishop Edmund de Courcy won recognition from the Italian Primate. The vicar general preferred not to mention these distasteful details in his Annals.

Edmund de Courcy won general recognition of his claims at the council of 1489. When the bishops assembled at that council had nominated the bishops of Meath and Ardagh to act as arbitrators in the disputed succession of O.386v.
Kilmore, with power to co-opt a third arbitrator, their choice fell on Bishop Edmund. Since the bishop of Meath was the English Dominican, John Payne, and the bishop of Ardagh was the warlike Irish chieftain, William O Farrell, their recognition of Edmund as bishop of Clogher would seem to imply that he had won the day in Ireland. But local opposition had yet to be overcome and Cathal MacManus—backed by the powerful Maguire connection—proved too strong for the new bishop. We hear no more of Bishop Edmund in Ireland for the next few years. He was absent from the Primate's provincial council of 1492, and we can only guess that he had gone abroad—either to England or to Rome. On September 26, 1494, Alexander VI provided him to his own native diocese of Ross, though he does not seem to have renounced his claims to the see of Clogher.[1]

Meanwhile some entries in the Roman archives give us a glimpse of priests from the diocese of Clogher who had made the long journey to Rome—either for their own personal interests, or to oppose the bishop's claims. On January 12, 1492, Innocent VIII provided James MacMahon, rector of the parish church of St. Tigernach in the diocese of Clogher, to the archdeaconry of Armagh and the rectory of Heynestown.[2] James MacMahon, who appears here for the first time in the Roman records, is very probably the James, son of Philip, son of the coarb James, who is men-

[1] Brady II, p. 108; Costello, p. 56.

[2] Costello, p. 10.

tioned by Cathal MacManus in his first entry for the year 1486.[1] I have already dealt with the complicated story of this intrigue, which arose from a quarrel between Primate Octavian and his archdeacon, Henry Corkeran.[2] A few days after this provision, which proved ineffectual owing to the Primate's opposition, the Pope gave orders that Donald MacCreever should be provided to the deanery of Armagh and the priory of the Culdees in Armagh, which are stated to be vacant by the deprivation of Peter O Mulloy.

Since James MacMahon and Donald MacCreever bound themselves in person for payment of their annates a few days after the dates of these provisions, it is certain that the two men were in Rome during the first two months of 1492. A third priest of the diocese of Clogher, James O Beirne (Ybruyn), obtained a similar provision to the abbey of Knock, near Louth, on May 17 of that year. The presence of these three Clogher priests in Rome at a time when Edmund de Courcy was still seeking to secure recognition as bishop of Clogher can hardly be an accidental coincidence. They seem to have obtained their preferments in Armagh on a doubtful title, and were unable to sustain their claims. They belonged to the powerful MacMahon sept, which had always contested the Maguire supremacy in the eastern portion of the diocese of Clogher. There was thus a three-cornered contest for control of the diocese during these years. In Rome Bishop Edmund was arguing his case on grounds of canon law, whilst James MacMahon and Donald MacCreever were willing to take whatever fortune might send in their way. Meanwhile the vicar general, Cathal MacManus, was in a strong position at home in Fermanagh. Whilst the Roman authorities made grants and cancelled them, he was content to govern his people and compile his famous Annals.

A chance entry in a consistorial record for November 5, 1494, mentions an otherwise unknown James as bishop-elect of Clogher. The presence of James MacMahon in Rome in

[1] See above, p. 163. [2] See above, p. 17-18.

1492 makes it very tempting to identify him with this *Reverendus Dominus Jacobus, electus Clocorensis.*[1] Having failed to make good his claim as archdeacon of Armagh, James MacMahon may well have stayed on in Rome, hoping for another chance. The provision of Bishop Edmund to the see of Ross in September, 1494, was an obvious opportunity. It is clear from the Roman archives that Edmund de Courcy hoped to retain his diocese of Clogher, whilst also holding the diocese of Ross—just as Bishop Thady O Reilly of Dromore held the two sees of Ross and Dromore for some years in the next generation.[2] In 1500, Alexander VI gave Bishop Edmund a coadjutor in Clogher named Andrew, whilst recognising his title as bishop of Ross.[3] The appointment of Bishop James in 1494 cannot easily be reconciled with these other entries. I can only suggest that James MacMahon was in Rome when Bishop Edmund secured his provision to Ross in September, 1494; that he immediately laid claim to Clogher as vacant by this translation; and that the Pope (Alexander VI) made a provision to Clogher which was afterwards cancelled at the petition of Bishop Edmund. These facts fit the known background well; but one curious anomaly must be noted. The unknown James who is styled bishop-elect of Clogher in November, 1494, had secured *in commendam* the Cistercian monastery of Maure (*de Fonte Vivo*) in the diocese of Ross.[4] James MacMahon would hardly have chosen a benefice in his rival's diocese—unless this commendatory benefice had already been held for some years by Bishop Edmund as a means of supplementing his nominal revenues from Clogher. The Roman authorities may have blundered in assuming that this abbey in Ross was in some way attached as a benefice to the vacant diocese of Clogher. Bishop Edmund's counter-appeal has not been preserved; but there is no doubt at all that Edmund was still bishop of Clogher and bishop of Ross six years later. Very probably

[1] Costello, p. 55—but a wrong date (1495) is given on p. 56.
[2] See above, p. 147. [3] Costello, p. 56. [4] ibid.

he was also commendatory abbot of Maure as well. On July 5, 1501, James MacMahon secured a provision as bishop of Derry. This time he was successful in making good his claim.[1]

This prolonged struggle for the see of Clogher during the last years of the fifteenth century throws light on the contemporary history of Ireland's most famous pilgrimage. As early as 1479 Sixtus IV had received a report that the priory of Loch Derg "was without prior or convent, and (what is worse) that divine worship is not celebrated there, its revenues being in undue possession of some powerful clerks."[2] The Pope then ordered the abbot of SS. Peter and Paul at Clones, the dean of Clogher and Charles MacManus, a canon of the same diocese (very probably the compiler of the Annals of Ulster), to cite these clerks. If the facts as reported to the Pope were found true, they were ordered to separate the rectory of Templecarne from the priory of Loch Derg, and to collate Nellanus Magrath, who had petitioned for this dissolution, to the rectory. We hear no more of the priory for the next few years. In 1485 Primate Octavian issued formal letters of protection for two French pilgrims from Lyons, who had spent two years in Ireland and had visited Croagh Patrick and the Cave of St. Patrick's Purgatory.[3] In 1494 a Dutch pilgrim, formerly an Augustinian canon of Eymstadt, came to Ireland in the hope of visiting the Cave at Loch Derg. His own account of his experiences is as follows[4]:

"The Brother came to the place and the monastery where the entry was said to be and he spoke with the president of that place (*præsidens illius loci*), revealing to him his desire. Who sent him to the diocesan (*ad diocesanum*), telling him it was illegal for him to admit any one without his bishop's consent (*sine assensu pontificis sui*).

[1] See below, p. 192. [2] Costello, p. 49.

[3] Sir Shane Leslie, *Saint Patrick's Purgatory*, p. 61.

[4] The Latin text is printed by the Bollandists in *Acta Sanctorum*, March, vol. II, p. 588. Sir Shane Leslie prints a translation: op. cit., p. 61.

The pilgrim went to the bishop (*adiit episcopum*), but, since he was poor and penniless, he was scarcely admitted by the servants. Falling at the knees of the bishop, he begged permission to enter St. Patrick's Purgatory; but the bishop demanded a certain sum of money, saying it was due to him of right from those who entered. The Brother replied that he was poor and had no money; and even if he had, that he would not dare to give it for fear of the taint of simony by thus obtaining it. After many prayers he at length persuaded the bishop, who granted him letters of admission and sent him to the prince of that territory (*ad principem territorii illius*). The prince also asked the Brother for money; but, as he could not get it from one who had no money, he admitted him in the end, though with much difficulty. The Brother then returned to the prior of the place of the Purgatory (*ad priorem loci Purgatorii*), and showed him the letters of the bishop and the prince. The prior read them, and said to him: 'Brother, you must pay our monastery the accustomed fee'; and told him the sum. The Brother replied that he had no money because he was a mendicant; and that it was not lawful for him to pay for such a favour, as it would be simony; but that he begged to be admitted into that famous place for the love of God and the salvation of his soul. Accordingly the prior ordered his sacristan (*sacristæ suo*) to admit him to the place."

The narrative goes on to recount the Dutch pilgrim's disappointment after his night's vigil, and his subsequent journey to Rome where he denounced the whole pilgrimage to the Pope as tainted with simony. Alexander VI took action within the next two years. Very probably he had consulted Primate Octavian meanwhile, and had received an unfavourable report from Armagh. The Annals of Ulster have this brief, but carefully worded entry for the year 1497: "The Cave of the Purgatory of Patrick was broken in this year by the guardian of Donegal and by the representatives of the bishop in the deanery of Loch Erne, under the authorisation of the Pope, about the Feast of Patrick in that year: it being understood by every one in general, from the

History of the Knight and other old books, that this was not the Purgatory Patrick got from God, although they were every one visiting it."

The Dutch pilgrim's narrative is thus confirmed on one important point by the contemporary evidence of the Annals of Ulster. But there are several surprising details in his story. Who was the bishop of Clogher to whom he was sent by the prior of Loch Derg ? Why did he not go to Primate Octavian, since other earlier documents (including Octavian's permit of 1485) make it certain that license to enter the Purgatory had to be granted by both the Primate and the bishop of Clogher ? Why does his description of the pit into which he was lowered by the sacristan differ from every other description that has come down to us from the medieval period ?

I think there can be little doubt that we have here a truthful, though not very edifying account of the customs observed at Loch Derg during the years when Cathal MacManus was acting as dean of Loch Erne and vicar general (*fer-inaid espuic*) of the bishop of Clogher in Fermanagh. There is no mention of the Primate in his narrative, for the simple reason that Primate Octavian recognised Edmund de Courcy as lawful bishop of Clogher in 1494. The Dutch pilgrim had the bad luck to come at a time when the diocese was without a resident bishop, and the " bishop " to whom he went can hardly be any one else save Cathal MacManus, who exercised episcopal jurisdiction (without the Primate's sanction) during all these years. The phrase which he himself uses as compiler of the Annals of Ulster in 1497 (*lucht inaid espuic a n-degantacht Locha h-Eirne*) makes it almost certain that Cathal MacManus took part in the formal ceremony of demolition in that year. One recent commentator has argued, with fair show of reason, that the Dutchman's description of his experiences proves that he was never brought to the true Cave of the Purgatory at all.[1]

[1] Alice Curtayne : *Loch Derg : St. Patrick's Purgatory* (London, 1944), pp. 50-54 ; see also Leslie, op. cit., p. xxix.

As we read the pilgrim's lively account of the stubbornness with which he refused to pay any fee to the prior, the bishop and the prince of the territory (presumably Mac Craith), we cannot help suspecting that he was made the victim of a deliberate and cynical fraud. If he would not pay, so the prior and the sacristan seem to have argued, then he had no right to expect admission to the Cave. The subsequent order from the Pope that the Cave was to be broken up suggests that there must have been some very genuine reasons for suspecting the good faith of those who were in charge of the pilgrimage at this time. The Pope's mandate had no permanent effect, and we hear of fresh pilgrims to Loch Derg within a few years of the date of this formal suppression. The pilgrimage thus went on until, purified in the fires of persecution, it became once more a support and strength to the Irish people in the dark years of the seventeenth and eighteenth centuries.

Cathal MacManus died on March 23, 1498. From the long obit which his son and successor, Thomas MacManus, entered in the Annals at this point, we learn that Cathal had been vicar general (*fer-inaid espuic*) for fifteen years before his death: that is to say, from the death of Bishop Ross Maguire in 1483 to his own death in 1498. He was also hospitaller (*biatach*) of Seanadh, a small island sanctuary at the western end of Loch Erne, canon of the two dioceses of Armagh and Clogher, rural dean of Loch Erne, and parson of Inis-cain, an island in Loch Erne. The vicar general was thus the dominant personality in the diocese of Clogher for fifteen eventful years. His eulogy in the Annals of Ulster contains a panegyric of all his Christian virtues. The evidence of his own narrative, combined with other contemporary records, makes it only too plain that he was negligent in some of the most serious obligations of his priestly state. He himself chronicles the birth of various sons and daughters who were born to him whilst he was vicar general of the deanery. Their mother was a daughter of the neighbouring O Farrell chieftain, whilst Cathal's own mother had been a daughter of the Maguire chieftain,

Tomás óg.[1] Cathal MacManus was thus, by birth and all the ties of family tradition, tenacious of old Irish custom, whether good or bad. His formal eulogy tells us that the bards and pilgrims and poor mendicants of Ireland were grateful to him and that he was full of grace and of knowledge in every science, both law and divinity, physic and philosophy, and also of the Gaelic tongue. All this may well be true, but his death must have removed a formidable obstacle to reform in the diocese of Clogher. It also opened the way to a final settlement of the prolonged dispute concerning the bishop's claim to the see.

On June 10, 1500, Alexander VI gave Bishop Edmund a coadjutor named Andrew, with right of succession to the see of Clogher.[2] Edmund was still bishop of Ross at this time. This attempt at a settlement seems to have failed, for reasons unknown to us. Andrew disappears from the scene and Bishop Edmund finally resigned his claims to the see of Ross. On January 24, 1502, Alexander VI provided an Irish Augustinian friar named Nehemias Clonin to the vacant see. But this new bishop-elect of Clogher seems to have resigned his claims to the troublesome diocese within the next two years. On March 6, 1504, a new Pope (Julius II) provided the abbot of Clones, Patrick O Connolly (Gilla Padraig O Conalaigh) to the vacant see.[3] None of the names hitherto mentioned are recorded in the Annals of Ulster, with the exception of this bishop-abbot. His obit is given under the year 1504: "The abbot of Clones, Gilla Padraig, son of Henry O Connalaigh, died this year, of the King's game[4] [the plague] after the bishopric of Clogher had been obtained for him."

The new bishop must have died soon after his provision. On April 4, 1505, Julius II made a provision that was to prove more permanent. He chose the dean of Clogher,

[1] A.U. a. 1486, 1515.

[2] Costello, p. 56. [3] ibid.

[4] Patrick O Connolly had been abbot of Clones since 1493: Costello p. 43.

Eugene MacCawell (Eoghan Mac Cathmhail) who belonged to a family that had given bishops and other dignitaries to the two dioceses of Armagh and Clogher for many generations.[1] Bishop MacCawell died in 1515 and the Annals of Ulster have this obit: "The bishop of Clogher, namely, Eoghan, son of Art, son of Eogan, son of another Art MacCawell, died this year." Eoghan was a fighting man, for the bull of his provision includes a dispensation from an irregularity owing to the loss of a finger of his left hand, "which he had lost in the defence of his church."

An entry for the year 1502—four years after the death of Cathal MacManus—tells us that "the coarb of Clones, namely, James, son of Rughraidhe MacMahon, died this year in an old age of ninety years."

This title "coarb of Clones" is misleading. In the earlier pre-Norman period the title was undoubtedly used to designate the abbots of Clones in succession to Tigernach, founder of this great monastery. There were still abbots of Clones in the fifteenth century, but the title "coarb" was now given to laymen who held the monastic revenues, and who are commonly called *rectores* or *plebani* of Clones in the contemporary papal documents.[2] Rughraidhe MacMahon, father of James, had at least eighteen sons, and died as king of Oirghialla in 1446.[3] James, his son Philip, and his grandson, the younger James, held the *corbania* of Clones for the greater part of the fifteenth century.

On August 8, 1477, when James must have been seventy-five years old, his son Philip lodged a petition against him in Rome, complaining that his father "James MacMahon, a layman of the diocese of Clogher, has usurped the fruits of the parish church of Clones for between thirty

[1] Costello, p. 56; Brady I, p. 251.

[2] Archdeacon Seymour has studied this *corbania* in his paper: "The Coarb in the Medieval Irish Church" (Proc. R.I.A., 1933), p. 222. But his evidence is most inadequate. The MacMahon family seem to have got control of Clones in the early fifteenth century.

[3] A.U. a. 1446: see also the Fermanagh genealogies printed in *Analecta Hibernica*, no. 3 (1931), p. 126.

and forty years."[1] According to the son's petition, the parish church of Clones "had been vacant for so long that there was no longer any certain knowledge as to the mode of its voidance." In other words the thirty years old tenure by the coarb James was now set aside as invalid and uncanonical, and Philip successfully petitioned for the collation of this valuable rectory to himself. The yearly value is given in this papal mandate as sixteen and thirty marks sterling. Sixtus IV commissioned the abbot of St. Mary's, Louth, to hear the case. Philip was already a canon of Clogher at the time of this petition. He must have won his case, for Cathal MacManus gives him the title "coarb of Tigernach" (that is to say, coarb of Clones, since Tigernach was the founder of this monastery) in his obit under the year 1486.

On Philip's death his place as "coarb" was taken by his son James, whilst Domhnall Maguire and Patrick O Connolly were rival abbots of Clones during the next few years.[2] Meanwhile there had been fighting at Clones. In his first entry for the year 1486 Cathal MacManus tells us that "Art, son of MacDonnell of Clann Cellaigh, was slain in Clones in a quarrel he made with clerics on Little Christmas Day" (January 6, 1486). The clerics who opposed Art are then named: "James, son of Philip, son of the coarb MacMahon; and the son of Donnchad MacMahon; and Gilla Padraig O Connolly, that is, the abbot." Eleven years later, within the lifetime of Abbot O Connolly, we find the obit of Domhnall, son of Bishop Ross Maguire, who died as "abbot of Clones" in the summer of 1497. This is a clear indication that the Maguire family were pressing hard on Clones, at a time when Cathal MacManus was still administering the diocese of Clogher in their interest. Domhnall Maguire failed to dislodge O Connolly, who survived him as abbot of Clones for another seven years.

A more successful effort was made in the early sixteenth century—very probably in the years immediately following

[1] C.P.L. XIII, p. 579.

[2] Costello, pp. 40, 43; A.U. a. 1497, 1504.

Abbot O Connolly's death. The famous Maguire chieftain known to history as "Cuchonnacht the coarb" first appears in the Annals of Ulster as "the coarb Maguire" in the year 1513.[1] He is named again in 1519 and 1522; and he was proclaimed Mag Uidhir in 1527. From that date to his death in 1537 he was the most formidable figure in Fermanagh and Monaghan.[2] His curious title has never been explained. I suggest that he had succeeded in establishing his claim, most probably by violence, to the *corbania* of Clones, which had hitherto been held by members of the MacMahon family or of their kindred septs. Even within the lifetime of the great Cuchonnacht, the MacMahon family had not renounced their claim to the monastery. Manus MacMahon died as abbot of Clones in 1536, according to an entry in the Annals of Ulster. The two families of MacMahon and Maguire were thus disputing their rival claims to the monastic revenues when Henry VIII set about suppressing all the Irish monasteries within his jurisdiction. The King's power did not extend as far as Clones and the monastery thus escaped immediate suppression. We hear no more of its history until we find a record of its former possessions in an Inquisition of 29 Elizabeth (1587).[3]

The seizure of the monastic lands of Clones by the Maguire chieftain must have meant a great shifting of power within the diocese.[4] The MacMahon interest had suffered a grievous blow and it is perhaps no mere coincidence that their most prominent ecclesiastical representative, James MacMahon the younger, left the diocese and accepted a provision to the see of Derry in 1501. Meanwhile the bishopric had passed in turn from Edmund de Courcy to

[1] See Father Paul Walsh's article: "The Maguire chieftains of Fermanagh" (cited below, p. 186, note 2).

[2] Cuchonnacht's name occurs once in Cromer's Register (fo. 52), when his aid was invoked on behalf of an appellant in 1530.

[3] Archdall, *Monasticon*, p. 584. Clones is not among the Irish monasteries whose "Extents" have recently been edited by Mr. N. B. White.

[4] The Annals of Ulster (a. 1537) describe this change when they say that Cuchonnacht had "placed under his obedience from Cluain-eois to Cael-uisce."

Patrick O Connolly and from Patrick O Connolly to Eoghan MacCawell. Bishop MacCawell died in 1515 and the see remained vacant for more than a year.

On February 11, 1517, Leo X provided an Irish Augustinian friar named Patrick O Cullen to the see of Clogher.[1] In the traditions of his order Bishop Patrick is remembered as an eminent prelate, learned, eloquent and devout. Little is known of the early years of his pontificate but in 1525 his name is associated with Rory O Caiside, archdeacon of Clogher, a noteworthy figure in the history of Irish sixteenth century learning. As early as September 2,
O.180. 1502, Archdeacon O Caiside was party to a suit before Primate Octavian's court at Drogheda in defence of his rights in the vicarage of Magheracross. Some years later—most probably soon after 1506—he seems to have acquired the manuscript version of the Annals of Ulster which is now known as the B-text of those Annals (Rawlinson MS. B. 489).[2] A note under the year 1541 records the fact that the archdeacon, who died in that year, " wrote this book for the greater part." The precise meaning of this phrase is open to doubt. A similar entry under the year 1528 records the death of Rory O Luinin " who wrote the choice part of this book." Rory O Luinin was undoubtedly responsible for the A-text of the Annals of Ulster (T.C.D. MS. H.1.8) which ends in 1504, and his handwriting can be identified as responsible for the bulk of the B-text, ending in 1506.[3] From that date onwards the B-text is continued in a series of annalistic entries, written by various scribes in succession. Rory O Caiside was probably responsible for the main section of the B-text, in so far as it is a very full summary, not a mere transcript of the A-text, and he is the most probable compiler of the entries which continue the record from 1504 to his own death in 1541.

[1] Brady II, p. 258-9.

[2] See McCarthy's edition of the Annals, vol. IV, pp. iii, ix.

[3] Dr. Best has kindly verified this fact for me from photostat copies, now in the National Library. McCarthy's description of this MS. (IV, pp. iii-v) is inaccurate.

Whatever may be the true interpretation of these puzzling entries, it is plain that Archdeacon O Caiside was an acknowledged authority on Irish history in the early sixteenth century. In 1525 he compiled a register of the diocese of Clogher, with a catalogue of all known bishops of Clogher, at the request of Bishop Patrick O Cullen. No copy of this register is now extant, but some notes have been preserved which tell us that the archdeacon was engaged on this work in 1525.[1] An earlier register of the diocese of Clogher had been compiled in the late thirteenth century by Bishop Mathew Mac Cathasaigh. It was still extant in the sixteenth century. Rory O Caiside made use of this earlier record and copied some valuable documents from it. To-day, neither the register of Bishop Matthew nor the register of Archdeacon Rory has survived; they were probably lost in the general disasters of the seventeenth century. Lynch, who wrote his *De Præsulibus Hiberniæ* towards the middle of that century, was able to use and quote Archdeacon Rory's register[2]; and we know that a register was in the custody of the Protestant Chancellor of the diocese in 1605.[3] Blessed Oliver Plunket visited Clogher in 1671 and saw there " an old parchment book, written many years ago, which contains the annals of that diocese."[4] If this vague phrase describes the Clogher register, we must presume that Oliver Plunket had been allowed to see it by the Protestant chancellor in whose custody it was. It has disappeared long since.

Bishop Patrick O Cullen was associated with his archdeacon in the work of compiling this register. A note that has been copied among the surviving extracts tells us that the bishop added an Office of St. Macartan to the register in 1528. Some entries in Cromer's register help us

[1] Dean Lawlor edited what remains of this register in the *Louth Archæological Journal* (1918), pp. 226-257, from T.C.D. MS. E. 3. 20, and other seventeenth-century copies.

[2] Lynch, *De Præsulibus Hiberniæ*, I, p. 200.

[3] *Analecta Hibernica* xii (1943), p. 105-6.

[4] Moran, *Memoir of Oliver Plunket*, p. 283.

to fix the bishop's movements in these years. The Primate
C.23 v. collated to two vacant rectories in the diocese in 1526. No
reason is given for this action, but the bishop was probably
non-resident at the time. On March 10 of a year that is
C.34 v. either 1527 or 1528 Bishop Patrick obtained a papal
dispensation to reside outside his see and appoint suitable
vicars.[1] The entry recording this dispensation is followed
immediately by a record of a case which came before the
Primate's court on July 7, 1528. Bishop Patrick had
probably gone to Rome in 1526 and had obtained his
dispensation early in 1527. In granting the dispensation
Clement VII states that the diocese of Clogher is now
worth scarcely 80 ducats a year, owing to wars, poverty and
other causes. The bishop had probably gone to Rome in
the hope of making some more adequate financial settlement.
The note in Archdeacon Rory's register makes it almost
certain that the bishop was back again in his diocese before
the end of 1528.

C.46. In June, 1530, another appeal came before the Primate's
court, which shows that Bishop Patrick was now active in
his diocese. The bishop had appointed Art MacCawell as
dean of Clogher and one of the priests in his diocese appealed
against this decision on the ground that the new dean was
C.51; 53 v; 58. unfit for his office. Three appeals from Clogher came before
the Primate's court within the next twelve months. They
are of no special interest, but they suggest that Bishop
C.61. Patrick was meeting with a good deal of local opposition in
his work throughout the diocese. In December, 1531, the
Primate collated to two more parishes in Clogher—
apparently in the bishop's absence. On November 7, 1533,
C.71. Bishop Patrick sought confirmation from the Primate of a
collation which he had made to the rectory of Kinawley,
now in the diocese of Kilmore, but stated in this entry to be
within the diocese of Clogher. Kinawley may, perhaps,

[1] The date has been partially effaced in the register, but 1527 is probable—since there would have been no need to record this dispensation in the Primate's register until the dispute in Clogher was referred to his court in July, 1528.

have been disputed territory between the two dioceses at this time and the bishop may have thought it prudent to obtain the Primate's confirmation for his collation.

Bishop Patrick O Cullen was dead before March 26,
1534, when the Primate nominated Richard Springan and C.74 v.
Cormac Roth as his two subcustodians of the vacant see.
Springan was prior of St. Mary's, Louth and Cormac Roth
was the Primate's archdeacon and official. On September 9,
1534, an appeal came before the Primate against the action C.78.
of his subcustodians. They had taken the part of the
Friars Minor of Monaghan in a local dispute which arose
from previous acts of violence within the lifetime of Bishop
Patrick. Conn O Neill and Patrick MacMahon, captains of
of their nations, with Bernard (Brian) O Neill, Conn's
brother and others, had raided and robbed the churches
and church-lands of Magheracloone, Carrickmacross and
Donaghmoyne, and also the lands of the priory of St. John
the Baptist, Ardee, in the diocese of Armagh. Bishop
Patrick had pronounced censures of excommunication and
interdict on the offenders, but the friars of Monaghan had
taken the part of the Irish chieftains and had admitted them
to Mass in their church despite the bishop's censures. They
had also given Christian burial to Patrick O Connolly,
Hugh Roe MacMahon and many others who had incurred
similar censures. Echoes of this border war can be found in
an earlier entry in Cromer's register (February 9, 1531), C.53 v.
and in the Annals of Ulster (a. 1535). The feud came to a
tragic end in 1540, when the English soldiery sacked the
convent of the friars in Monaghan, beheading their guardian
and several members of the community.[1]

The two appellants who are named in the entry for
September 9, 1534, were Remund MacMahon and Patrick C.78.
Sigh. Patrick Sigh is named in the earlier entry of
February 9, 1531. Remund MacMahon occurs here for the C.53 v.
first time. He is almost certainly the future bishop of
Clogher, who was provided to the see by Paul III on

[1] A.F.M., a. 1540.

August 27, 1546.[1] But we must go back to the situation created by the death of Bishop Patrick O Cullen in 1534.

More than a year after the bishop's death Paul III provided Hugh O Carolan (Odo or Aodh O Cearbhallain) to the vacant see of Clogher.[2] The new bishop had been a chaplain to Conn O Neill, one of Remund MacMahon's opponents in 1534. Hugh O Carolan surrendered his papal bulls to Henry VIII in 1542 and did fealty for the temporalities of his see.[3] Whether he went further in his renunciation of allegiance to the Pope is not clear, but Paul III was not satisfied with his loyalty. On August 27, 1546, he provided Raymund MacMahon to the see of Clogher, ignoring his own previous provision and stating that the see was still vacant by the death of Bishop Patrick. In this bull Raymond is given the title of "canon of Clogher." It is a pity that the entry in Cromer's register for September 9, 1534, has been mutilated at the edges of the folio so that we can no longer read the name of Remund's benefice. His fellow-petitioner, Patrick Sigh, is described as the herenagh of Magherosse (Carrickmacross). Remund MacMahon was most probably vicar of Donaghmoyne or Magheracloone. If he is identified with the Raymund of August 27, 1546, he had acquired a canonry in the diocese between 1534 and 1546.

A minor puzzle may be considered here. In 1526 a
C.23 v. clerk of Clogher, named Patrick O Syke (or O Syge) in Cromer's register, was commissioned by the Primate to induct Donatus O Caalan, a priest of the diocese, into the vicarage of Magheracloone. He himself had been collated
C. 47v. to the vicarage of Carrickmacross before July 9, 1530, but had lost his right to this benefice owing to his failure to receive Holy Orders. A Patrick O Sigh, vicar of Carrickmacross, had died in Rome before September 16, 1530.[4] Almost certainly he was the clerk whom the Primate had

[1] Brady I, p. 252-3. [2] Brady I, p. 252.

[3] *State Papers* III, p. 429 ; see also the extract from T.C.D. MS. E.3. 13, printed by E. Curtis in *J.R.S.A.I.* LXII (1932), p. 30.

[4] Costello, p. 44-45.

deprived of his vicarage and who died fighting his case in Rome a few months later. Who then was Patrick O Sigh, the herenagh of Carrickmacross, who appealed to the Primate in the autumn of 1534? I can only conjecture that he was a kinsman of the dead vicar, and that he was most probably a layman, who had inherited the traditional rights of the herenagh of this parish. A clerk of the diocese, whose name is spelt Thomas Mackaj in the Roman archives, was granted the vicarage when it was left vacant by the death of the earlier Patrick O Sigh in 1530.[1]

One last observation may be made about the numerous entries concerning the diocese of Clogher in Primate Cromer's register. The diocese includes to-day almost the whole of the county of Fermanagh, and the mention of the parish of
Kinawley as within the diocese in Bishop Patrick's day C.71.
suggests that even that portion of the modern county which lies now within the diocese of Kilmore was then part of the diocese of Clogher. None the less, it is remarkable that practically all the churches named in Cromer's register for these years are situated in the modern county of Monaghan.
There is one entry of October 19, 1530, in which Cormac C.51-2.
Roth, acting as vicar general for the absent Primate, addresses an inhibition to the prior and canons of Lough Derg (*Lacus Ruber*); and the Primate collated a vicar to
the parish of Derrybrusk in August, 1535. All the other C.90 v.
names mentioned in Cromer's very detailed register belong to the eastern portion of his diocese: Aghavea, Tullycorbet, Donaghmoyne, Magheracloone, Carrickmacross, Clones, Muckno, Clontibret. Some of these names occur more than once in the register. The almost total absence of Fermanagh names suggests that Primate Cromer and Bishop Patrick O Cullen exercised a very much more effective jurisdiction over the territory of MacMahon than over the more distant territory of Maguire.

There is a curious passage in the Inquisition of 1609, in which the local jurors bear witness to the unchallenged control of the Maguire sept over all the ecclesiastical benefices

[1] Costello, loc. cit.

and lands in the western portion of the diocese of Clogher.[1] I quote this passage in full, though it is of later date, for it throws unexpected light on the general situation towards the end of the Middle Ages :

" Moreover the said jurors do upon their oaths say and present that in every of the parsonages and vicarages within the said county of Fermanagh (excepting such as are impropriate) the bishop in whose diocese the said benefice shall be void did and might, within the next six months after the vacancy, collate to the benefice being void, and that if the bishop collated not within six months, that then the said collation came to the archbishop of that province ; and that if the said archbishop collated not within other six months, that then the said collation came to the Pope ; but the said jurors say that they have heard that great Coconnagh McGuire, grandfather to Brian óg now living, had all advowsons, presentations and rights of patronage of all parsonages and vicarages within the said county, until the Pope, by the General Council of Trent, took them from him ; but the said jurors have not seen it in their time."

The " great Coconnagh " mentioned in this Inquisition is the younger Cuchonnacht, son of Cuchonnacht the Coarb. We know that he promulgated the Decrees of the Council of Trent in his territory a year or two before his death in 1589.[2] The older jurors of 1609 could thus easily remember a state of discipline which had been unknown for no more than twenty or twenty-five years. Brian óg, Cuchonnacht's grandson, who was still alive in 1609, must be added to the list of the Maguire chieftains of Fermanagh which the late Father Paul Walsh compiled with such care.[3] The customs abolished by the Council of Trent may be assumed to have been in full force during the lifetime of Cuchonnacht the Coarb, and most probably for all the fifteenth century.

[1] *Inquisitions*, s.v. Fermanagh (towards the end of the depositions).

[2] Renehan : *Collections on Irish Church History* (Dublin, 1861), p. 139.

[3] Paul Walsh : " The Maguire Chieftains of Fermanagh," in *Irish Ecclesiastical Record* XIX (June, 1922), pp. 598-613.

8. DERRY

The diocese of Derry includes almost the whole of the modern county of Derry, with the peninsula of Inishowen and a large portion of northern Tyrone. Its territory lies partly within the lordship of O Neill, partly (in Inishowen) within the lordship of O Donnell. Historically it has always been closely connected with the neighbouring diocese of Raphoe. Under Henry VIII the diocese is of very special interest, since its bishop, Rory O Donnell—with the support of his cousin, the chieftain Manus O Donnell—was for a brief moment able to rally all the Irish and Catholic forces of the North against the King's new religious policy.

Derry was ruled by Irish bishops throughout the fifteenth century, with one exception. On February 21, 1466, Paul II provided Nicholas Weston to the see, in succession to Bartholomew O Flanagan who had died in the previous year.[1] Nothing is known of this new bishop beyond the fact that he had already obtained a canonry in Armagh with the prebend of Ballyclog.[2] Since Ballyclog lies in the Irish-speaking territory of Armagh, it is probable that Bishop Weston was a member of some " Old English " family which had become familiar with Irish ways of life and Irish speech. English settlers of this name occur in the official records of the fourteenth century, mainly in Kilkenny, and a John Weston is named as holding land in the eastern portion of Meath under Henry VI.[3] These records do not suggest any contacts outside the Anglo-Irish Pale ; but Bishop Weston may perhaps have come from the

[1] Costello, p. 228 ; C.P.L. XII, p. 695. In the bull of provision Paul II states that the see is vacant by the death of John (O Gibbon) who had been bishop from 1433-56. He thus ignores Bishop Bartholomew O Flanagan, though he was duly provided to this see by Calixtus III in 1457, and ruled the diocese for eight years : C.P.L. XI, p. 341 ; XII, pp. 25, 118, 227, 548.

[2] C.P.L. XII, p. 659.

[3] *Rotulorum Patentium et Clausorum Cancellariæ Hiberniæ Calendarium* (Dublin, 1828), p. 240.

"Old English" colony in Co. Down.[1] His name is spelt in a curious phonetic form (*Sar Nicol Uasdun*) in the Annals of Ulster at the time of his death (1484). Whatever the truth as to his origins, it is plain that this bishop of Derry was both resident and active in the diocese for almost twenty years. He was abroad, most probably in Rome, during the
O.238. autumn and winter of 1469-70 and Primate Bole appointed Art MacCawell as his subcustodian of the diocese during the bishop's absence at this time. A series of papal mandates issued during the months of December and January of that year granted him the necessary dispensations and faculties for certain cases in which he had sought to remedy some long-standing-abuses.[2]

More important than these mandates is a grant dated December 14, 1469. The Pope, at the request of the bishop, grants an indulgence of seven years for all who are willing to help in the rebuilding of Derry cathedral.[3] Bishop Weston had reported to the Pope that the cathedral was all but roofless; that the bishop had no house in which he could fittingly reside; that there was only one chalice, made of tin, for the use of the priests who served the cathedral, and that the church was in need of chalices, books, vestments and all other ecclesiastical requirements. An earlier petition of 1466 lets us see that there were no resident canons and no prebendaries in the diocese.[4] Bishop Weston was present
O.385. at the first of Primate Octavian's provincial councils at Drogheda on July 5, 1480. His death is recorded by Cathal MacManus in the Annals of Ulster, under the year 1484: "The bishop of Derry, namely, Sir Nicholas Weston, died shortly before Christmas."

Bishop Weston's immediate successor was an Irish Observantine Friar Minor named Donald O Fallon

[1] Father MacErlean has called my attention to the existence of two townlands called *Ballyvaston*: one west of Belfast, the other in Lecale, Co. Down.

[2] C.P.L. XII, pp. 336, 717-8, 748; *cf.* also the mandate of December 14, 1469 (p. 691).

[3] Costello, p. 222; C.P.L. XII, p. 717-8.

[4] C.P.L. XII, p. 548.

(Domhnall O Fallamhain). He was provided to this see by Innocent VIII on May 16, 1485.[1] As bishop-elect of Derry he attended the provincial council which Primate Octavian held on July 10, 1486; but he was still bishop-elect in the summer of 1487, when he was one of two prelates whom the O.288. Primate commissioned to visit the diocese of Dromore.[2] There seems to have been some local opposition to the new bishop, but it soon died away. Bishop Donald was present as consecrated bishop of Derry at the provincial council which the Primate held at Drogheda on July 6, 1489. Opposition to the new bishop can be explained only on the assumption that some local dynastic claim was being urged against him. It was certainly not due to any lack of virtue in the bishop-elect, for this is the prelate of whom Cathal MacManus writes in the year 1486: "Domhnall O Fallamhain, a Friar Minor of the Observance and the preacher that did most service to Irishmen since Patrick was in Ireland, was at that synod (July, 1486), endeavouring to release his letters for the bishopric of Derry, which had been granted to him at that time from Rome." In their panegyric of this Franciscan bishop at the time of his death (a. 1500) the Four Masters tell us that "for the period of thirty years he diligently taught and preached throughout Ireland." Assuming that this calculation includes the period of his episcopal rule, Brother Donald must have been preaching throughout Ireland for some fifteen years at the time of his provision to the see of Derry.

These contemporary judgments are confirmed by a papal mandate which Sixtus IV issued to the abbot of Derry on May 9, 1482.[3] The Pope informs the abbot that "on account of the rich fruits which the Friars of the Observance had brought to the people of Ireland by their exemplary lives, their preaching and other good works, and since the devotion of the faithful towards them daily increases so much that they are ready to build new houses for them in suitable places," he has empowered the Irish Friars of the Observance

[1] Costello, p. 228. [2] See above, p. 145. [3] C.P.L. XIII, p. 744-5.

to build or receive two houses in Ireland, with church and cemetery attached to each. The Pope orders the abbot to see that this indult is put into execution.

These witnesses to the impression created by the fervour of the early Observantine Friars in Ireland throw some light on a problem that must occur to any student of this period. In the twelfth century, when all Ireland was affected by a nation-wide movement for ecclesiastical reform, Derry produced one notable figure in the monastic reforming abbot, Flaithbertach O Brolchain; and Bishop Muiredach O Cobhthaigh, who died in 1173, is one of many saintly Irish prelates of this period.[1] There follows a long period during the thirteenth and early fourteenth century, when the diocese of Derry disappears almost entirely from our view in the general confusion of those long years of strife. When our documents become more abundant in the latter portion of the fourteenth and the early fifteenth century, the little that we hear of Derry lets us see that the diocese had fallen on evil days.[2] Bishop Weston's report to the Pope in 1469 confirms this impression, so far as the external fabric of the cathedral is concerned. How then did it come to pass that Derry gave Catholic Ireland a leader within the next two generations? Bishop Weston himself set about remedying some of the financial confusion into which the diocese had fallen. He seems to have been in Rome during the winter of 1469-70, when he presented his report on the state of his cathedral and obtained an indulgence for those who should be willing to help towards its restoration.[3] The published Papal Letters make it plain that he was active in his diocese for the first three or four years of his pontificate, and we must presume that he continued to do his best in troubled times. But he was an Englishman, resident in a diocese that was remote from ordinary English influence. His career is unintelligible unless he had acquired Irish ways

[1] See Annals of Ulster, a. 1150-64, 1173-5, 1185.

[2] See in general the registers of Primates Sweteman and Fleming, and the visitation of Primate Colton in 1397.

[3] C.P.L. XII, p. 744-5; *cf.* also (of same date) XII, p. 691.

and a working knowledge of the Irish language, but he must have found it hard to adapt himself to the traditions and customs of his subjects.

The movement initiated by the Friars Minor of the Observance brings us very much closer to the ordinary life and customs of these northern lands. Hugh Roe O Donnell brought the Friars Minor to Donegal in 1474 and a chapter of the Friars of the Observance was held there in 1488.[1] The monastery of Donegal seems to have been a centre of the new movement from the day of its foundation; and the contemporary Annals of Ulster bear witness to its success. On August 14, 1497, sixteen friars of this community left Donegal for Carrickfergus, where they took possession of the former Conventual friary in the name of the Observance. Hugh Roe O Donnell did not die until July 11, 1505. He was then buried at his own request in the monastery which he had founded at Donegal. Three years earlier (1502) the Friars of the Observance had taken possession of the friary at Cavan, where Bishop Thomas MacBrady was buried in 1511. The death of another famous preacher of the Observance, Patrick O Feidhil, is recorded by the Annals of Ulster under the year 1505. Niall O Neill, who had brought the Observantine friars to Carrickfergus in 1497, died in 1512, and was buried in their monastery. Bishop Menelaus Mac Carmacan, who died with the reputation of an earnest and saintly bishop of Raphoe in 1515, was buried at his own request in the habit of a Friar of the Observance, within the precincts of the monastery of Donegal.[2] Bishop Rory O Donnell, who gave a courageous leadership to the Catholics of Tir Conaill and Tir Eoghan, died in 1550. He was buried in the same Franciscan habit and within the precincts of the same monastery.

These names bring us to the very heart of the new reforming movement in Ireland and it is plain that a large

[1] A.F.M. a. 1474; A.U. a. 1488. For the first Observantine foundations in Ireland, which date from the period 1449-60, see Little-FitzMaurice, *Materials*, p. xxxii; and Michael O Clery's list of foundations, edited by Fr. Paul Walsh in *I.E.R.* (Feb., 1922, p. 223).

[2] See below, p. 201.

share of the credit for this new movement must go to the friars whom Irishmen of that day recognised as an inspiration and an example.[1] We know very little of the actual episcopal work of Bishop Donald O Fallon, but it is not rash to conjecture that he must have done much during the fifteen years of his rule (1485-1500) to prepare the way for a true religious revival in his diocese. He died at Trim and was buried in the Franciscan monastery there. The Annals of Ulster describe him in their obit as "one who was laborious and successful in preaching throughout Ireland for thirty years before that time." It would thus seem probable that the bishop continued his apostolic work as a missionary preacher, inside and outside his diocese, to the end of his life.

Bishop Donald's immediate successor was James MacMahon, grandson of the coarb of Clones who died at the age of ninety years in 1502. The younger James was provided to the see of Derry by Alexander VI on July 5, 1501.[2] If I am right in my conjecture that the new bishop of Derry is to be identified as the James MacMahon who was intriguing for preferment in Rome during the years 1492-4, Derry is not likely to have gained by this provision.[3] Alexander VI died on August 18, 1503, and the bishop's bulls had not been expedited at that date. So long a delay suggests strong opposition to the provision, but Julius II, who was elected on November 1, 1503, expedited the bishop's bulls on November 26. The bishop was not present at the
O.287. provincial council which Primate Octavian held at Drogheda
on July 8, 1504; but he was present at the council of
O.404. July 12, 1507. Sir James Ware tells us that he was also commendatory abbot of the monastery of SS. Peter and Paul at Knock, near Louth.[4] It is very doubtful whether he was ever a resident bishop of Derry. The Four Masters, who had a special interest in this diocese, never mention his

[1] The decision by which the Franciscan chapter general of 1517 finally separated the Observantine friars from the Conventuals is recorded as a victory in the Annals of Ulster.

[2] Costello, p. 228-9. [3] See above, p. 171. [4] Ware-Harris I, p. 291.

name. The Annals of Ulster, with their special interest in the MacMahon sept, tell us that he died in 1519.

Bishop James MacMahon's successor was Rory O Donnell, who was provided to the vacant see by Leo X on January 11, 1520.[1] The new bishop had been dean of Raphoe at the time of his appointment, and he was allowed to retain his deanery in Raphoe for some years after his promotion to the see of Derry.[2] Bishop Rory's appointment was unquestionably due to the influence of the O Donnell sept, which was then at the height of its power in Tir Conaill. The bishop's grandfather was Aodh Ruadh, the chieftain who had brought the Friars Minor to Donegal in 1474 and who died in their monastery in 1505. Aodh Dubh, who succeeded to Aodh Ruadh as lord of Tir Conaill and who died in 1537, was the bishop's uncle. Manus, son of Aodh Dubh, who succeeded to his father's lordship in 1537 and who died in 1563, was the bishop's cousin.[3] These family ties were to have an important bearing on Bishop Rory's whole administration. They gave him the opportunity of becoming for a time a national leader in the movement of Irish resistance to King Henry.

Bishop Rory's name occurs seldom in Primate Cromer's register, though he was bishop of Derry during the whole of the Primate's rule in Armagh. This silence of the register is most probably a sign that the normal life of the diocese was continuing without interruption under a bishop who understood his people and was able to win their respect as being one of the ruling dynasty. The few cases that do occur are of interest as showing the type of problems that commonly arose in the more purely Irish dioceses of this period.

An appeal from the diocese of Derry came before the Primate's court on September 19, 1529. Bishop Rory had C.42 v.
heard a case between two clerks of his diocese: Maurice MacSorly and Thomas MacCawell. The bishop had given

[1] Costello, p. 229. [2] Costello, p. 271.
[3] See Bishop Rory's obit. in A.F.M. a. 1550.

judgment against MacSorly, who now appealed to the Primate. Cromer appointed three canons of the diocese of Derry to hear the case in his name. This commission suggests that he was unwilling to interfere in the bishop's jurisdiction.

C.81 v. On February 8, 1535, another appeal came before Primate Cromer from Bishop Rory's diocese. Two priests of the diocese, Maurice MacCawell and Felim MacSomnagh, were involved in a dispute concerning their rights in the vicarage of a church called here *Dorsorathie*, which can be identified as the parish of Drumragh, including the town of Omagh.[1] Bishop Rory had given sentence against Felim, and had pronounced him unfit to hold this or any other vicarage in his diocese, but had been unable to dislodge him from the parish. The Primate again referred the case back to a court of Derry priests, including Bishop Rory's own official, and he empowers the judges, should they find Felim guilty of the charges brought against him, to remove him from the vicarage and to collate his rival, Maurice MacCawell. Once more, it is plain that the Primate is content to leave this Derry case to a Derry tribunal.

C.91-2. Another appeal from Derry came before the Primate's court about the same time (September 20, 1535). It is very much more instructive. Two priests of the Derry diocese whose names are given in the register as Magonius Ogarquinclayder and Torroletus McAeder, had appealed to the Primate. By good fortune we get the other side of their story from a bull of Paul III, who had made a provision which was the original cause of this trouble.[2] We are thus able to watch the proceedings from both sides. We can also identify *Ogarquinclayder* as an exceptionally erratic spelling of O Gormley (*O Gairmblegayd* in the corresponding Roman entries).

The Irish section of the Armagh diocese had long been familiar with the type of Irish clerk or priest who went

[1] I am indebted to Rev. Professor J. F. O'Doherty, of Maynooth College, for help as to local names in this diocese.

[2] Costello, p. 225.

abroad to Rome and there secured some coveted benefice by papal provision.[1] Derry was as familiar with this type of schemer as Armagh and a Derry priest named Hugh or Odo MacAbarde is the central figure in this minor drama of sixteenth-century Ireland. One of the best parishes in the diocese of Derry was Urney (spelt *Furnayed* in these entries), to which were then attached two chapels in the parish of Urney and the rectory of St. Maolruba in the island of Islay. In 1535 these two chapels were held by two Derry priests, Neillanus O Gormley and Torroletus McHugh (MacAodha); whilst the rectory and vicarage of Urney were divided between three priests of the diocese, Torroletus McHugh, Magonius O Gormley and Nellanus O Carolan. The rectory of St. Maolruba was held by two Scottish priests, Patrick Roisse and Macolinus Macamiradhy (?). Odo MacAbarde had his own view as to the better organisation of all these benefices, which (so he alleged) were held without sufficient canonical title. His plan was that these scattered benefices should be united into a single canonry and prebend, and that he himself should be the first beneficiary of this scheme—a plan for which many parallels can be found in the extant papal documents of this period.

Odo probably went to Rome in the summer or autumn of 1534. He had obtained a provision in his favour during the winter of 1534-5 and bound himself for payment of the customary annates or first-fruits on January 7, 1535.[2] Armed with this papal provision, he came back to Derry in the spring or summer of 1535. Magonius O Gormley and Torroletus McHugh, who describe themselves in the entry of Cromer's register as vicar and rector of Urney, appealed to the Holy See and the Primate on September 20, 1535. Their appeal was not directly against the intrusion of Odo into their parish—that was a matter which they must first have taken up with the bishop of Derry—but against the sentence of a special court of three judges who had been delegated by the Holy See to hear the case in Ireland. The two appellants disputed the validity of the apostolic letters

[1] See above, p. 13-15. [2] Costello, p. 209.

by which these judges claimed to have jurisdiction to hear the case. The names of the three judges are given in
C.91-2. the Primate's register as Edmund O Gallagher, dean of Derry; Art O Friel (O Fyrgall), canon of Raphoe; and Maurice MacClusky, who is here described as subdelegate for the bishop of Sodor. This last name seems at first to be strangely out of place in a lawsuit concerning a Derry parish and a word of explanation is needed. There were two bishops of Sodor at this period: one whose see lay in the Isle of Man, the other whose full title was *episcopus Sodorensis et Insularum* and whose usual residence was in the island of Iona.[1] In 1535 Bishop Farquhard Hector or Farquhard Farquhardson was bishop of the Isles, whilst an Englishman named Thomas Stanley had been consecrated bishop of Sodor and the Isle of Man in 1531.[2] Maurice MacClusky was thus most probably acting in this Derry lawsuit as subdelegate for Bishop Farquhard of the Scottish Isles.

Cromer's register tells us no more than that the Primate accepted the appeal of the rector and vicar of Urney and that he granted them his protection. He issued the customary
C.91 v. letters tuitorial on behalf of the two appellants on September 20, 1535. By that time Henry VIII had already renounced his allegiance to the Roman Pope and Primate Cromer knew well that trouble was coming in Ireland. Whether the appeal was ever forwarded to Rome in these troubled times, is more than doubtful. The Primate also appealed for protection to the secular arm. His appeal is directed to Odo (Aodh Dubh) O Donnell as captain of his nation and to his son Magonius (Manus). Eoghan O Gormley (Eugenius Ogarquielayd) is also named as captain of the nation to which one of the two appellants belonged. The Primate
C.92 v. adds a special appeal to the bishop of Derry, which is worded very much more respectfully than is customary in

[1] See a letter of July 31, 1542, printed by Father E. Hogan in *Ibernia Ignatiana*, p. 8: "which bishop lyeth of Icolm Kille, between Scotland and Ireland." See also below, p. 251.

[2] Brady I, pp. 106-9, 162-3.

entries of this kind elsewhere in Cromer's register. The bishop of Derry was plainly a force to reckon with in his own diocese.

9. RAPHOE

The diocese of Raphoe includes almost all the modern county of Donegal, with the exception of the peninsula of Inishowen which had belonged to the diocese of Derry since the middle of the twelfth century. It lay within the O Donnell lordship of Tir Conaill, but the family of O Gallagher had established an almost hereditary claim to many of the most important benefices in the diocese. One sept of this family claimed descent from Lochloinn, the earlier of two bishops of this name who ruled the diocese of Raphoe during a large part of the fifteenth century. The diocese lay remote from the centres of ecclesiastical authority and discipline was relaxed.

Bishop Lochloinn I became bishop of Raphoe in 1420, when his election was confirmed by Martin V at the end of the Great Schism.[1] He had been dean of Raphoe for more than twenty years before his election as bishop, and the future fortunes of his family must be traced back to his activities at a time when the Great Schism had fatally weakened the government of the Church throughout all Western Europe.

Two years after Bishop Lochloinn's death Eugenius IV provided Cornelius MacGillabrighde to the vacant see.[2] This new bishop was dead before June 18, 1442, when the same Pope provided a second Lochloinn O Gallagher to the see of Raphoe, with a dispensation *ex defectu natalium*.[3]

[1] Costello, p. 287-8. [2] Costello, p. 288 ; C.P.L. IX, p. 127.
[3] Costello, p. 288 ; C.P.L. IX, pp. 284, 319, 336.

Irish genealogical tables make it certain that this Bishop Lochloinn II was in fact the grandson of Bishop Lochloinn I. In his bull of provision, Eugenius IV states that the chapter of Raphoe had humbly supplicated him by letters patent on behalf of the bishop-elect. The Roman authorities may not have been aware of the full truth concerning the new bishop's parentage. They can have known little also of his
O.246. personal character. In March, 1470, Primate Bole, then on his visitation of the city of Armagh, dispensed Bishop Lochloinn from various censures which he had incurred by his misdemeanours. The papal letters of Sixtus IV contain evidence which makes it only too plain that Bishop Lochloinn was, from first to last, unworthy of his priestly character. In 1476 he visited Rome in person, and was then absolved by a special court of judges.[1] But the records of this period, so far as they have survived, show that the diocese of Raphoe was in a sad state of confusion under Bishop Lochloinn's rule. He died in 1478 or 1479: none of the Irish annals mention his name.

On November 21, 1479, Sixtus IV—who had just sent Primate Octavian to Ireland—provided an Italian named Giovanni de Rogeriis to the see of Raphoe. This bishop-elect had died before November 4, 1483, when the Pope provided Menelaus MacCarmacan as his successor.[2]

Bishop Menelaus took his oath of obedience to Primate Octavian in the cathedral of Armagh on July 16, 1484.[3] He ruled the diocese of Raphoe for thirty troubled years. The official Roman documents make it plain that the power of the O Gallagher septs was still predominant in the diocese through all this period. The appointment of Menelaus had vacated the deanery of Raphoe, which was then granted to Nicholas Omechkayn (probably an erratic spelling of the family name, O Miadhachain).[4] Within

[1] C.P.L. XIII, p. 512. [2] Costello, p. 288; C.P.L. XIII, p. 119.

[3] The full text of this oath is in Octavian's register (fo. 317). The Primate was not present at the ceremony, but was represented by the dean of Armagh and all the Irish dignitaries of the chapter.

[4] C.P.L. XIV, p. 70.

little more than a year, Lochloinn O Gallagher, one of the numerous sons of the dead bishop, had petitioned against this provision on the grounds (true or false) that the new dean was blind of one eye, a public fornicator, a perjurer and under sentence of major excommunication. Lochloinn had succeeded in getting a dispensation for himself *ex defectu natalium*, and the appointment of a commission of three judges delegate from the diocese of Derry who were to hear the case and collate him to the vacant deanery, should his charges against Nicholas be proved true. We hear no more of this case, which may very well have been no more than a shameless attempt to oust the dean. In his petition to the Pope, Lochloinn complains that he is unable to meet his judges within the city or diocese of Raphoe for fear of the dean and his supporters. Public opinion was outraged by the conduct of the dead bishop's son; and we shall find further proof of this healthy reaction from such abuses.

Another of the bishop's sons, named Art O Gallagher, gave similar trouble in his persistent efforts to get control of the Cistercian abbey of Assaroe. This abbey had fallen vacant in 1476, when John O Gallagher resigned his position as commendatory abbot in favour of a canon of the diocese whose name is spelt John Olasci or Olasti in the contemporary Roman documents; the true form (O Laisdi) is given in the Annals of Ulster (a. 1502).[1] John O Laisdi owed his canonry to Bishop Lochloinn II and he was one of three judges delegate who were empowered to absolve the bishop from the censures he had incurred in the summer of 1476.[2] Six years later O Laisdi obtained two more benefices in the diocese of Raphoe, by provision of Sixtus IV.[3] But his position was challenged in the winter of 1483-4, when he was denounced to the Holy See as having incurred excommunication for his conduct. His accuser, Edmund O Rafferty (*Orobfartyn*) was seeking to oust him from the abbey of Assaroe.[4] We hear no more of this case

[1] C.P.L. XII, p. 574; XIII, pp. 479, 532; Costello, p. 267.
[2] C.P.L. XIII, p. 512. [3] C.P.L. XIII, p. 259.
[4] C.P.L. XIII, p. 161; Costello, p. 268.

until August 28, 1486, when Niall O Gallagher lays claim to this abbey, for which John O Laisdi and Edmund had been contending for the past two years.[1] Niall O Gallagher disappears at this stage in the complicated story and his place is taken in 1489 by Art, the dead bishop's son, who maintained his family's hereditary rights for the next thirteen years.[2] Death put an end to this long struggle in the year 1502, when the Annals of Ulster have this obit: "Two abbots who were long in contention respecting the abbacy of Assaroe, namely, Art, son of bishop O Gallagher, and John O Laisdi, died within two days and a night of each other."

This Art O Gallagher, who claimed to be abbot of Assaroe, is most probably to be identified as the father of Edmund, who died as dean of Raphoe in 1538. Yet another son of Bishop Lochloinn was named Brian. He was the father of another Edmond, who was first dean of Derry and then bishop of Raphoe. We shall meet these names again in the history of these two dioceses.[3]

There is little in our surviving records to throw light on the personal character and achievement of Bishop Menelaus MacCarmacan. A manuscript *Catalogue of the Bishops of Raphoe,* which was composed in the early seventeenth century, tells us that Bishop Menelaus died in the habit of a Grey Friar (Friar Minor of the Observance) on the seventh of the Ides of May, 1515, and that he was buried in the Franciscan monastery at Donegal.[4] Sir James Ware tells us, on the authority of Anthony Wood, that the bishop had studied theology in Oxford.[5] His immediate successor was also a graduate of the university of Oxford, but there seems to have been some undue haste in securing his provision. Bishop Menelaus is said to have resigned his see in 1514, but

[1] C.P.L. XIV (unpublished galley-proofs); Costello, p. 269.

[2] Costello, p. 269; Octavian's Register, fo. 78.

[3] See below, p. 204-7.

[4] Brit. Mus. Add. MSS. 4797, formerly in the collection of Sir James Ware.

[5] Ware-Harris I, p. 274.

there were doubts as to the fact of this resignation and consequently as to the validity of the following provision.

Leo X provided Cornelius O Cahan, who is described as a clerk of the diocese of Derry and a bachelor in the decretals, to the see of Raphoe on February 13, 1514. In his bull of provision the Pope states expressly that he has made this appointment at the request of "his dearest son in Christ, Henry, the illustrious king of England."[1] The new bishop belonged to a family whose lordship extended over the northern portion of the modern county of Derry. For the next forty years Bishop Cornelius was to make it plain to all the world that he was a King's bishop, first and foremost.

Some light is thrown on this provision by an entry in the consistorial records of 1534. Bishop Cornelius had been seeking to establish himself as bishop of Raphoe for twenty years at that date, but opposition to his claims had become stronger with increasing knowledge as to the policies of the King of England and Paul III had determined to set aside the provision of 1514. In the record of his new provision it is stated that the see of Raphoe had been vacant "for about seventeen years" since the death of Bishop Menelaus.[2] This calculation plainly ignores the rights of Bishop Cornelius, who had been provided to the see two years before the death of his predecessor. If we go back to the terms of the bull by which Leo X provided Cornelius to the see in 1514, we find that a commission of Cardinals had reported to the Pope that Bishop Menelaus was too old and infirm to discharge the duties of his office and that he had freely resigned his see into the Pope's hands.[3] There may have been some undue haste in assuming the fact of this resig-

[1] Costello, p. 288; Brady I, p. 306.

[2] Brady I, p. 307: ". . . . vacanti per obitum Menelai Marcoman. extra Romanam curiam defuncti, et devolut. ob. no. nominationem Regis, et vacavit ab annis xvii circiter." I am puzzled by the clause *devolut. ob. no. nominationem Regis.*

[3] Costello, p. 288: "Cum Rdus. . . . Menelaus epus. Rapothen. senio confectus et viribus sui corporis destitutus curam et administrationem ecc: Rapot. . . . gerere et exercere non valens. . . ." Bishop Menelaus was dead within little more than a year of the date of this report.

nation, or the party which were opposed to the succession of Bishop Cornelius may have held that the bishop's resignation had not been voluntary. English influence at the papal court was strong in those early years of Henry's reign, and the King was obviously anxious to secure the appointment of a bishop on whose loyalty he could count. Whatever the cause, there is no doubt at all that the provision of 1514 had been challenged for some years before it was set aside by Paul III in his new provision of 1534. Cromer's register throws some new and welcome light on the situation in the diocese during these critical years.

C.29 v. Bishop Cornelius is first mentioned in the Primate's register when the Primate commissions him to visit the diocese of Raphoe in his name on December 3, 1527. On
C.35 v. July 10, 1528, an appeal from judgment of Bishop Cornelius came before the Primate's metropolitan court. William, the Cistercian abbot of Assaroe, had appealed against the bishop over a dispute between his community and Maurice O Clery, with his brethren, "concerning the revocation of the perpetual alienation of certain lands and a house, vulgarly called *Inteaghcloich* within the cloistral part of the said monastery, made by one of the abbot's predecessors."[1] The Primate delegated John O Gallagher the younger and Dermitius O Leyner, both canons of Raphoe, to hear the
C.35 v. case. On the same day the Primate heard an appeal by John O Gallagher, clerk of Raphoe—who seems to have been distinct from the canon of Raphoe—concerning a charge brought by John against the vicar of Clondavaddy, Bernard McKarni, which Bishop Cornelius had refused to admit in his diocesan court. The Primate referred this case to yet a third John O Gallagher, archdeacon of Derry, and to two canons of Raphoe. The mention of these names is sufficient to illustrate the difficulties that must have confronted any bishop of Raphoe, once he had incurred the enmity of the O Gallagher septs.

[1] This alienation may perhaps have been made by Thady O Reilly, the bishop of Dromore, who was also abbot of Assaroe from 1511-26; see above p. 147.

Two years later Bishop Cornelius is mentioned again in the Primate's register. On June 22, 1530, Niall (Nelanus) O Neill, son of Art óg, complained before the Primate's court that certain ecclesiastics, whose names are given as O Mellan, O Corre, O Keylte, O Molchallyn, Maguoyrke and McGillgowb, had " most illegally disturbed him " by fasting and ringing bells against him. These are the names of local erenaghs who were resisting Niall's claims in the border parishes of Derry and Armagh.[1] The Primate commissioned the bishop of Raphoe and the official of Raphoe to inquire into the case, with power to punish the offenders. C.46 v.

There is only one further entry in Cromer's register concerning the diocese of Raphoe. On July 3, 1535, the Primate heard an appeal from the vicar of Clondahorky, whose name is given as Dunselemini (Donnshléibhe) O Shyryn, against the unlawful intrusion of another priest of the same diocese, Torroletus MacSwiney, into the rectory of Clondavaddy. Torroletus, so Dunselemini complained, had been deprived by the ordinary of his diocese *in actu capitulari*. Dunselemini seems to have had some hope of receiving the rectory of Clondavaddy himself, but it was first necessary for him to expel this intruder. Bishop Cornelius was unable to help him and he now appealed to the Primate—who referred the case back to a commission of five local judges. The names are of interest: the dean of Raphoe, who is unnamed; John O Gallagher, abbot of Assaroe; the commendatory of the same monastery; Art O Friel, canon of Raphoe[2]; and the rector of Clondahorky, who is unnamed. John O Gallagher was provided to the abbey of Assaroe by Clement VII on August 2, 1530. with a canonry and prebend in the cathedral of Raphoe.[3] C.85 v.

The provision of John O Gallagher as abbot of Assaroe in 1530 is one of many signs that the septs of this great family were gaining ground at the papal court during

[1] I am much obliged to Dr. Séamus O Ceallaigh who helped me to locate and identify these names.

[2] This is most probably the future archbishop of Tuam: see below p. 238.

[3] Costello, p. 271.

these years. In January, 1528, Clement VII issued a bull in favour of two members of this sept. John O Gallagher, who may very well be identical with the John who became abbot of Assaroe in 1530, was then vicar of Drumholme; and Ludovicus (probably Lochloinn) O Gallagher was a canon of Raphoe and vicar of Raymoghy.[1] The two men had exchanged their benefices. They now pray the Pope to free them from any ecclesiastical censures they may have incurred by this unlawful exchange. Since trustworthy witnesses have given testimony on behalf of Lochloinn, the Pope now directs that three local prelates whom he names as judges delegate, should inquire into the present tenure of the archdeaconry of Raphoe and the rectory of Raymoghy—which were held by John O Devany and Thady Otaimud (?). Should these two benefices be found to be void or irregularly held, they are to be united into a single benefice and conferred on Lochloinn O Gallagher, together with the perpetual vicarage of Raymoghy which he already held.

There is thus clear evidence that the O Gallagher septs were growing yearly more powerful in the diocese of Raphoe. This increase in their strength—rather than any new objection to the canonical position of Bishop Cornelius—was probably the reason why they took the final step of challenging the bishop's authority in Rome. Their success in this last manœuvre is apparent in the provision of a new bishop of Raphoe by Clement VII on May 11, 1534.

The identification of this new bishop of Raphoe is complicated by a whole series of minor errors and confusing statements. In the actual text of the provision the Bishop's name is given as *Edmundi Ogalembarys* in one version, whilst *Edmundi* has been corrupted to *Odomuchi* in another version.[2] This Bishop Edmund died in 1543. His obit is given in the Annals of Loch Cé as follows: *Espuc Ratha Both .i. Emonn mac Briain mic in espuic I Ghallchubair do*

[1] Costello, p. 285.

[2] Brady I, p. 307. The Italian scribe of the Vatican MS. wrote two forms of this name: *Odomuchi, Odormich*.

ég ar bfhághail choinntinne móire a timchell a thigernuis ("The Bishop of Raphoe, that is, Edmund, son of Brian, son of the Bishop O Gallchubhair, died, after having had great opposition regarding his lordship.") The Four Masters have the same obit for this year, with the addition of the exact date (February 26), but they omit the clause stating that Brian was son of Bishop O Gallagher. The manuscript Catalogue of the Bishops of Raphoe, which dates from the early seventeenth century, gives less accurate information: "Edmund died before the controversie was ended, soe that Connor O Kahane was bisshop both before and after him."[1] Father Paul Walsh seems to be justified in his conclusion that the authority of the Annals of Loch Cé is here the more reliable authority. He includes Bishop Emonn as a grandson of Bishop Lochloinn II in his complicated pedigree of the O Gallagher septs.

The text of the papal provision contains yet another puzzling clause. In the consistorial record the new bishop of Raphoe is entered as having been dean of Raphoe at the date of his provision (*decani illius*). But this statement is not easy to reconcile with other contemporary documents. In Cromer's register "Edmund O Gallcubar dean" is C.91-2.
mentioned in an entry for September 20, 1535, as having been appointed by the Holy See shortly before that date to hear a case in the diocese of Derry. The wording of this entry is somewhat obscure and it is not clear whether this Edmund was dean of Derry or Raphoe. The Holy See must have recognised Edmund, son of Brian, as bishop of Raphoe at this date. Edmund O Gallagher, who was dean in 1535, must, therefore, be distinct from Edmund, son of Brian. A probable solution is to assume that the unnamed dean, "son of Art, son of Lochloinn O Gallagher" whose death is recorded under 1538 by the Annals of Ulster, was Edmund, son of Art and grandson of Bishop Lochloinn. This unnamed dean must have been dean of Raphoe, not of Derry. We know from two letters of King James V of

[1] Leslie, *Raphoe Clergy*, (1940), p. 4.

Scotland, dated July 22, 1536, and July 1, 1538, that Art O Gallagher, son of Felim, was dean of Derry during these years.[1] If we assume that Edmund, son of Art, was dean of Raphoe in 1535 and that he died in 1538, it follows that Edmund, son of Brian, who became bishop of Raphoe in 1534, had been dean of Derry before his provision. The statement in the Roman consistorial record that he had been dean of the diocese to which he was provided as bishop (*decani illius*) is thus to be explained as an error for which a papal scribe, writing in Rome, may easily be excused.

This conjecture is supported by another entry in C.85 v. Cromer's register for July 3, 1535. Here the Primate issues his official letters to the dean of Raphoe and other dignitaries of that diocese, but does not mention the dean's name. If we assume that this dean of Raphoe was the son of Art who died in 1538, there is no difficulty at all. If we identify him with Edmund, son of Brian, it becomes impossible to reconstruct the story. For the Primate supported Bishop Cornelius O Cahan throughout all these years as the sole canonical bishop of Raphoe. In his eyes Edmund, son of Brian (the rival bishop in 1535) was no more than an intruder. It seems incredible that the Primate could have included this dean among the clergy of the diocese to whom he addressed his letters. The easiest solution is to assume, as I have suggested, that Edmund, son of Art, was dean of Raphoe in 1535, and until his death in 1538 ; that Edmund, son of Brian, was dean of Derry until his provision to the see of Raphoe in 1534 ; and that Art, son of Felim, was dean of Derry from 1534 (when a vacancy occurred by reason of this provision) until 1547, when he was himself provided by Paul III to the see of Raphoe, in succession to Edmund, son of Brian. If these calculations are correct, Edmund, son of Art, and Edmund, son of Brian, were first cousins ; both were grandsons of Bishop Lochloinn II. Nothing is known of Brian, the father of Bishop Edmund. Art, father of Dean

[1] *Analecta Hibernica*, no. 12 (1943), pp. 179-181 ; Fr. Paul Walsh, loc. cit., p. 197.

Edmund, is certainly Art, son of Bishop Lochloinn, whose death as abbot of the Cistercian monastery of Assaroe is recorded by all the Irish Annals under the year 1502. The Annals of Ulster state expressly that this Art was son of Bishop Lochloinn.

These facts make it plain that the O Gallagher septs must have been exceedingly powerful in Raphoe during these critical years. The threat of their new attack on his position as bishop of Raphoe explains the unexpected collation of Bishop Cornelius to a vicarage in the diocese of Meath about this time.[1] Yet their power did not go unchallenged. Dr. G. A. Hayes-McCoy has recently published some valuable extracts from an unpublished letter-book of King James V of Scotland. Two of these letters deal with the problem of the disputed succession in the diocese of Raphoe.[2] In the earlier of these letters, dated July 22, 1536, King James writes to Paul III on behalf of a third candidate, whom he describes as *Derensis ecclesie decanus Arturus Ogaltnit vir non minus doctus quam probus*. Art, who was finally provided to the see of Raphoe in 1547, died in 1561. The Four Masters, in their obit, state that he was son of Felim Fionn, and Father Paul Walsh's pedigree shows us that this rival candidate was a member of a rival sept (*Sliocht Aodha*).

The King's letter opens with the statement that the diocese had been troubled with the contest between two rival bishops for some time past (*iamdiu*). The two rival claimants were both acting as bishops of Raphoe, but the King has been informed from Ireland that neither claimant had any true right to the see. He adds that his own candidate, Dean Art of Derry, was preparing to set out for Rome to seek confirmation from the Holy See and that he had the support of the chapter of Derry. The King begs the Pope to name judges to hear the case in Ireland and suggests the bishop of Derry (Rory O Donnell) and the official of Moyle as most suitable. If their judgment is in

[1] See above, p. 128.

[2] *Analecta Hibernica*, no. 12 (1943), pp. 179-181.

favour of Art, the King petitions the Holy See that his election may be ratified without further delay, and that the new bishop of Raphoe may be consecrated by Bishop Rory of Derry and some other prelate.

This letter was not written in vain. Two years later (July 1, 1538) James V wrote again to Paul III on behalf of Art O Gallagher. This second letter lets us know that the Pope had in fact granted the King's request and had commissioned Bishop Rory of Derry to examine the whole problem as to the lawful succession in Raphoe. Bishop Rory had made a full inquiry and had reported to the Holy See that neither of the two rival candidates had any strict right to the see. We should welcome further details, but the King's letter contains no more than a bare summary of the bishop's conclusions. Since Clement VII's provision of May 11, 1534, was of recent date and of unquestioned authenticity, we can only conjecture that Bishop Rory found reason for believing that the Holy See had acted on false or insufficient information. Very possibly the true facts as to the new bishop's parentage and ancestry had been concealed by Bishop Emonn's agents in Rome. Whatever the motives alleged by Bishop Rory, his verdict left the way open for a new papal provision, and King James writes once more and more urgently, on behalf of his own candidate. " We urgently request Your Holiness and we even beseech you," writes the King to the Pope, " that you may crown your former graciousness in our regard by granting this vacant bishopric, which has been so long without a lawful pastor, to Dean Arthur of Derry."

Art O Gallagher set out for Scotland in this same summer, but his ship was " wynde dryven " into Drogheda haven. In a letter which the King's Council sent from Ireland on August 22, 1538, they report the capture of " the dean of Dirry of O Donnell's country," and add that he had recently " obtained the bishopric of Raphoe by commendation of the king of the Scots."[1] Until the

[1] *State Papers* III, Part 2, p. 253; see also *Letters and Papers* XIII, Part 2, no. 159.

publication of the extracts from the letter-book of King James, this statement served only to add to the existing confusion. Students were bound to conclude that the dean of Derry here mentioned as having obtained the bishopric of Raphoe was Edmund O Gallagher. The King's letters make it plain that he was acting in opposition to Bishop Edmund throughout these tortuous negotiations. The dean of Derry whom the English captured in the summer of 1538 was undoubtedly Art O Gallagher, whose claims to the see of Raphoe are here stated with fair accuracy. Though his election by the chapter of Raphoe had not yet been confirmed by the Holy See, he had the support of Bishop Rory O Donnell, who had been appointed by the Holy See to inquire into this matter. He had also the support of the King of Scotland. His arrest in 1538 was no more than a passing episode in his career. The dean was released by Lord Leonard Grey within the next few months, and he appears as one of the witnesses to the agreement between Manus O Donnell and Tadhg O Connor on June 23, 1539.[1] But Paul III was not yet prepared to take action on behalf of a third candidate to the disputed see of Raphoe. He preferred to temporise and waited until the death of Bishop Edmund in 1543 had removed one of Art's two rivals. By that time, as we shall see, the situation in Ireland had altered for the worse from the Pope's point of view and the claims of Cornelius O Cahan were not easily challenged. Not until the death of Henry VIII and the succession of Edward VI had sharpened the conflict between the Pope and the English King, was Paul III at last induced to take strong action against Cornelius O Cahan. He provided Art O Gallagher to the see of Raphoe on December 5, 1547.[2] The see was then declared to have been vacant since the death of Edmund, "of good memory."

[1] *Letters and Papers* XIII, Part 2, no. 658; see below, p. 243.

[2] Brady I, p. 307.

Colaiste Oideachais Mhuire Gan Smal
Luimneach

PART IV

THE YEARS OF CONFUSION (1535-47)

I. THE DUBLIN PARLIAMENT OF 1536-7

The last entry in Cromer's register is most significant. The King had issued a writ ordering the clergy to elect proctors who should appear on their behalf at a parliament summoned for January 20, 1536.[1] At the same time a warning had been sent by one of the King's Council in Dublin that henceforth public prayers would not be permitted for the Pope as Supreme Pontiff or for his college of Cardinals. In England the breach with Rome had been consummated, and Henry VIII was now beginning to push his anti-papal policy in Ireland. George Browne, the first schismatic archbishop of Dublin, had not yet been appointed in succession to Archbishop Allen, but negotiations had already begun to that effect. The outlook was thus black for prelates like Primate Cromer, who depended on the King's favour for the security of their position in Ireland.

At the summons of the Primate a convocation of clergy met in the church of the Holy Trinity at Termonfeghin on
December 22, 1535. The entry in Cromer's Register notes C.93 v.
that all the clergy who had been summoned attended, with the exception of the dean and chapter. The dean of Armagh, Edmund McCawell, resided permanently in Armagh *inter Hibernicos*, and was not accustomed to attend the meetings of convocation *inter Anglos*. This

[1] For various reasons this parliament did not meet until May, 1536: see R. D. Edwards, *Church and State in Tudor Ireland*, p. 6.

entry is thus unusual. Formal notification must have been sent on behalf of the dean and chapter, stating that they were not prepared to attend. Even more remarkable is the fact that Cormac Roth did not preside in the absent Primate's place. The archdeacon was an important member of the chapter, and his abstention must have been deliberate. William Mann, who had been rector of Manfieldstown and vicar of Ardee for some years past, presided over the meeting. After some hesitation and deliberation Master William Hamling, the new vicar of St. Peter's, Drogheda, was chosen to represent the clergy of Armagh at the forthcoming parliament. He himself lodged an objection, as did also the proctors of the Lanthony community as proprietors of the vicarage of St. Peter's; but we are not told whether their objection was made effective. The clergy present then proceeded to elect three collectors of the King's subsidy, for the three deaneries of Dundalk, Drogheda and Ardee.

Where was the Primate during the session of this fateful convocation? His absence may have been deliberate, and due to caution. But we are told expressly in this entry that the meeting had been summoned on the date assigned by the Primate, and the official entry of its proceedings in his register makes it certain that these proceedings must have met with his approval. Primate Cromer was probably unable to attend owing to ill health, for he had been a sick man since the autumn of 1534. Some months before the date of this convocation (April 30, 1535) the new Deputy, Sir William Skeffyngton, wrote to excuse himself for an apparent lack of zeal in fulfilling the King's wishes: "Concerning your gracious pleasure for the attaching of the body of the archbishop of Armachan, and the examining of him upon certain articles of treason, and the justifying of him according your laws, I could not accomplish the same hitherto for such diseases and sickness as the said Archbishop hath been detained with, so as he could not in proper person repair to me, nor your Council."[1]

[1] *State Papers* II, p. 243.

Primate Cromer was indeed a sick man, sick in heart
and sick in body. Proof of his long illness can be found in
the last entries of his register, which suggest that he was
confined to his manor at Termonfeghin for more than a year
before the convocation of December 22, 1535. On June 30,
1534, less than three weeks after the dramatic session of the C.76 v.
King's Council in Dublin at which Silken Thomas had
renounced his allegiance to the King, the Primate presided
in person over a synod of the English clergy at St. Peter's,
Drogheda. That is the last record of any public appearance
outside Termonfeghin. On October 1 his letters in favour C.79 v.
of Cormac Roth were issued from his manor; and it was at
his manor that Lord Dunsany and his three Anglo-Irish
companions sought him out in October with a view to C.80 v.
obtaining his pardon as chancellor. About the same time
Master John Aleyn, whose letter to Thomas Cromwell we
have already quoted, was acting for the Primate as
chancellor in Dublin "during his sickness."[1] News of the
attack on his manor in Armagh must have reached the
Primate during his illness. His letters on this subject are
dated February 16, 1535. Sir William Skeffyngton's letter C.82-3.
proves that Cromer was still a sick man in April of that year.
On July 6 a synod of the English clergy met at St. Peter's, C.90.
Drogheda; but Cormac Roth presided over its sessions in
the name of the Primate. On September 17 the same C.91.
English clergy were summoned to meet the Primate in
convocation at the church of the Holy Trinity, Termonfeghin. Sister Mary Cusack and Abbess Margaret Silk
appeared before the Primate at Termonfeghin in October and C.92.
November. The evidence of these entries is thus consistent.
Cromer was no longer able to transact his duties as Primate
outside his manor at Termonfeghin or its immediate
neighbourhood.

The entry concerning the convocation of December 22 is clear proof of divided counsels in the diocese at this moment of crisis. The Primate must be held personally

[1] See above, p. 71.

responsible for the decision to send a proctor as the representative of his clergy at the forthcoming parliament in Dublin. His own health would no doubt be sufficient excuse for his absence from that parliament, but he must have made up his mind to attend by proxy, if he could not attend in person ; and his clergy, after some hesitation and formal protests, agreed with his policy. Any other decision would in fact have been an open defiance of the King's authority in Ireland. But that simple fact throws new light on the abstention, almost certainly the deliberate abstention, of the dean and chapter of Armagh, including the Primate's own faithful official, Archdeacon Cormac Roth. The day had come for a grave decision. The Irish clergy in Armagh had no doubt as to the course they ought to pursue. Cormac Roth had a more difficult choice to make, and the thought of his many wealthy benefices in the two dioceses of Armagh and Down must have weighed heavily in the scales on the side of caution and worldly prudence. That he found some way of saving his benefices for the last five years of his life is certain, for he held them until his death in the winter of 1539-40. But at this moment when a critical decision was forced upon him, he seems to have thrown in his lot with the Irish Catholic party. Master John Aleyn had been well informed when he included the official of Armagh "with certen other papistis" as prominent among the supporters and counsellors of Silken Thomas.[1]

The parliament that had been convoked for January 20, 1536, did not actually meet until the following May ; but preparations for its work had been actively pushed forward since the summer of 1535. The fate of the Geraldine cause had been decided by the capture of Maynooth Castle on March 23 of that year. Silken Thomas was still at large, and a potential menace to the English Government, until his unexpected surrender in the following August. The sudden collapse of his power in Ireland opened the way for a

[1] See above, p. 71.

more vigorous English policy; and the King was not slow to insist that the anti-papal legislation which he had forced through the English parliament in the past two years should now be made law for Ireland also.[1] Poynings' Law had made the procedure in Ireland more cumbersome, but also very much more satisfactory for the English government. No bill could now be submitted to the Irish parliament until the King's representative in Ireland and the Irish council had first sent a draft of the proposed measures to England under the great seal of Ireland. We know from a letter of the Deputy and council, dated June 16, 1535, that "certain Articles to pass in Ireland by Acts of Parliament for the King's advantage and the common weal of the land and reformation" were sent over to England at that time for examination and approval.[2] Of these the second was summarised as follows: "The King to be Supreme Head of the Church, and to have the domination of all dignities in Ireland."

Details of this first draft are lacking, but we may be sure that Thomas Cromwell knew the King's mind and had his own views as to the legislation that should now be submitted to the Irish parliament. Twice within the next few months we find Henry VIII writing to his Deputy in Ireland (Skeffyngton) urging that "our parliament there be summoned, with all convenient diligence, and that ye use such means, industry and policy that the causes to be moved there for Us may take effect"; and that the King counts on his active co-operation for "the advancement of our causes in our parliament, with that diligence and dexterity as We may see the success to follow of your fruits and doings, that We daily expect, in and about the effectual increase of our strength, jurisdiction, revenues, and profits there, according to your many persuasions and writings unto us."[3] But the work of preparing for the sessions of an Irish parliament depended more on the Deputy's success in stamping out the

[1] For what follows, see Edwards, op. cit., pp. 6-10.

[2] *Letters and Papers* VIII, no. 880.

[3] *State Papers* II, pp. 281; 294.

last remnants of the Geraldine armed forces within the Pale than on the skill of any lawyer. The entry in Cromer's register is our first indication that parliament had been summoned for January 20. Further delay proved unavoidable, and it was not until May 1 that parliament actually met in Dublin. Writing to Cromwell on May 7, Lord Leonard Gray (who had now taken Skeffyngton's place) reports that " the parliament began here the last Monday; and such matters as yet hath ben preferred for our sovereign Lord the King goeth forward without any stop."[1]

A letter to Cromwell from Brabazon, the King's " Treasurer for War," dated May 17, gives us our first detailed list of the acts that were passed by the commons in this first session: the Act of Attainder against the adherents of the Geraldine cause; the Act of Succession; the Act of First Fruits; the Act of the Supreme Head; the Act of Slander (against the King or his heirs); the Act of Appeals; and an Act which dealt with " the spiritualities as well as the temporalities of such religious houses in England as had any possessions, tithes or other hereditaments here." Brabazon adds: " The proctors of the Spiritualities somewhat do stick in divers of these Acts; and loth they are that the King's Grace should be the Supreme Head of the Church."[2] This is the first sign of resistance to the new legislation, and it is significant that it comes from the proctors of the clergy. Primate Cromer may well have had this purpose in view when he ordered his clergy of Armagh to meet at Termonfeghin and elect a proctor for the coming parliament.

A word of explanation is here needed. In England there had formerly been an estate of clerical proctors, which sat in parliament as well as in convocation—though they seem to have been summoned, not by royal writ, but at the summons of their own bishops.[3] Since the immediate summons from the Crown was lacking, these clerical proctors

[1] *State Papers* II, p. 314. [2] ibid. II, p. 315-6.
[3] Pollard, *Evolution of Parliament*, p. 199; Edwards, op. cit., p. 9.

dropped out of parliament in England and contented themselves with the sessions of convocation, where they could make decisions that were communicated to parliament by their prolocutor (speaker) or by the bishops in the upper house. In Ireland a separate estate of proctors had been maintained as part of the normal structure of parliament. The entry in Cromer's register shows us the system by which such proctors were summoned to the Irish parliament—as it happened, for the last time. Henry VIII was not the man to suffer obstruction from a body of this kind, and the resistance offered by the clerical proctors in this parliament of 1536-7 provoked an act which abolished their estate for the future.

The presence of these proctors in parliament is important, as they were to take a more active part in the sessions of the next few months than the bishops, who prudently safeguarded themselves from the King's wrath whilst encouraging the proctors to make technical objections. And here we come to a question that is not easily answered. How many of the Irish bishops were present at the sessions of this Dublin parliament ?

It is not safe to assume that only those bishops came to Dublin whose dioceses lay within the narrow limits of the English Pale. This same Dublin parliament was prorogued in July to meet first at Kilkenny, and then at Limerick—though these meetings seem never to have taken place, for the second session was held again at Dublin in September.[1] At the end of the year the King's commissioners dissolved parliament, giving as one reason that many of the members were in danger, " coming thereunto, constrained to pass the countries not very obedient to the King's Majesty."[2] Bishops like Rory O Donnell of Derry or Emonn O Gallagher of Raphoe would not come to Dublin, and it is doubtful whether a formal summons was issued to these more distant dioceses. A recent study of the Irish parliamentary system during the fifteenth century has led a competent

[1] *State Papers* II, pp. 344-5 ; 365 ; 380.

[2] ibid. II, p. 534.

scholar to the conclusion that Dublin, Kildare, Meath and Armagh were the only dioceses regularly represented in the parliaments of this period.[1] Ferns, Ossory, Limerick, Waterford and Lismore were occasionally represented, but it would be rash to assume the presence of their bishops at any single session. Of the monastic prelates, the abbots of St. Mary's and St. Thomas's, Dublin, Baltinglass and Mellifont, with the priors of Connell and Kilmainham, were usually present either in person or by proxy.

If we apply these conclusions to the parliament of 1536-7, we may guess that Bishop Staples of Meath and (perhaps) Bishop Nugent of Kilmore were among the small gathering of prelates who represented the province of Armagh on this occasion. Derry, Clogher, Ardagh and Clonmacnois were ruled by Irish prelates who were not likely to answer the summons at any time. Raphoe may perhaps have been represented by Cornelius O Cahan, who received his grant of English liberties about this time and was henceforth resident within the Pale.[2] It is hard to add another name. Blyth of Down and Connor was an absentee in England, and Dromore was still vacant. Some abbots attended this Parliament, and we may count Abbot Comptor of Mellifont as almost certainly present. The Primate himself must have been summoned, but he had already found a valid excuse for not answering the Deputy's summons on the ground of his age and many infirmities. We may guess that he used the same good reason for absenting himself from a parliament that was certain to cause trouble for any Primate of All Ireland.

Parliament met in Dublin in September, 1536; and again in January, 1537. In the earlier of these two sessions opposition was made, even in the house of commons, to the suppression of the Irish religious houses. One of Cromwell's agents in Ireland reported to his master that Sergeant

[1] H. G. Richardson: "The Irish Parliament Rolls of the Fifteenth Century," in *English Historical Review* 58 (Oct., 1943), pp. 455-7.

[2] See above, p. 128.

Patrick Barnewall had been bold enough to argue in public debate that " he wold not graunte that the Kynge, as Hedd of the Churche, had soo large power as the Bysshop of Rome."[1] By the following January word had gone round the Pale that Silken Thomas and his fellow-prisoners in the Tower were about to be released and sent home. There was general alarm among all those who had reason to fear a revival of the Geraldine power ; whilst the former adherents of Kildare took heart again. Lord Gray reports to Cromwell that the commons were " so astonyed " by this report " as it shuld seame, of the ruffle which hath been ther, as they litell regard to passe anny thinge."[2] Faced with this new spirit of opposition to the proposed acts, the Deputy once more adjourned parliament to May 1. But Henry's patience was wearing thin, and he sent a letter to the Deputy and council on February 25 which contains this open threat[3] :

" And We wold you shul all thinke that We have such a zeale to the advauncement of the good of that cuntrey, that like as We propose ernestly to devise for the reformacion thereof, and the reducing of it to a perfite civilitie, soo let every man, whom We there put in trust, be assured, that if We shall find he hath against our expectacion, directly or indirectly, divised or practised the let, hinderance, or impechment of this our purpose for any respecte, whereunto We woll not fayle to have a special eye, We shall soo loke upon him, what degre soever he be of, for the same, as other shall, by his exemple, beware howe they shal misuse their Prince and Sovereigne Lorde, and transgresse his most dradd commandment."

Only two bishops signed the letter sent by the Council in answer to this reproof : George Browne of Dublin, and Staples of Meath. Browne had been consecrated in London on March 19, 1536. He had reached Dublin in the middle of July, coming too late for the first sessions of parliament.

[1] *State Papers* II, p. 372. [2] ibid., II, p. 407.
[3] ibid., II, p. 425-6.

From the first he had been a zealous supporter of the royal policy. His presence in Dublin must have been, of itself, a powerful motive for keeping the Primate away from the capital. But Archbishop Browne who had served the King so well in England as his principal agent in the suppression of the English monasteries did not satisfy Henry in Ireland. He and Staples were, to Irish eyes, unduly subservient to the King, their master. To Henry and Cromwell they seemed to be lacking in the ruthless energy that was needed to push the new programme for reform in face of every obstacle. On July 31, 1537, the King sent a sharply worded reproof to the archbishop and the bishop.[1] Browne was bidden remember the days " bifore your promotion and advauncement to that ordre, dignite, and auctoritie of an Archebishop " when he " shewed an apparaunce of suche entiere zele and affection " in the furtherance of the King's work. He is reprimanded for his " lightnes in behaviour " and is bidden curtly to " reforme yourself, therfore, with this gentle advertisement." Should this warning fail to amend him, " should you persevere in your fonnde foly and ingrate ungentilness," the King would have Browne remember " that We be as hable, for the not doing therof, to remove you agayn, and to put an other man of more vertue and honestie in your place." Staples received a similar reproof, in language that was no less plain and no less alarming.

Why did the King not send a similar letter of reproof to Primate Cromer ? As an Englishman and a former royal chaplain, the Primate would seem to Henry no less bound than his brethren of Dublin and Meath to show all possible zeal and deference towards his royal will. There seems to be only one possible explanation of this surprising omission.[2] For one reason or another (and the most plausible reason is the Primate's real or alleged physical infirmities) Henry VIII must have been satisfied that Cromer was no longer a man

[1] The letter to Browne is in *State Papers* II, p. 465. The letter to Staples is summarised in *Letters and Papers* XII, Part 2, no. 377.

[2] See the comments of Dr. Edwards, op. cit., p. 28, note 1.

on whom he could count for active work on his behalf in Ireland. Cromer's register lets us see that the Primate stayed at home in his manor at Termonfeghin for the whole of 1535. From the complete obscurity that surrounds his acts and movements during the next seven years we must conclude that he remained in his manor, a voluntary prisoner or an invalid, for the rest of his life.

None the less, Primate Cromer must have watched the manoeuvres of the clerical proctors in Dublin with close interest, and his advice may have been taken from time to time, as to the possibility or wisdom of further resistance. Parliament met again in May, 1537. The proctors were now organised as a solid block against the new religious laws. Gray and Brabazon, reporting to Cromwell on May 18, complain: "The frowardnes and obstynacye of the Proctours of the Clergy, from the begynnyng of this Parliament, and at this cession, bothe of them the Bishops and Abbotis, hathe bene soche, that we thinke we can no les do than advertise your Lordship therof."[1] When parliament met, so they say, "some billis were passed the Comon House, and by the Speker delyvered to the Highe House, to be debated there." It is a pity that Cromwell's two correspondents are not more explicit. What were these bills which provoked the last determined opposition of the bishops and proctors of the clergy? From a comparison of various lists of acts that passed the Irish parliament during these two years, Dr. Edwards has argued that the final stand was probably made on the debate concerning an act against the authority of the Pope, and the act against bringing papal dispensations into Ireland.[2]

The few bishops who attended this parliament were plainly afraid to declare their views in public debate. They took the line that they would not allow the debate to proceed, until the position of the state of proctors had been fully recognised. The Deputy—"perceiving that, by this means, thei sought an occasion to denie all thinges that

[1] *State Papers* II, p. 437-8. [2] Edwards, op. cit., p. 15.

shuld be presented unto the Upper House "—summoned a meeting of the Council to discuss the constitutional rights of the estate of proctors. The opinions " of the lerned men of Ingland " were brought forward to support the view " that the said Proctours had no voice in the Parliament " ; and the argument was also put forward from entries on the rolls that the denial or assent of the proctors could not be held necessary to legislation on spiritual issues since " it was written undre divers Actes *Procuratores Cleri non consenserunt*, and yet were the same Actes good and effectuell in lawe."[1]

Since the legal position seemed doubtful, Gray and Brabazon reported their difficulties to Cromwell. The bishops, they added, were playing a game of obstruction. They had a majority in the upper house, when they were all present. But some were abstaining from attendance ; others would seek license to depart, and would then appear unexpectedly and act as a solid body—" contynued (of a sett course) holly togethers, every day, in the Parliament House." It was time, the Deputy thought, that an end should be put to these tactics. " And therfor, my Lord, it were well doon, that some mean be devised, wherby thei may be broute to remember ther duties better." If the proctors are not " put from voice " in parliament, " ther shall but feue thinges passe for the Kinges profit." The Deputy is quite clear, however, that the proctors were acting on the advice and with the secret support of the bishops. " It dothe well appere," he wrote to Cromwell, " that it is a crafty case, divised betwixt their masters the Bishoppes, and them."[2]

Cromwell had a ready answer to this appeal for help. On July 31, 1537, little more than two months after the date of this letter, a commission was issued by the King to four commissioners (Anthony Saintleger, George Poulet, Thomas Moyle, and William Berners), giving them full powers and

[1] *State Papers* II, p. 438.
[2] ibid., II, p. 439.

instructions to provide "for the ordre and establishment to be taken and made touching the hole state of our lande of Ireland, and all and every our affaires within the same, bothe for the reduction of the said lande to a due civilitie and obedyens, and the advauncement of the publique weale of the same."[1] On their arrival in Dublin these commissioners sent messages to both houses of parliament, ordering the members to conform themselves to whatever proposals should be brought before them. It was at this juncture also that the King sent his sharp reproof to Archbishop Browne and Bishop Staples.

The royal will was now so plain that no further resistance was offered to the last stages of the proposed anti-papal legislation. An Act was passed (28 Henry VIII, c. 18) terminating the parliamentary rights of the estate of proctors, and with the dissolution of this separate body clerical resistance to the new measures collapsed. The commissioners were able to report to Cromwell on January 2, 1538, that their work was completed and that they had dissolved parliament before the end of the year.[2] The Act of Supremacy, the Act against the power of the Pope, and all the other measures of Henry's anti-papal programme were now, so far as the King's power reached, the law of the land.

2. IRISH PLANS FOR RESISTANCE

Whilst those of the Irish bishops who accepted the King's authority were thus yielding to royal pressure, the chieftains and bishops whose territory lay remote from the King's control, and whose people were not subject to his laws, began to send messages to Rome asking the Holy See

[1] *State Papers* II, pp. 452-63.
[2] ibid. II, p. 534.

for help in this crisis. Our first clear indication that messages of this kind were being sent is to be found in the embassy of Charles Reynolds and Richard Walsh during the winter of 1534-5.[1] During the next two years we hear less of such negotiations. The sudden collapse of the Geraldine power in Ireland must have disheartened many who had looked to Silken Thomas as their leader. His execution, together with the execution of several of his kinsmen, was delayed until the spring of 1537. The letters of the King's council in Dublin during the eighteen months following the surrender of Silken Thomas make it plain that the Englishry in the Pale feared nothing so much as the return of the Geraldine prisoners. Their execution in 1537 was the final blow to the party which had been formed around the Earl of Kildare and his impetuous son.

On January 14, 1538, Cranmer sent a letter to Cromwell with an enclosure from one of his agents in Spain.[2] The news from Spain was in fact news from Rome through Spain, and we must allow a considerable interval for the transmission of this message, from Rome to Seville and from Seville to London. The story, as it was finally told to Cranmer by a man who had formerly been his servant in England and had then taken service with Cardinal Ghinucci, was that " there came to the Holy Father a canon from Ireland, and His Holiness confirmed to him certain letters with compassion." This canon had brought letters to the Pope from " a powerful gentleman in Ireland, who has three brethren, with great kindred, and who, by the recent death of his father, enjoys possession of the royalty, by which he is bound to be at the King's Deputy's commandment; but he has never come to the King nor his Deputy, and writeth (to the Pope) that the King's Deputy and his father with great power hath procured to take him and to have him brought to the King, which they never succeeded in doing, by reason of his power, nor yet any of his three brethren."

[1] See above, p. 129-30.

[2] *Letters and Papers* XIII, Part 1, no. 76-77.

There can be no doubt at all as to the identity of this Irish lord. Aodh Dubh O Donnell had died on July 5, 1537. A full account of his power and military success can be read in the long notice of his death by the Four Masters. Aodh Dubh had long been on bad terms with his son and heir, Manus O Donnell, who now succeeded him as lord of Tirconnell. The three brothers of Manus who are mentioned in this letter, were Aodh Buidhe, who died as heir to the lordship of Tirconnell in 1538; Domhnall, who was slain in 1548; and Conn, who was sent as a hostage to England in 1543. That last episode took place after the submission of O Neill and O Donnell in the winter of 1542-3. There was no question of O Donnell sending hostages to England in 1537. As Manus proudly wrote to the Pope, "neither he nor his brethren will go near the King or his Deputy; and no King of England to this day has put governance among them, but they have always lived without order, with great charge of conscience."[1]

Cromer's register throws some light on the probable identity of the Irish canon whom Manus O Donnell sent to Rome soon after his father's death, in the summer or autumn of 1537. Canon Art O Friel is twice mentioned in the register for 1535, and he was plainly one of the most C.85 v.
prominent priests in the diocese of Raphoe. In 1535 Paul III nominated him as one of three papal judges in the lawsuit concerning the benefices of Aodh MacAbarde in 1535.[2] C.91-2.
On October 7, 1538, Paul III provided Art O Friel, canon of Raphoe, to the see of Tuam, on the report of Cardinal Ghinucci.[3] This is the very Cardinal whose letter to his brother of Seville had been betrayed to Cranmer twelve months earlier. This unexpected provision of a priest from Raphoe to the archbishopric of Tuam is most easily explained if we assume that Art O Friel had been in Rome for the past year: having come there as the agent of Manus O Donnell in 1537, and having stayed at the papal court as

[1] I quote from the English summary in *Letters and Papers*, loc. cit., but the wording is here obscure.

[2] See above, p. 196. [3] Brady II, p. 133; see below, p. 238.

an accredited representative of Irish interests. The King had nominated Christopher Bodkin, bishop of Kilmacduagh, to the vacant see of Tuam early in 1537. This counter-provision of Art O Friel to the metropolitan see in Connacht is, as we shall see, the first step in a new and bolder papal policy in Ireland.

What was the nature of Manus O Donnell's appeal to Rome in 1537 ? Cranmer's information seems to have been fairly detailed and trustworthy. He quotes from the letter which Cardinal Ghinucci sent to Seville, reporting the substance of O Donnell's letter :

" That now the King has taken on him the whole power of the Pope, with the consent of his bishops (in England) ; and they make order at their own will, insomuch that the realm of England is in division, the great masters being against each other, fathers against their sons, husbands against their wives, and the commonalty one against another." The Pilgrimage of Grace had threatened Henry's position at home in 1536, and exaggerated news of its success seems to have reached O Donnell in Ireland. " There was a division in England in the field in one part," he writes to the Pope ; " fifty thousand to maintain the constitutions of His Holiness, and as many more against them." He himself, when the news had come to him (this must have been some months before his father's death) " had been with a great part of Ireland to know their minds, and also with the bishops and religious houses, and finds them all ready to rise against the King of England at the bidding of the Apostolic See, because they will not be governed after the order of the Church of England against that of the See Apostolic." " He and the rest of Ireland," Manus continues " are in dread that the Anti-christ of England will come or send his power, to put such order in the churches of Ireland as he has done in England." He " writes for the discharge of his soul, and begs the Holy Father to give him help to uphold the Apostolic See ; which if His Holiness will do, he will fulfill these promises following, and trusts that the stones, the trees, the fowl in the air and the fish in the sea will rise to aid him, and much more the people who are very Christians."

Here is a bold programme of open resistance to the King's power in Ireland. Manus, however, was promising the Pope more than he could actually perform. If His Holiness will send him "certain ships with galleys and pinnaces of Biscay, with some men of Biscay, artillery and powder," thirty thousand men of war, led by himself and his kinsmen, will join them on landing. These will be sufficient for the conquest of Ireland. Meanwhile O Donnell undertakes to reimburse the Pope for all the expenses of the campaign. It is his intention, if he captures any of the Englishry who have caused such damage to Ireland, "to use them as Moors, as reason is." After the first year he will be bound to pay the Pope 100,000 ducats of gold out of the land, "and he will deliver to His Holiness so many Moors of England that their ransom alone will suffice to bear all the costs." Lord Leonard Gray's seasoned troops, with their better discipline and more modern equipment, were soon to make an end of these illusions. But Manus O Donnell had at least offered leadership to the Irish Catholic cause. His letter to Paul III lets us see that many bishops and other prelates in Ireland were far from assenting to the weak subservience of those who attended the King's parliament in Dublin.

The Pope was plainly moved by this appeal from Ireland. The Cardinal's letter to Seville reports that the Holy Father was planning to negotiate a peace between the Emperor and the King of France, so that the way might be clear for a General Council at which he would "desire all Christian princes to aid the good Christian people of Ireland." Failing their active support, the Pope will try to raise funds for an expedition to Ireland, and will appeal to the Christian King of France and to the King of Scots for aid, "as their kingdoms are near Ireland."

Scotland was indeed the kingdom to which the Irish of Tirconnell looked with most confidence for aid at this time.

There was much coming and going between Ireland and Scotland in the summer of 1538. On July 20, 1538, Ormonde writes to Robert Cowley in London, telling him that " Bishop O Donyll, James Delahide, Mr. Lurous and Robt. Walshe are gone to the Scotch King from O Donnell, O Neill and young Gerald [the brother of Silken Thomas] to ask aid."[1] The Geraldine cause was now without effective leadership, and the two northern chieftains begin to stand forth as the most important champions of the Irish Catholic cause. Just one month later, three of the King's council were able to report to Cromwell that they " have taken of late the dean of Derry, of O Donnell's country, who has by commendation of the King of Scots obtained the bishopric of Raphoe here, and who confesses that O Donnell has now messengers in Scotland to obtain battery pieces."[2] This dean of Derry is, as we have seen, Art O Gallagher whom the King of Scotland was then recommending to the Pope as his candidate for the see of Raphoe. His later release by Lord Leonard Gray was used by the Deputy's enemies in Dublin as one of many arguments by which they sought to discredit his loyalty to the King.[3] But Gray was a shrewd diplomat as well as a very competent soldier, and he probably had sound reasons for believing that the dean would be more useful to him as an intermediary with O Donnell than as a prisoner in his hands.[4]

Bishop Rory O Donnell must have come back to Ireland from Scotland in the summer or autumn of that same year. He was in Derry on the following New Year's Eve, when he sent a letter to Pope Paul III, dated from Derry on December 31, 1538.[5] The bishop's letter is now in the London Record Office, having fallen into the hands of

[1] *Letters and Papers* XIII, Part 1, no. 1429. Mr. Lurous (not Lurons) is Thomas Leverous, later bishop of Kildare; Robert Walshe is the " Parson Walshe " of 1534-5.

[2] ibid. XIII, Part 2, no. 159; see above, p. 207-9.

[3] Art was released before June 23, 1539, when he witnessed the agreement between Manus O Donnell and Tadhg O Connor: see below, p. 243.

[4] *Letters and Papers* XV, no. 830; Edwards, op. cit., p. 44.

[5] ibid. XIII, Part 2, no. 1164.

Cromwell's agents in England. The story of its adventures gives us yet another glimpse into the constant coming and going between Ireland, Scotland and Rome in these stormy and fateful years. Bishop Rory commends his messenger to the Pope as an honest and discreet monk, named Roger O Spellan. The same messenger carried a letter from young Gerald FitzGerald to Cardinal Pole dated from Donegal on December 7, 1538.[1] In this letter Gerald describes his messenger as Ruoric O Spealayn, " a monk of the monastery of Collis Victoriæ." This is the official Cistercian name for the monastery of Knockmoy in Co. Galway. Bishop Rory's messenger was thus an Irish Cistercian monk named Rory O Spillane, of the community at Knockmoy.

The bishop's messenger must have crossed over to Scotland from Derry early in January, 1539. On his way through Scotland he got in touch with the abbot of Melrose, from whom he received letters to the Pope and other friends in Rome.[2] The next stage of his journey was by ship from some port on the eastern coast of Scotland to France. Rory was no longer alone, but sailed in company with an Irish friar (whose name is given, in the act of attainder which sentenced them both to execution, as John Macyvaroill) and an English priest named Robert More. More was from Primate Cromer's native diocese of Chichester; he had escaped from an English prison at Hexham, and was now on his way to France and Rome.[3] The three refugees were most unfortunate. A storm blew their ship into the mouth of the Tyne, and they were captured by English officers at South Shields.[4] Within the next few weeks their names were included in a general act of attainder; they were probably executed before the end of that summer.

Bishop Rory's letter has survived, and gives us a vivid picture of the Irish scene as it appeared to the bishop of

[1] *Letters and Papers* XIII, Part 2, no. 999.

[2] ibid. XIV, Part 1, no. 516.

[3] ibid. XIV, Part 1, no. 867.

[4] The first news was sent to Cromwell early in March: ibid. XIV, Part 1, nos. 455; 481.

Derry within three years of the collapse of the Geraldine revolt. The King's Deputy in Ireland, so he tells the Pope, refuses to recognise the Pope's authority. His men go through the country, burning houses, destroying churches, ravishing Irish maids, spoiling and killing the innocent. They kill any priest who prays for the Pope, or else seek to compel him to erase the Pope's name from the Canon of the Mass. They torture all preachers who do not repudiate the Pope's authority. It would fill a book to tell all their cruelties.

Bishop Rory then passes to graver news. The four archbishops in Ireland, so he informs the Pope, have withdrawn their obedience from Rome; and the English have subdued almost the whole of Ireland to their wicked laws. Bishop Rory then begs the Holy Father to grant him authority to remove unworthy bishops and clergy from their benefices, and to put others in their places. He asks also for special faculties to reconcile heretics, schismatics, etc. Finally he asks that credence may be given to his messenger. Rory O Spellan—" an honest and discreet monk." With that last petition the letter ends.

Not every detail in Bishop Rory's letter need be taken as strictly accurate. He was writing at a moment of great crisis, when bad news of every sort was coming to the north from all over Ireland; and bad news, then as always, lost nothing in the telling. But there is one item of information in this letter which is worthy of special note. The Bishop's statement that every one of the four archbishops in Ireland had renounced the Pope's authority can hardly have been made without sufficient grounds for so grave a charge. Two of the archbishops at this period were unquestionably committed to the King's cause in Ireland. George Browne of Dublin had come to this country in the summer of 1536 as the King's nominee. He had no provision from the Pope, and he was known as a strong supporter of the Royal Supremacy in Ireland. Bishop Christopher Bodkin of Kilmacduagh, whom Henry VIII had translated to the see of Tuam in 1537, was less of a King's man than Browne of Dublin. But he had accepted nomination to Tuam without seeking the pallium from the Holy See, and he was now faced with the opposition of a papal candidate—for the provision of Art O Friel to the see of Tuam took effect a few weeks before the date of this letter.[1] In Cashel Edmund Butler belonged to a family who were the hereditary enemies of the Geraldines of Kildare. James Butler, heir to the Earl of Ossory, was at this time the most actively anti-papal nobleman in Ireland. There is some doubt as to how far Archbishop Butler had committed himself to an acknowledgment of the Royal Supremacy at this period, but it seems probable that he was suspect at least, perhaps actually guilty of disloyalty to the Holy See in 1538-9.[2]

There remains the Primate of All Ireland. Had Primate Cromer committed himself openly to recognition of the Royal Supremacy by the end of 1538? We shall see that the Pope had no doubts as to his defection early in 1539, and it is difficult to believe that the bishop of Derry could have made this statement in an official letter to the Holy See, were he not certain of the attitude taken up by his own metropolitan. The act prescribing the Oath of Supremacy, which included a formal rejection of the Pope's authority in Ireland, was part of English law in Ireland from the end of 1537. This oath was seldom enforced at this early stage of the new religious policy. In a letter which Archbishop Browne sent to Cromwell on January 8, 1538, he complains that, since his arrival in Ireland eighteen months earlier, he has been unable to persuade or induce any one, either religious or secular, "to preache the Worde of God, or the juste title of Our moste illustrious Prince."[3] As usual, he blames his failure on the Lord Deputy's hostility to himself, but it is obvious that opposition to the new measures, even in Dublin, made their enforcement impracticable. During

[1] See below, p. 237.

[2] Edwards, op. cit., pp. 33-35; Canon Jourdan, in *History of the Church of Ireland* (1933) II, p. 209.

[3] *State Papers* II, p. 539.

the years 1538 and 1539 sporadic efforts were made, by the Deputy and by other members of the council, to enforce the new legislation, and in particular to administer the Oath of Supremacy in various parts of Ireland. How far these efforts were strictly legal, is matter of dispute ; for there is no authentic record of what was done.[1] We may hazard a guess that the Oath of Supremacy was tendered to Primate Cromer at his manor in Termonfeghin at an early date. In a memorandum drafted in September, 1537, by John Aleyn, then master of the rolls in Dublin, it is suggested that the Oath of Supremacy " be offerid untill every of the Kinges subjectes by Commyssioners in every countye, and all the Lordes to be sworne thereunto at the next Parlyament."[2] It is plain that the oath had not yet been put into execution at the date of this memorandum. The Primate had been an absentee from the sessions of parliament in 1537, but it seems hardly credible that he would not have been required to make some formal declaration, binding himself to acknowledge the King's " juste title " in Ireland. Conformity on that occasion would have been a public renunciation of the Pope's jurisdiction ; and would have justified the bishop of Derry in his report to the Pope that the four archbishops, including the Primate of All Ireland, had withdrawn their obedience from the Holy See.[3]

3. THE POPE TAKES ACTION

In his letter to the Cardinal of Seville, Cardinal Ghinucci had reported that, when the Irish canon arrived in Rome in the autumn of 1537, " His Holiness confirmed to him certain letters with compassion." These " letters " may perhaps have been the bulls granting a new indulgence, of

[1] Edwards, op. cit. pp. 85-90 and in *Irish Ecclesiastical Record* Fifth Series, vol. 45 (January, 1935), pp. 39-60.

[2] *State Papers* II, p. 480.

[3] For Primate Cromer's open recognition of the Royal Supremacy in 1541, see below, p. 255.

which George Browne complains in his letter to Cromwell of January 8, 1538: "Theire is of late comen in to Ireland from Rome a pardon, motche consonante to a pardon graunted by Julious the Seconde, in tyme of the warres bytwene the French King and hym; and that was, that they that wolde enjoie it, shulde faste Wensday, Friday, and Saturday next after they hard furste of it, and on the Sunday consequentlie ensuying to receyve the Communyon. And many, as it is reaported, hath receyved the same."[1]

An indulgence of this kind could do little more than encourage the Catholics of Ireland to hold firmly to the ancient Faith, hoping for better times.[2] What was needed, more and more desperately as year followed year without any change in the King's anti-papal policy, was the provision of trustworthy and courageous bishops to fill the vacant sees in place of those who had proved unworthy of their trust. It was for this that Bishop Rory O Donnell had appealed to Rome in 1538. We must now consider the position of the Irish hierarchy as a whole during the years 1535-39.[3]

When the storm of the Geraldine revolt first heralded the coming of a greater storm in the King's open attack on papal jurisdiction in Ireland, several Irish sees were vacant and others were held by absentee prelates. In the province of Armagh the see of Dromore had been vacant since 1526, whilst Down and Connor were held by the absentee Bishop Blyth. Clogher fell vacant in the winter of 1534-5.[4] Dublin fell vacant in the summer of 1534 with the murder of Archbishop Allen. In the province of Cashel the two united dioceses of Ardfert and Aghadoe fell vacant at some date earlier than 1536, by the death of Bishop John FitzGerald. The two united dioceses of Cork and Cloyne fell vacant soon afterwards, by the death of Bishop John Bennet in 1536.

[1] *State Papers* II, p. 540.

[2] For the effect of similar indulgences in Clonfert, see *State Papers* II, p. 516; III, p. 51.

[3] For what follows I have been much assisted by the excellent tables printed by Dr. Edwards in *Irish Eccl. Record* (February, 1935), pp. 196-205. I have made one or two minor corrections.

[4] See above, p. 182.

The situation was more complicated in the province of Tuam, where the diocese of Elphin had been held by an absentee English bishop, John Max or Maxey, since 1525. Clonfert fell vacant at some date earlier than 1534 by the death of Bishop Denis O More, whilst the absentee Bishop Maxey died in 1536. The metropolitan of this province, Archbishop Thomas O Mullally, also died in 1536. It is probable (though not certain) that he had also ruled over the small diocese of Enaghdun near Galway, of which the last recorded bishop, whose name is given as Francis, had been provided by Alexander VI as far back as 1496.[1] Finally, the small see of Mayo was held by an absentee Bishop John Bel, who had been provided in 1493 and was dead before 1541.[2] After the death of Archbishop O Mullally in 1536 there were thus only three resident bishops in Connacht: Christopher Bodkin of Kilmacduagh, Richard Barrett of Killala, and Cormac O Coyn of Achonry.

There was thus much room for action by the Pope and the King as rival nominating powers in the first years of the Henrician schism. Clement VII had already challenged a King's bishop by his provision of Emonn O Gallagher to the see of Raphoe on May 11, 1534. His action, as we have seen, was due mainly to local causes; none the less, it is significant of the Pope's attitude at a time when Henry had already broken with the Holy See in England. About the same time—certainly before the death of Clement VII in the autumn of that year—the Dominican Roland de Burgo, a kinsman of the Clanrickarde family, was provided to the see of Clonfert; but he does not seem to have taken up residence in his diocese until 1537.[3] On August 6, 1535, Paul III provided Hugh O Carolan (Aodh O Cearbhallain) to the see of Clogher, within a few months of the death of Bishop Patrick O Cullen.[4] No other papal provision has been recorded for this year, though we must always remember that our surviving records are exceedingly imperfect.

[1] Brady II, p. 152. [2] Brady II, p. 154.

[3] Lynch, *De Præsulibus* II, p. 313; see below, p. 236-7.

[4] Brady I, p. 252.

The King made no appointment to any Irish see during these two years. In Raphoe he supported Cornelius O Cahan against the newly consecrated Emonn O Gallagher, and we know that he did not recognise Roland de Burgo as bishop of Clonfert. His policy seems to have been at first the negative policy of refusing recognition to any candidate whom the Pope might provide, unless that candidate surrendered his papal bulls to the King and did fealty for the temporalities of his see.[1] On this ground Henry did not recognise Hugh O Carolan as bishop of Clogher until 1542, when the bishop conformed to this recognition of the King's authority in Ireland.

The year 1536 was marked by several appointments to Irish sees: some by provision of the Pope, others by the King's authority. On May 29 Paul III provided the Dominican Quintin Cogley to the see of Dromore, which had been vacant for the past ten years.[2] The King did not recognise this appointment, but made no appointment of his own. On August 15 the Pope provided James Fitz-Maurice to the sees of Ardfert and Aghadoe, which had been vacant for some time.[3] Once again, the King did not recognise this appointment, but made no effort to nominate a King's bishop for Kerry.

Meanwhile the King had nominated George Browne, the prior provincial of the Augustinian friars in England, to the see of Dublin which had been left vacant by both Pope and King for more than a year and a half. Browne was appointed on March 12, and was consecrated on March 19, 1536.[4] This was the first instance of a direct royal nomin-

[1] On this question, see Dr. Edwards in *Irish Eccl. Record* (Jan., 1935), p. 52 foll.; but I cannot agree that the surrender of papal bulls was no more than a continuance of the medieval custom by which each bishop, in seeking restitution of temporalities, was expected to renounce those clauses in the bull of provision which were prejudicial to the King's temporal authority. The King was now claiming spiritual jurisdiction and the demand for surrender of papal bulls was the symbol of this claim.

[2] Brady I, p. 299.

[3] Brady II, p. 53.

[4] Ronan, *Reformation in Dublin*, p. 17.

ation to an Irish see, without reference to the Pope in Rome. The new archbishop of Dublin was never recognised by the Pope, but Paul III made no effort to provide a rival candidate to the metropolitan see of Dublin. He seems to have judged it imprudent to expose his authority to contempt in a see where no Pope's bishop could hope to exercise effective jurisdiction during the reign of Henry VIII. George Browne came to Dublin in the summer of 1536. Soon afterwards—most probably at Browne's suggestion—Richard Nangle, the prior provincial of the Augustinian friars in Ireland, was nominated by the King to the see of Clonfert.[1] This is the first instance of a candidate nominated by the King in opposition to a papal candidate, though Bishop Roland de Burgo does not seem to have come to Clonfert until 1537.[2] Finally, the King nominated Dominic Tirrey, rector of Shandon church in Cork, to the united sees of Cork and Cloyne on September 20, 1536.[3] The Pope does not seem to have challenged this appointment until 1540, when he provided an Irish Friar Minor named Lewis MacNamara. After his death, which occurred within a few days of his provision, the Pope again provided John Hoveden, canon of Elphin, to these two sees which were adjudged vacant since the death of Bishop John Bennet.[4]

By the end of 1536 all the vacant Irish sees had thus been filled, either by the King or by the Pope, with the exception of the two western sees of Tuam and Elphin. The Pope had filled vacancies in Dromore, Clogher, Clonfert, Ardfert and Aghadoe; the King had filled vacancies in Dublin, Clonfert, Cork and Cloyne. Setting aside the exceptional case of Raphoe, there had not yet been any instance of an open clash between two rival candidates to the same see. For the King in nominating Richard Nangle to the see of Clonfert may have been ignorant of the fact that the Pope had already provided Roland de Burgo to

[1] Morrin I, p. 27. The exact date is not known.

[2] *Calendar of Carew MSS.* I, p. 136; *State Papers* II, p. 516.

[3] Morrin I, pp. 24; 26.

[4] Brady II, p. 84-5; *Letters and Papers* XVI, p. 231.

that see. When the Pope's bishop reached Clonfert in the summer or autumn of 1537, he was successful in contesting the claims of Richard Nangle, just as Emonn O Gallagher had been successful in contesting the claims of Cornelius O Cahan in Raphoe.

In the summer of 1538 Robert Cowley, one of Cromwell's agents in Ireland, sent the following complaint to his master in London: ". . . . General recourse is daily to Rome by religeous men of Irish nacion and papisticalles; soo that where, in tyme past, they repayred to the Kinges Highnes, to opteyn His Graces denominacion, they goo now immediately to Rome, and optaine whate they pursue, soo that there be now lately 5 Bisshoppis in Irland by the Bisshop of Romes auctoritie, besides Abbotes and Priors. And never so mouche suyte from Irland as nowe to Rome, all by permyssion and sufferance, without any prosecuting."[1]

Like George Browne, Cowley was seeking arguments to discredit the Deputy in England, and his statement of the facts may not be strictly accurate. But Cowley had probably heard, as his master Cromwell had heard, of Manus O Donnell's message to Rome and his appeal for help from the Holy See. The five Pope's bishops whom he names are probably Emonn O Gallagher of Raphoe, Quintin Cogley of Dromore, Hugh O Carolan of Clogher, Roland de Burgo of Clonfert, and James FitzMaurice of Ardfert and Aghadoe. The Pope had certainly not been idle, though he had not yet been able to restore the shattered hierarchy of Connacht. Here Roland de Burgo had driven the King's bishop to take shelter in Galway. But Tuam and Elphin were vacant, whilst Mayo was still held by the absentee Bishop John Bel.

The King was the first to act in 1537. On February 15 he nominated Bishop Christopher Bodkin of Kilmacduagh to the vacant metropolitan see of Tuam.[2] Bodkin seems to have retained his see of Kilmacduagh for some years under this arrangement, and it is certain that he also claimed

[1] *State Papers* III, p. 51. George Browne had the same story to tell: ibid. III, p. 104.

[2] Morrin I, p. 31.

jurisdiction over Enachdun as being canonically united to the see of Tuam.[1] The Pope must have got word of this attempted translation during the following twelve months, but he took no action for more than a year. Finally (October 7, 1538) he provided Canon Art O Friel of Raphoe to the vacant metropolitan see.[2] This surprising nomination is, as we have seen, to be explained by the fact that Art O Friel had been in Rome for some months past as the representative of Manus O Donnell, and was perhaps the best informed Irish clerk in Rome at that date. The new archbishop of Tuam was back in Ireland before June 23, 1539, when he is named as one of the witnesses to an agreement between Manus O Donnell and Tadhg O Connor.[3]

No record has survived of the papal provision of John O More to the see of Enachdun; we first hear of it from an English source in 1540.[4] Bishop John had reached Ireland at some unknown date, had been arrested by the English and released by Lord Gray as Deputy before Gray's departure from Ireland in the spring of 1540. We can only conjecture that the Pope, probably with the intention of contesting Bodkin's authority in Connacht, had decided to revive the separate see of Enachdun, and had appointed a bishop who could and would rally the Pope's supporters in the country round Galway and Kilmacduagh. The exact date of this provision is unknown, but it was probably made soon after the provision of Art O Friel to the archbishopric of Tuam.

The Pope was thus beginning to take strong action in the province of Tuam; but he met with no more than partial success. Roland de Burgo was able to oust his rival from Clonfert, but Bodkin held his own in Tuam and Kilmacduagh. Art O Friel was too much of a stranger in Connacht to be able to count on local support, though he played an important part in the negotiations between

[1] Lynch II, p. 232.

[2] Brady II, p. 133; see above, p. 225-6.

[3] See below, p. 243.

[4] *Letters and Papers* XVI, p. 304 (ii).

Manus O Donnell and Tadhg O Connor in the summer of 1539.[1] Bishop John O More fell into the hands of the English soon after his arrival in Ireland, but he was not long held a prisoner. In the end he was able to hold his own in Enachdun, and we find him recognised as bishop of the diocese in an English grant of July 28, 1551.[2] He had most probably surrendered his papal bulls before that date.

Elphin was still vacant at the end of 1538, and two new Irish vacancies occurred during this same year. Quintin O Huigin, the Franciscan bishop of Clonmacnois whose lamentable failure is recorded in Cromer's register, and Quintin Cogley, the newly consecrated Dominican bishop of Dromore, died in 1538. The King made no effort to fill any of these vacancies; but the Pope took action to fill the three vacancies at a consistory held on June 16, 1539.[3] Richard Hogan, an Irish Friar Minor, was provided to the see of Clonmacnois; William Magne (? Maginn), a canon of Dromore, was provided to the see of Elphin; and Rory Macciath (? MacAodh), vicar of Killaie, was provided to the see of Dromore. It is perhaps worth noting that this rapid provision of a new candidate for the vacant see of Dromore, coupled with the provision of a canon of Dromore to the see of Elphin, suggests the presence of some adviser from that diocese in Rome. William Magne, who was provided to the see of Elphin, may perhaps have been this adviser. Rory Macciath was never an effective bishop of Dromore. He was dead, or had resigned his see, before April 16, 1540, when the Pope provided Art Magennis to that see.[4]

The consistory of June 16, 1539, at which Paul III filled the three remaining vacancies in Ireland (always excepting Dublin, and the two united dioceses of Cork and

[1] There is an interesting account of Archbishop Bodkin's administration of Tuam, and the failure of his rival from Raphoe, in Lynch II, pp. 230-33.

[2] *Fiants, Edward VI* (Appendix to Deputy Keeper's Eighth Report), p. 112, no. 808.

[3] For these three provisions see Brady I, p. 245; II, p. 198; and I, p. 299.

[4] Brady I, p. 300. No mention is made of Rory Macciath in this provision.

Cloyne) was notable for a more unusual act on the part of the Holy See. For the first time since the open breach between Henry VIII and Rome an Irish bishop was deprived of his two sees for unworthy conduct, and another bishop was deprived of jurisdiction over his diocese, which was now entrusted to an administrator nominated by the Holy See. These two sentences were soon to be followed by similar action against the Primate of All Ireland, whose conduct during the crisis of the past five years had made him suspect of heresy in Rome.

In Down and Connor Robert Blyth had been an absentee since his provision in 1520. There is no doubt that he had conformed to the King's new legislation, and had recognised Henry as Supreme Head of the Church of England.[1] The Pope now set him aside, without naming the offences which had caused his deprivation, and provided Eugene Magennis, archdeacon of Down, to the two sees of Down and Connor.[2] This provision was never challenged by the King, who ended by recognising Eugene as bishop of Down and Connor after he had surrendered his papal bulls in 1541.[3]

There remains one puzzling provision. In the bull by which Paul III provided Richard Hogan to the see of Clonmacnois on June 16, 1539, he also entrusted to Bishop Hogan the administration of the see of Killaloe.[4] James O Corrin had been bishop of Killaloe since 1526. He was one of the small group of Irish prelates whom Master John Aleyn denounced to Cromwell at the end of 1534 as having been, " with certen other papistis," the " lerned counsaill-ours " of Silken Thomas " in all theis maters against the King and his Crowne."[5] We hear no more of him during the next four years, but it seems hardly credible that a prelate who was so actively engaged in the Geraldine cause

[1] Blyth was abbot of Thorney in Cambridgeshire and received a pension at its dissolution : see above, p. 138.

[2] Brady I, p. 263. [3] Morrin I, p. 91.

[4] Brady I, p. 245 ; II, p. 117.

[5] *State Papers* II, p. 219-220 ; see above, pp. 71 ; 214.

during the winter of 1534-5 should have been disloyal to the Pope by an act so public as to provoke his suspension in 1539. Yet the provision of Bishop Richard Hogan as administrator of Killaloe was in effect a sentence of suspension against Bishop James O Corrin; and the Pope's sentence was renewed and confirmed before the end of that same year. For Bishop Hogan was dead before December 5, when Paul III made a new provision, appointing another Irish Friar Minor, Florence Kirwan, to the two sees of Clonmacnois and Killaloe.[1] In both these provisions James O Corrin is ignored. The see of Killaloe is stated to be vacant by the death of Bishop Terence O Brien, who had died before 1526.

Five weeks after the Consistory of June 29, 1539, Paul III took decisive action against the Primate of All Ireland. To understand the full purpose of his action we must remember the existing political situation in Ireland during the spring and summer of 1539.

Writing to Robert Cowley in London on July 20, 1538, Ormonde reported that Bishop Rory O Donnell of Derry, James Delahide, Thomas Leverous (later bishop of Kildare) and Robert Walshe had been sent to Scotland on behalf of Manus O Donnell, Conn O Neill and young Gerald FitzGerald, to seek aid from King James V.[2] Bishop Rory O Donnell was back from that embassy by the end of the year, for he addressed his appeal to the Pope from Derry on New Year's Day, 1539. Meanwhile Dean Art O Gallagher, had been captured by the English on a similar mission in the summer of 1538, and had been released by Lord Leonard Gray soon after his arrest.[3] On April 17, 1539, a former servant of the Deputy, who had since taken service with young Gerald FitzGerald, was examined at Dublin Castle. He had been arrested on his way back to the north from a mission to O Toole in Wicklow.[4] His examination yielded

[1] Brady I, p. 245-6.

[2] See above, p. 228.

[3] *Letters and Papers* XIII, Part 2, no. 159; and XV, p. 830.

[4] *State Papers* III, p. 139, note 1.

valuable evidence as to the Irish plans for the coming summer. Among other items he admitted that the bishop of Derry, accompanied now by Abbot O Siaghail, had gone back to Scotland about mid-Lent; and that the dean of Derry had been sent to MacDonald of the Isles by Manus O Donnell. A month or two later a Galway merchant named Thomas Lynch gave the Council a vivid description of the constant comings and goings at the Irish headquarters in Assaroe and Donegal, where Manus O Donnell (who had married Lady Eleanor FitzGerald in the previous year) was now acting as the recognised head of a nation-wide Geraldine League.[1] Lynch seems to have known little or no Irish, and had difficulty in identifying the various messengers whom he saw coming and going on their mysterious errands. But he knew enough to alarm the council, and he was able to give them the name of John Kate, a Bristol merchant, who was then at Assaroe, and who "can speke and understande Yrishe." From him the council could get more accurate information.[2]

A rare good fortune gives us some very much more authentic information as to what was afoot in Donegal during that summer. At the end of a small Irish vellum MS. of the early sixteenth century (now MS. R.I.A. 23 F 21) an unknown scribe has copied in full the text of a treaty between Manus O Donnell and Tadhg óg O Conor, which was signed at Donegal on June 23, 1539.[3] The autograph signatures of several witnesses are appended to this document, which thus appears to be an original and authentic instrument. Manus O Donnell and Tadhg óg were the representatives of two Irish septs that had long been at enmity one with another, the chief cause of their enmity being the disputed possession of Sligo Castle. Twelve months before this date news had reached Ormonde in Kilkenny (who had duly relayed it to his English friends

[1] *State Papers* III, p. 140, note.

[2] ibid. III, p. 142, note.

[3] This text has recently been edited by Mrs. Carney in *Irish Historical Studies* III (1942-3), pp. 282-96.

in London) that Tadhg had broken off his former alliance with O Conor Sligo, and had entered into an alliance with O Donnell.[1] That was in June, 1538—soon after the marriage of Manus O Donnell to the Lady Eleanor Fitz-Gerald. The fruits of this new alignment of forces in the north-west were visible in the following December, when Manus O Donnell—now supported by Tadhg against O Conor Sligo—captured Sligo Castle which his father had lost to O Conor some years earlier.[2] By June 23, 1539, six months of negotiation had passed since the taking of Sligo Castle. The text of the treaty which has been preserved by this lucky chance is concerned with the future rights of Tadhg O Conor and Manus O Donnell over this all-important key to the north-west.

The witnesses to this treaty between two Irish chieftains are as interesting as the terms of the treaty itself. The principal surety named by the two parties is the new archbishop of Tuam, Art O Friel, who had been Manus O Donnell's trusted agent in Rome for the past year and more.[3] The archbishop's presence in Donegal is proof that he must have left Rome soon after his provision and consecration, and his active interest in this treaty-making between two rival Irish chieftains is in keeping with all that we know of papal policy in Ireland during these years. One other bishop witnessed the treaty: Emonn O Gallagher, the bishop of Raphoe whom Manus had recently sent on a mission to MacDonald of the Isles. With him was also the abbot of Derry, who is not named. Bishop Rory of Derry and Abbot O Siaghail of Ballysodare do not witness this treaty: they were still in Scotland at this date. The other witnesses include the dean of Derry, who is not named, but who was certainly Art O Gallagher, a future bishop of Raphoe; the guardian of the Friars Minor at Donegal with all his community; Conchobhar Ruadh Mac an Bhaird,

[1] *State Papers* III, p. 52.

[2] A.F.M., a. 1538.

[3] The archbishop is named as surety and witness; but his signature does not appear at the foot of the document.

O Cleirigh and Fearghal son of Domhnall Ruadh Mac an Bhaird, as representing the professional literary class.[1]

We have here the immediate background for the Pope's action in suspending Primate Cromer from the exercise of his jurisdiction as archbishop of Armagh. Paul III entrusted the administration of the primatial see of Ireland to a Scottish prelate, " blind " Master Robert Wauchop. All through that winter and spring and summer high ecclesiastics of Ulster, in union with several other Irish prelates and chieftains, had been negotiating for peace in Ireland and an alliance with Scotland. The treaty between Manus O Donnell and Tadhg O Conor had been preceded (about Easter, 1539) by a similar treaty between O Neill and O Donnell.[2] We may guess that the prelates who were so active in the second treaty had as full a share in the first. That they were in touch with Rome at this crisis is certain—even though we know that some of their letters did not always escape the vigilance of Cromwell's officers and spies. Paul III must have consulted these Irish prelates before he made his final decision as to his future policy in Armagh. His choice of Robert Wauchop as administrator of Armagh is in harmony with all that we know of Irish policy during these fateful months. Hopes of aid from Scotland and the Empire ran high in Irish circles during the winter of 1538-9. They were doomed to disappointment, Lord Leonard Gray's superior military skill and equipment brought all these high plans to ruin in the autumn of that year, when the Deputy met and defeated the troops of O Donnell and O Neill at Bellahoe.

The Pope's decision to suspend the archbishop of Armagh and to appoint an administrator in his place was announced at a public consistory held on July 23, 1539. On this occasion Paul III thought fit to state the reasons which had moved him to adopt this new policy ; and a summary of his statement survives in the consistorial

[1] The *literati* bound themselves by the terms of this treaty to satirize Tadhg, should O Donnell order them to do so.

[2] A.F.M., a. 1539.

record of his act.[1] Cardinal Ghinucci, whom we have met already as the correspondent of the Cardinal of Seville in 1537 and as the Pope's adviser on Irish matters in October, 1538, had reported to the Holy See that "the archbishop of Armagh has been publicly defamed as a heretic by good and grave men." The Pope provides an administrator in his place, "until such time as the archbishop shall have canonically purged himself of this defamation, or (if he has failed to purge himself or has not attempted or completed his purgation) until such time as he shall have resigned the rule and administration of his diocese, or until he shall have died." The Pope's sentence was thus not formally a sentence of deprivation. None the less it had the effect of suspending Primate Cromer from all canonical jurisdiction over his diocese. Cromer paid no heed to this sentence of suspension, and continued to exercise his episcopal functions in Armagh until his death in 1543. But his position as Primate of All Ireland and Metropolitan of the Province of Armagh had been shaken. His last years were clouded by the suspicion of heresy, and by this formal sentence of the Pope's condemnation.

There can be no doubt as to the truth of the charges which Paul III brought against the Irish Primate. In Dowdall's register there is a letter from Cromer to Henry D.17 v.
VIII, dated June 26, 1541, in which the Primate appeals to the King for a settlement of a dispute between himself and the bishop of Meath. This letter is explicitly addressed to the King as "Supreme Head on earth of the English and Irish Church" (*in terris Ecclesiæ Anglicanæ et Hibernicæ Supremo Capiti*).[2] Bishop Rory O Donnell's letter of New Year's Eve, 1538-9, had been seized by the English at South Shields and was never read by the Pope. But other letters from Ireland must have got through to the Pope in Rome, and the Primate's defection must have been matter of common knowledge.

[1] Brady I, p. 216.
[2] See below, p. 255.

The more interesting problem is to decide why Paul III took this drastic action against the Primate, whilst taking no action against prelates such as Archbishop Browne of Dublin and Bishop Staples of Meath, whose active support of the royal supremacy in Ireland was known to all. The most obvious solution of this difficulty is to assume that Paul III, being a statesman with a sense of what was actually possible at a given moment, decided that action in Armagh might be beneficial, whilst action in Dublin and Meath could only expose his authority to contempt. Even in Tuam, where the Pope's candidate might have hoped for the support of Irish Catholic opinion, Art O Friel failed to oust Archbishop Bodkin, who enjoyed the support of Clanrickarde. Paul III must have wished to strike hard against the Primate in Ireland as a warning to other prelates. He must also have had hopes of local support in Armagh. The diocese was divided between the English and the Irish, and there was strong support for the Pope's cause among the "Old English" clergy of the diocese. But the appointment of a Scots prelate to Armagh, like the provision of Art O Friel to Tuam, was an error of judgment. Paul III was to learn from the bitter experience of the next few years that local support in Ireland could only be won by the provision of local candidates.

The Irish provisions made by Paul III in 1540 and 1541 suggest that he was beginning to learn this lesson. They cannot be fully discussed here, for most of them concern other provinces than the province of Armagh. We may note, however, the provision of Art McGuinness to the see of Dromore in April, 1540; and the provision of John MacBrady to the see of Kilmore in November of the same year.[1] Here Paul III was challenging the actions of Bishop Edward Nugent, who had been provided to this see by Clement VII in 1530. Nugent must have conformed in some public manner to the King's new policy; he certainly surrendered his priory of Tristernagh to the King's officers in 1539.[2] The Pope took stronger action here than he had

[1] Brady I, p. 279; 300. [2] Morrin I, p. 136.

ventured to do in Armagh, for he provided John MacBrady to the see without any reference to Bishop Nugent's claims. This was in effect a formal sentence of deprivation. But in Kilmore, as elsewhere, local influence backed by the King's authority proved too strong for the Pope's policy. John MacBrady was unable to oust Nugent from the see of Kilmore, and he abandoned any effort to interfere with his rival until Nugent's death in 1550. He then surrendered his papal bulls, to be cancelled by the King's authority; and was thereupon recommended to the King by the council as Nugent's successor in the see.[1]

A word must also be said about the position in Ardagh. Here Bishop Rory O Malone died in 1540. Both the King and the Pope attempted to nominate a successor. On May 2, 1541, Henry VIII appointed Richard Farrell as King's bishop of Ardagh.[2] Paul III countered this stroke on November 14, when he provided Patrick MacMahon to the vacant see.[3] Here two local candidates were again opposed to one another, and each was probably supported by a rival faction. Richard Farrell seems to have been more successful than the Pope's candidate, who failed to establish himself as bishop of Ardagh. In 1545 we find the King's council recommending Patrick MacMahon for the next small bishopric that might fall vacant.[4] It would seem that the council were satisfied that this bishop would cause them no trouble, but were not willing to recognise him as bishop of Ardagh in opposition to the King's nominee.

The situation was very similar in Clogher. Raymond MacMahon was provided to this see by Paul III, in opposition to Hugh O Carolan, on August 27, 1546[5]; and these two rival bishops disputed the right of succession for a quarter of a century.

[1] Shirley, *Original Letters and Papers of the Church in Ireland*, no. 18.

[2] *State Papers* III, p. 303; *Fiants, Henry VIII*, no. 215.

[3] Brady I, p. 290.

[4] *Letters and Papers* XX, Part i, no. 475. See also Dr. Edwards in *Irish Ecclesiastical Record* (February, 1935), p. 205.

[5] Brady I, p. 252.

4. THE FIRST JESUIT MISSION TO IRELAND

The vigorous action taken by Paul III in 1539 suggests that the Holy See was becoming more confident of success in Ireland, once the first shock of the King's schismatical actions had been overcome. Robert Wauchop, the new administrator of Armagh, seems to have had no intention of visiting his diocese in person at this time. His purpose was rather to remain in touch with the Holy See, and direct a general plan of campaign in Ireland from Rome. He himself was actively engaged in important diplomatic work for the Papacy in Germany during the next few years. From 1545 to 1547 he was engaged on no less important theological work during the first sessions of the Council of Trent.[1] An active promoter of the Roman Counter-Reformation during these critical years, it is not surprising that he should turn to the newly founded Society of Jesus for help in the work of securing Ireland for the Holy See.

The full story of the first Jesuit mission to Ireland need not concern us here, but some mention of its work is necessary. We first hear of the scheme in a letter which St. Ignatius Loyola gave to St. Francis Xavier as an introduction to his own brother, Don Beltran de Loyola, in Spain.[2] Francis Xavier had been nominated for the new mission to the Far East early in 1540—a few months before the formal confirmation of the Institute of the Society of Jesus by Paul III (September 27, 1540). In his letter to Don Beltran the Jesuit founder alludes to the Irish project as one of many reasons why he cannot write more fully to his brother. " Owing to the great urgency and haste with which we have been asked to send some of our men to the

[1] See his letters, printed with a brief biographical notice by Moran, in *Spicilegium Ossoriense* I, pp. 13-32

[2] This letter has been printed in the *Monumenta Historica Societatis Jesu : Epistolæ S. Ignatii* (Madrid, 1903), I, p. 155 ; a Latin translation has been printed by Father E. Hogan, S.J. in *Ibernia Ignatiana* (1880), p. 1.

Indies, others to Ireland, and others to every part of Italy, it is not possible for me to write in full, as I should have wished." This letter is dated March 16, 1540. Robert Wauchop had thus lost little time in pressing for a Jesuit mission to Ireland. Ignatius alludes again to the request for men to be sent to Ireland in a letter which he wrote in the following August, but no final decision was taken until April 24, 1541.[1]

Meanwhile, Conn O Neill had written to the Pope on October 31, 1540. His letter has been lost, and we know no more of its contents than can be learned from the Pope's reply. O Neill told the Pope something of the devastation that was being caused in Ireland by the English armies, but protested his own loyalty and the loyalty of his countrymen to the cause of the Holy See. Paul III sent the Irish chieftain an encouraging reply to this letter.[2] He commends O Neill for his loyalty, and assures him that help will be forthcoming. In a formal brief, dated April 24, 1541, and addressed to all the archbishops, bishops and other prelates and lords of Ireland, the Pope renews the expression of his sorrow at the tidings he has heard from Ireland, and commends the two special nuncios whom he has chosen to act as his representatives in Ireland. Their names were John Codure and Alphonsus Salmeron, two of the Jesuit Fathers then in Rome. It was hoped that they would be able to leave for Ireland within a few weeks, and the Pope gave them full powers to confer many indulgences and other privileges on the Catholic faithful in Ireland. But Father Codure died unexpectedly on August 29, 1541, and his place on the mission was taken by another of the Jesuit Fathers in Rome, Paschasius Brouet. Brouet was a Frenchman by birth, Salmeron a Spaniard.

Further delays kept the two Jesuit nuncios waiting in Rome until the middle of September. They left the city on

[1] *Monumenta*, loc. cit., p. 159; Hogan, op. cit., p. iii.

[2] Fr. Hogan has printed this letter: op. cit., pp. 2-3. The full text is in Raynaldus, *Annales Ecclesiastici* xxi, ad ann. 1541, nos. 37-40. There is an English abstract in *Letters and Papers* XVI, no. 755.

September 10, 1541, with a long letter of instructions from Ignatius, now the first Father General of the Society of Jesus.[1] They went first to Scotland, where they heard news from Ireland that was of ill omen for their mission. Lord Leonard Gray had won a last, and decisive, victory over the Irish forces at Bellahoe in the summer of 1539.[2] O Neill and O Donnell did their best to continue the struggle for another year. Gray was recalled from Ireland early in 1540, but the new Deputy, Anthony St. Leger, inherited the advantage of his victories, and the Irish cause was soon desperate. Conn O Neill submitted to the Deputy in the winter of 1541-42. His submission was soon followed by the submission of Manus O Donnell, the most active spirit on the Irish side.

News of these disasters was well known in Scotland, and King James did his best to persuade the two papal nuncios from risking their lives in a country where they could hope for no effectual support. But the Jesuits held to their course. They left Scotland with letters of commendation from King James on February 13, 1542, but found little to encourage them in Ireland. O Neill and O Donnell were now unwilling even to meet the Pope's representatives, for fear of involving themselves in a policy which might be construed as treason by the Deputy or the King. Ignatius gives a brief account of the experiences and ill-success of this first mission in a letter which he addressed to all the Fathers of the new Society of Jesus. It is dated June 1, 1542, when he had just received letters from his two sons in Ireland.[3]

" The principal matter," he writes, " is that, by God's grace and special providence, they have come to Ireland, and remained there for thirty-four days during Lent." The two Fathers " had suffered not a little for the Lord." They

[1] Printed by Hogan, op. cit., pp. 4-5 ; also in *Monumenta*, loc. cit., pp. 174-81.

[2] For the general situation in Ireland at this time, see Philip Wilson : *The Beginnings of Modern Ireland*, pp. 227-294.

[3] The full Italian text has been printed by Hogan, op. cit., p. iii-iv. See also *Monumenta*, loc. cit., p. 203.

had helped souls by hearing confessions and granting indulgences. They had also granted dispensations freely to the poor, whilst they had imposed a fine on those who could afford to pay a penalty for their unfaithfulness. The money so received had been distributed to the poor in the presence of the local bishop, and some of it had been set aside for the repair of the churches. "None the less," writes Ignatius, "things are going so badly there, owing to our sins, that even the news from Germany is less alarming. All the princes, except one, have bound themselves to the King of England; and the one who remains is about to do the same. They have taken an oath to the King as Head *in spiritualibus et temporalibus*, and have sworn to destroy all letters that may come to them from the Apostolic See; and also, 'should they find any men of this way,' to send them bound as prisoners to England, or to the King's Deputy in Ireland. In such circumstances they could hope for no fruit, and they have returned safe and sound to Scotland."

Ignatius sent a letter to the two Jesuit Fathers, bidding them remain in Scotland until further orders. But this letter did not reach them in time to delay their return. They were in France, on their way through to Rome, by the middle of the summer. William Paget, the English ambassador in France, wrote home to the King from Lyons on July 31, 1542[1]: "There hath lately bin in yor Majestys land of Ireland two Freres Spaniardes sent thither by the Bishop of Rome to practise with O Donnell against your Majesty. They passed through Scotland with letters of commendation to the King of the Scots. With them was sent for that purpose the Bishop of the Isles' brother, that is, Farquhard Farquhardson, which Bishop lyeth at Icolm Kille, between Scotland and Ireland. The two Spaniards and the Bishop's brother be arrived within these two days in this town on their return from Ireland where, as they say, they have done no good, because the Scottish King kept not his promise. And this confession have these two Freres

[1] Hogan, op. cit., p. 8; also in *Letters and Papers* XVII, no. 554.

made to the Lieutenant of this town, for here they were arrested for spies."

The failure of this first Jesuit mission did undoubtedly discourage the Roman authorities for some time, and no further effort to send a papal mission to Ireland was made until after the death of Henry VIII. It has often been said that the report sent home by the two Jesuit Fathers was unduly pessimistic, and that their brief visit to this island made it impossible for them to judge the situation in Ireland with any accuracy. There is, of course, some truth in these criticisms ; but it is always easy to be wise after the event. In the spring of 1542 few observers would have cared to risk a forecast that Ireland would remain constant in her loyalty to the Holy See. What Ignatius wrote in the summer of that year was literally true. The Irish princes, one by one, were surrendering to the victorious Deputy, and were compromising their faith by acceptance of the King's claim to rule the Church as Supreme Head *in spiritualibus et in temporalibus*. These were the years when a nameless Irish poet was writing his fierce satire on these same princes : *Fúbún fúibh, a shluagh Gaoidheal : ni mhair aoineach agaibh* (" Shame on you, O race of the Gael : there is no life in one of you ").[1] The bishop who welcomed the two Jesuit nuncios to Ireland, and who helped them proclaim their indulgences and distribute their alms, was almost certainly Bishop Rory O Donnell, to whose territory in Derry they would most easily have taken ship from Scotland. It is pleasant to think that this patriot Irish bishop, who had sent his urgent appeal to Rome just four years earlier, had the courage to meet the nuncios when they did at last come to Ireland ; but Bishop Rory was a solitary figure of resistance in 1542. St. Ignatius had good reason to exclaim that " for our sins, even the news from Germany is less alarming." The Irish Catholic cause did in fact look desperate to all observers in that year. Primate

[1] Aodh de Blacam : *Gaelic Literature Surveyed* (Dublin, 1929), p. 125-7 ; from a transcript made by Dr. Douglas Hyde.

Dowdall's register, to which we must now turn, fully confirms the accuracy of the news sent back to Rome by the two Jesuit nuncios.

5. PRIMATE CROMER'S LAST YEARS

The first portion of "Dowdall's Register" is in fact a continuation of Primate Cromer's episcopal register. It gives us the record of Dowdall's activity as the Primate's official during the last three years of Cromer's life.[1] From the evidence of these entries it is plain that the prelates and clergy of the province of Armagh paid little heed to the sentence of suspension, by which Paul III had hoped to deprive the Primate of all effective jurisdiction. They still looked to this English archbishop of Armagh as the source from whom judgment might be obtained or jurisdiction confirmed in doubtful cases.

In almost all the dioceses of the northern province the King's authority had been formally acknowledged before the arrival of the Jesuit Fathers in the spring of 1542. Bishop Florence Kirwan of Clonmacnois and Bishop Eugene McGuinness of Down and Connor had both surrendered their papal bulls in September, 1541.[2] Hugh O Carolan, who was bishop of Clogher since 1535, did the same in October, 1542.[3] In Raphoe Emonn O Gallagher still strove to hold his own as Pope's bishop, with the support of his clan, but Primate Cromer was able to send Bishop Cornelius O Cahan and three other prelates as his commissaries to visit the diocese of Raphoe in the summer of 1541.[4] In Ardagh Richard

[1] Dowdall's original register has been lost, and the entries in the surviving seventeenth-century copy are not in chronological order. Apparently the leaves of the original register had been misplaced when the copy was made.

[2] Morrin I, p. 82 ; 91.

[3] *State Papers* III, p. 429.

[4] See below, p. 257.

O Farrell was established as the King's bishop since the summer of that same year. In Kilmore Edmund Nugent held his diocese against the Pope's bishop, John MacBrady, who had been provided to this see in November, 1540. In Meath Staples was still without a rival claimant to his episcopal authority. Derry and Dromore were the only two northern dioceses in which the King seems to have made no effort to establish a bishop of his own nomination. Of the two, Derry was beyond all doubt the more important and the more influential; but the exact position of Bishop Rory after the submission of Manus O Donnell is obscure. He is named as one of the eight bishops whom the King authorised to assist at the schismatical consecration of Primate Dowdall in 1543.[1]

Dowdall's register, which has come down to us in an
imperfect copy of a mutilated original, contains the record
of his own administration as Primate Cromer's official from
March, 1540 to March, 1543. For the five years that
separate these first entries from the last entry in Cromer's
episcopal register (December 22, 1535), there is only one
D.105-6. casual, but significant entry. On January 9, 1539, the
Primate registered at Termonfeghin a matrimonial dispensation from the impediment of consanguinity, which had been
granted to two citizens of Drogheda by the archbishop of
Canterbury. This official recognition of Cranmer's jurisdiction in matrimonial causes does not, it is true, constitute
a formal recognition of the King's supremacy *in spiritualibus;* but in practice recognition of the one must have
come very close to recognition of the other. Dowdall's
register for 1541 contains another entry which places the
matter beyond any doubt. Acting as the Primate's
D.115. commissary, Dowdall held a formal visitation of the diocese
of Meath at St. Mary's, Drogheda, on February 9, 1541.
Bishop Staples, who seems to have resented the new
official's activity in his diocese, sent in a formal excuse for
his absence on the grounds of ill health, but appointed

[1] See below, p. 262-3.

Bishop Cornelius of Raphoe, with his own official and the rector of Ardmulghan, as his proctors. A few months later (May 29, 1541) Bishop Staples appealed to the King against the rights which Dowdall had claimed as the Primate's commissary during this visitation. The Primate counter-appealed in a letter which he sent to the King from Termonfeghin on June 26, 1541. This letter is addressed to Henry as "King, by the grace of God, of England and the Supreme Head on earth of the English and Irish Church" (*Serenissimo ac invictissimo Principi nostro Henrico Octavo Dei Gratia Angliæ Regi, ac in terris Ecclesiæ Anglicanæ et Hibernicæ Supremo Capiti*). Here is clear proof that both Cromer and Dowdall accepted Henry VIII as the Supreme Head of the Church in Ireland.

D.16.

D.17 v.

Yet Dowdall's register makes it plain that this surrender to the royal claims had not, so far as we can judge, done much to weaken the Primate's position in the province of Armagh. Apart from a long series of entries which record the usual collations and institutions in the English-speaking half of the diocese, there are several entries which show us that the Primate continued to exercise effective jurisdiction over the Irish clergy. On May 19, 1540, the Primate collated John O Culean to the vicarage of Derrybrux, now part of Killyman. On March 8, 1542, the Primate collated Dermitius O Conwey to the vicarage of Derryluran, and on the same day he collated Malachy Kelly to the vicarage of Monterheney or Tamlaghlege (Tanderagee). Both of these benefices are stated to have become vacant by the death of Felim O Neill, who had obtained them by lay influence (*per potentiam laicalem*). Dowdall, as the Primate's official, was here restoring the normal jurisdiction of the Primate in an area which, for a time, had been administered without regard to his customary rights. On June 10, 1542, the Primate collated Maurice McCamill to the vicarage of Clonoe. On the same day he appointed Malachy O Kelly, the new vicar of Monterheny, and Dermicius O Conwey, the new vicar of Derryluran, as his two chaplains in Armagh; and charged them with the duty of assisting the

D.13.

D.21 v.

D.23.

D.24.

dean and the master of the fabric in the work of attending
to the maintenance of the cathedral at Armagh, since the
Primate was now too old and infirm to attend to these duties
D.1. himself. Finally, on July 27, 1542, the Primate collated
George Dowdall himself to the rectory of Killeavy, which
had been held—like Derryluran and Monterheny—by
Felim O Neill *per potentiam laicalem.*

These entries make it plain that Cromer's authority, as exercised in his name by a vigorous and energetic official, extended to the Irish territory of the diocese during the last two or three years of the Primate's life. His authority seems also to have been accepted without challenge in most of the suffragan sees at this time.

Ardagh fell vacant early in 1540 by the death of Rory
D.6. O Malone. The Primate collated Magonius O Kane to a
church in this diocese on May 29, 1540.

On November 2, 1540, the Primate collated an Irish
D.10 v. canon of Clogher to a rectory in the diocese of Clogher.
He made two more collations to benefices in Clogher in May,
D.13; 15; 31 v. 1541, and yet another on September 28, 1541. This
regular series of collations seems to imply that the Primate
refused to recognise Hugh O Carolan as bishop of Clogher
until he had surrendered his papal bulls to the King in the
autumn of 1542.

I have already noted the visitation of Meath which
Dowdall made in the Primate's name in 1541. The Dues of
St. Patrick were regularly collected in the deaneries of
Meath during this period by the Primate's collectors.
D.9. There is a note in this section of the register which defines
the powers of these collectors. They were commissioned,
in the name of the Primate and the Church, "to seek, levy
and receive the first-born of cattle, the first-crops of corn
and their market-dues, and the principal quarter of every
animal dedicated (*nominati*) to the gracious Confessor and
blessed Apostle and Patron of Ireland"; and also to
receive all alms bequeathed by the faithful in each deanery.

The Primate's commission was addressed to all rectors and vicars, with or without cure of souls, in the deaneries; and an injunction was laid on the bishop of Meath to assist the collectors. It would be interesting to know how far Bishop Staples was willing to co-operate with the Primate's collectors in this traditional levy. The unusually detailed statement of the rights and duties of these collectors in this entry suggests that their authority had recently been challenged.

During the winter of 1540-41, a metropolitical visitation D.12.
was held in the diocese of Connor, and the Primate collated Kellan O Hele to the archdeaconry of Connor during this visitation. On October 12, 1541, the Primate passed D.32.
sentence in a dispute concerning certain benefices in Down which had been united to the Cathedral of Down by an earlier bishop of the diocese.

Finally, there is an interesting entry concerning the diocese of Raphoe. On August 31, 1541, the Primate issued D.31 v.
a commission to four prelates, empowering them to hold a visitation of Raphoe in his name with the usual full powers. The names of the four commissioners are given in the sole extant copy of the register as Henry, bishop of Kildare; Cornelius, bishop of Raphoe; Hugh Scheyll, the Primate's chaplain; and Conocius Scheyll, abbot of Kildare. There are strong reasons for suspecting an error in the copyist's text of this entry. William Miagh was the King's bishop of Kildare from 1540-48; and Thady Reynolds was the Pope's bishop of the same diocese. Only one Bishop Henry is known in Ireland at this period: Henry de Burgo, whom the Pope provided to the see of Enaghdun on April 16, 1540.[1] Kildare (*Darensis*) and Derry are often confused in the Latin records of this period. "Henry of Kildare" is probably a copyist's error for "Rory of Derry."[2]

On April 22, 1542, the Primate issued a commission to D.27 v.
all his suffragans to consecrate Richard O Farrell, the King's

[1] Brady II, p. 152.

[2] *Roricus darensis*: the original entry is, of course, lost.

nominee as bishop of Ardagh, since he himself was prevented by his age and infirmities from officiating in person. On
D.2 v. July 24, 1542, the Primate collated Patrick Magerrigan to the vicarage of Moybolg in this diocese. On this occasion the collation is stated to belong to the Primate *per viam devolutionis*, since Geffredus Magerrigan who held this vicarage and was also herenagh of the vill of Moybolg, had failed to be promoted to holy orders within the statutory time.

No similar collation occurs for the diocese of Derry; but the Primate was evidently in receipt of his customary rents from the primatial lands in this diocese. On
D.34. September 4, 1541, he appointed Hugh Scheyll, one of his commissaries for the visitation of Raphoe, and Art O Hagan, his official in the deanery of Tullaghog, to act as his receivers for the rents due to him from the diocese of Derry. If I am right in my conjecture as to the true identity of "Bishop Henry of Kildare," then there is no doubt that Bishop Rory O Donnell accepted the Primate as his lawful metropolitan in 1541 after the submission of his cousin, Manus O Donnell.

It will be noted that Dromore and Clonmacnois are the only dioceses not expressly mentioned in these entries of Dowdall's register. Since the entries are of a casual nature, the absence of these two small dioceses calls for no comment. We may take it that Primate Cromer, though under suspicion of heresy and formally suspended from the exercise of his jurisdiction by decree of the Holy See, was none the less effectively recognised as archbishop of Armagh and Primate of All Ireland at a time when Robert Wauchop, the absentee papal administrator, was vainly hoping that he could restore the Pope's authority by the presence in Derry of two Jesuit nuncios.

The first impression to be gathered from this section of Dowdall's register is that Henry VIII's anti-papal policy had won unqualified success in the province of Armagh. The history of the next ten years was to show how far this temporary success was in fact an illusion. The King was not an old man in 1540; but his health was broken by many diseases, and there were few who thought that his reign could last for more than a few years. What would happen on his death? Would the Protestant party in England prove victorious? Or would the Princess Mary become the centre of a Catholic restoration? Questions such as these were in every man's mind during the last years of Henry's reign; and the temptation to compromise in the hope of better days was never greater.

6. A NEW PRIMATE

The entries in Dowdall's register for the years 1540 to 1543 make it plain that Primate Cromer was physically unable to bear the burdens of his office. In April 1542, Cromer excused himself on the ground of his infirmities D.27 v.
from officiating at the consecration of the new bishop of Ardagh. In the following June he nominated two chaplains D.24.
to represent him on the work of maintaining the fabric of the cathedral at Armagh, since he himself was too old and too infirm to take an active part in this work. As early as the winter of 1540-41 the new Deputy in Ireland (Sir Anthony St. Leger) and his Council were urging the King to prefer "the son of the late baron of Delvin" to the archbishopric of Armagh, which was evidently expected to fall vacant in the near future.[1] These indications suggest that the Primate's part in the activities of these last three years must have been little more than a nominal acquiescence in the proposals and actions of his new official.

George Dowdall was not slow to take advantage of this position. On November 2, 1540, Primate Cromer collated D.10.
Dowdall to the rectory of Carnteel, which was vacant by the death of the late commendatory of the monastery of

[1] *State Papers* III, p. 299.

D.1. SS. Peter and Paul in Armagh. On July 27, 1542, he again collated Dowdall to the rectory of Killeavy, which was vacant by the death of Felim O Neill. Finally, on March 7,
D.20 v. 1543, little more than a week before the Primate's death, there is an entry in the register recording the collation of Dowdall to the rectory of Clonmore, vacant by the privation of Octavian Rownsell. Six days after this grant, there is
D.21. yet another entry recording the collation of the Primate's chaplain, Hugo Scheyll, to the parish church of St. Nicholas, Heynestown, vacant by the death of Ralph Solei. Those who were in the immediate neighbourhood of the dying Primate seem to have been determined to take no risks for their own future!

Primate Cromer died, after twenty-two years of a very troubled pontificate, on the Eve of St. Patrick's Day: March 16, 1543.[1] The question of succession depended ultimately on the King's favour, but there was probably
D.19. little doubt in Armagh. On July 3, 1543, Edmund McCawell, who had been dean of Armagh since 1505, presided over the annual synod as *custos spiritualitatis* of the vacant see. Beside him sat George Dowdall, no longer the Primate's official, but *subcustos spiritualitatis*. Since the dean was now a very old man, we may presume that the administration of the diocese during the short vacancy was almost entirely in Dowdall's hands. Four
D.19 v. months later (October 29, 1543) George Dowdall presided over the annual convocation of the English clergy; he was now archbishop elect as well as *subcustos spiritualitatis*.
D.20. In that capacity he presented Patrick O Loghran to the vicarage of Donnaghmore. His election had been approved by Henry VIII before November 28, 1543, when the King issued his mandate for the Primate's consecration.[2] The actual date of consecration is uncertain, but it must have
D.24 v. been earlier than December 18, 1543, when Dowdall, now Primate of All Ireland, collated Patrick O Loghran to his

[1] Ware-Harris I, p. 91. There is no record as to the place of Cromer's burial, but he was probably buried at Termonfeghin.

[2] Morrin I, p. 103; see below, p. 262.

vicarage. On the following day the new Primate appointed Dermicius McDywyn—no doubt a kinsman of his predecessor, Senekyn McDewyn[1]—as his official in the city of Armagh and the deanery of Orior, giving him full powers to hear and judge all matrimonial cases in that area. D.25.

Dowdall's election and consecration are of interest from more than one point of view. As compared with his two immediate predecessors, he was no Englishman by birth, but one of the " Old English " families of the Pale. Indeed he could claim kinship with the most famous of the older Anglo-Irish archbishops of Armagh, Richard FitzRalph, whom the theologians of the later Middle Ages knew as " Armachanus."[2] The policy of choosing members of these Old English families to rule the see of Armagh had prevailed, almost without interruption, from the election of Richard FitzRalph of Dundalk in 1346 to the provision of John Prene in 1439. After Prene's death in 1443 Armagh was ruled by a succession of English-born Primates, some of whom were absentees. It was to remedy the confusion caused by their misrule that Sixtus IV provided the Italian Octavian de Spinellis to the primatial see in 1479. Octavian had been followed by two more Englishmen, John Kite and George Cromer. George Dowdall's election was thus a reversion to an older tradition ; but the appointment of a " mere Irishman " to the primatial see would have been thought impossible in 1543.

The new archbishop of Armagh had been a prominent figure in the diocese for twenty-five years before his election. His name occurs frequently in Alexander Plunket's register of the metropolitan court as one of the lawyers commonly employed in the court's business during the years 1518-20. Dowdall is usually given the title " Master " in Plunket's register, which implies that he had studied in some University ; but he is described as *frater conventualis* of the priory of St. John the Baptist, Ardee, in an entry for December 4, P.60 v.
1522. The friars of Ardee were commonly known as the

[1] See above, p. 96-7.

[2] See my article in *Studies* (September, 1933), pp. 393-4.

"Crouched" or "Crutched Friars," and George Dowdall
seems to have joined their community about this time. He
C.13 v. was prior of St. John's in 1524, as appears from an early
entry in Cromer's register; and he held this office until the
suppression of the priory in 1539. Dowdall is not mentioned
more than casually in Primate Cromer's register until May
C.62 v. 4, 1532, when he is one of the two commissaries appointed
by Cormac Roth to visit the diocese of Meath. He was
appointed as one of the collectors of the subsidy from the
English clergy at the convocation of December 4, 1533; and
C.74; 91. again at the convocation of September 17, 1535. He
surrendered his priory to the King's officers on December 6,
1539, receiving in exchange a pension of twenty pounds
yearly until he should be preferred to some benefice.[1]
Preferment came without delay. He took the place of
Cormac Roth as the Primate's official and president of his
metropolitan court after Archdeacon Roth's death in the
winter of 1539-40. He appears for the first time with these
D.7. titles in the register for March 5, 1540.

The King issued his mandate for the consecration of Dowdall on November 28, 1543.[2] No record of the actual ceremony has survived; it must have taken place either in Armagh or in St. Peter's, Drogheda. There is no means of knowing how many of Dowdall's suffragans were present at his consecration. In the royal mandate eight bishops were mentioned by the King as "prelates in whose fidelity we confide," and any three or more of these were commissioned to consecrate the Primate and invest him with the insignia of Armagh and the pallium.[3] The eight bishops to whom this commission was issued were Edward Staples of Meath; Cornelius O Cahan of Raphoe; Rory O Donnell of Derry; Eugene McGuinness of Down and Connor; Edmund Nugent of Kilmore; Hugh O Carolan of Clogher; Florence Kirwan of Clonmacnois; Richard O Farrell of

[1] Archdall, p. 447-8.

[2] Morrin I, p. 103, no. 17.

[3] Printed by Rev. T. Gogarty in *Archivium Hibernicum* I (1912), pp. 253-7.

Ardagh ; and Thady Reynolds, the Pope's nominee for the see of Kildare whom the King how recognised as a suffragan of Archbishop Browne.[1] In the mandate it is expressly stated that Dowdall had taken the Oath of Supremacy, and it is difficult to see how any of these eight bishops could have been present at this consecration without incurring the formal guilt of schism from the Holy See. If all the bishops named in this mandate were present at the ceremony, then Henry VIII could justly maintain that he had established his claim to Royal Supremacy in every diocese of the province of Armagh except Dromore. But the absence of any official record makes such a conclusion no more than a doubtful conjecture.

Meanwhile the Holy See decided to take an action that seems to have been unaccountably delayed for two full years after Cromer's death. As we have seen, Paul III had deprived Cromer of his episcopal and primatial jurisdiction by the consistorial decree of July 23, 1539. By the same decree he had appointed Robert Wauchop administrator of the see of Armagh, until the Primate should have satisfied the Pope as to his orthodoxy. That position remained unchanged, so far as Wauchop was concerned, by the death of Cromer in 1543. But the Pope's administrator had been detained on the Continent by his work for the cause of ecclesiastical reform.[2] On March 23, 1545, more than two years after Cromer's death, Paul III granted the pallium to Robert Wauchop by a consistorial decree, in which Wauchop is given the title "Elect of Armagh."[3] He had been consecrated six weeks before this date. The new Primate attended the sessions of the Council of Trent from December, 1545 to the spring of 1547 ; and did not come to Ireland until the winter of 1549-50. He then spent some weeks in his native Scotland, and paid a hasty visit to Derry where he

[1] See above, p. 130. Thady Reynolds is probably the Bishop Thadeus who is entered in Dowdall's register (fo. 46v) as having sung the Mass at the synod of July 3, 1548.

[2] Moran, *Spicilegium Ossoriense* I, p. 13.

[3] Brady I, p. 217 ; Stuart, *Memorials of Armagh* (ed. Coleman), p. 153.

met O Neill and O Donnell. Dowdall, who was watching his rival's movements closely from Drogheda, wrote to the chancellor and council in Dublin on March 22, 1550, to report on Wauchop's movements: he describes his rival in this letter as "a very shrewd spy, and a great brewer of war and sedition."[1] But the danger was soon past. Wauchop went back to Rome in 1550, where he made preparations for a more fruitful apostolate in the near future. Julius III granted the Primate legatine powers for his forthcoming mission to Ireland on July 3, 1551; and Wauchop set out for his distant diocese.[2] But he died at Paris on November 10, and his death left the way open for Dowdall's reconciliation with the Holy See. For English policy had meanwhile become more and more openly Protestant in Ireland; and Dowdall was forced out of the country just at the time when Wauchop was preparing for his entry into Armagh as Primate of All Ireland and Legate of the Holy See.

7. PRIMATE DOWDALL'S POLICY

Dowdall's register tells us little of importance concerning the first two or three years of his pontificate, and almost nothing at all of the years 1547-52. This latter gap may be due to the loss of some leaves from the original register, for it is plain that the volume had fallen into a sorry state of confusion and mutilation when our extant copy was made in the seventeenth century. The entries for 1544 and 1545 record the usual routine business of the diocese *inter Anglos*.
D.34 v; 44. Synods were held on July 1, 1544, and on June 20, 1545.
D.25 v; 41 v. The Dues of St. Patrick were rented as usual for these two years. There is no record of the usual annual convocations, but we may presume that they also were held. Dowdall

[1] Shirley, *Original Letters*, p. 38.

[2] Moran, *Spicilegium Ossoriense* I, p. 14.

was evidently a keen business man, with a sense of the value of his diocesan rents and properties. The most important entries in his register are lists of the rents due to the Primate from various sources, which seem to have been drawn up for his use in 1541 and 1544. They are not complete ; and here again we must assume the loss of some leaves. Even in their imperfect state, they give us welcome information as to the revenues of the Primate from some of his lands *inter Hibernicos ;* from the proxies due to him in the deaneries of Ardee, Dundalk, Drogheda, and Tullaghog ; from the cottiers on his estate at Dromiskin, Kilmone, and Primatestown ; and from other sources.[1]

Like many of his predecessors in Armagh, Primate Dowdall found it necessary to assert his rights of possession as against the O Neill of his day. The Irish text of an agreement between the Primate and Conn O Neill has been preserved in the sixteenth-century Antiphonary of Armagh.[2] The text, as here copied, states that the agreement was made at Armagh in December 1535 ; but internal evidence shows that its true date must be December, 1555, a few months after Dowdall's return from exile. A dispute had arisen between the Primate and O Neill as to the ownership of some lands which lie in the parishes of Armagh, Eglish, Tynan and Derrynoose. They are defined in the text as the lands of Muintir Corra and Muintir Eachadha ; the country of Muintir Casalaidh ; four townlands of the country of the physician O Casaide ; and four sixths of the Cabraidhe, " in which the children of Sean (*clann tSean*) were sometime

[1] These lists will be found, edited by Fr. Murray, in *L.A.J.* VII (1929), pp. 82-95 ; (1930), pp. 260-75.

[2] The text of this agreement has been printed by Dr. Myles Ronan from T.C.D. MS. B.1.1., in *J.R.S.A.I.* LXVII (1937), pp. 239-41. The date is written in full in the Irish text : *mile coig cead cuig bliadhna deag.* But Dr. Ronan is fully justified in his conclusion that the scribe who copied this text into the Antiphonary " either misread 1555 for 1535, or omitted *da* before *fiche* by an oversight." A Latin copy of this agreement is included in Dowdall's register (ff. 76v-77) ; but the text, at least as copied in the surviving transcript, is full of inaccuracies and obvious blunders. The date is here given as December 16, 1515.

tenants of the Primate."[1] Conn O Neill had seized these lands, possibly during the Primate's absence in the reign of Edward VI ; and he had also seized the rents of Eanach Moy and Maeygere, as penalty for the murder of one of his men. The dispute was not finally settled until three trustworthy witnesses—Eoin O Cuilen, lecturer (*fear leighenn*) of Armagh, Seinicin MacDeimin, official (*oifisdel*) of Armagh, and Eoin MacGillamura, master of the works (*maigistir saoithir*) of Armagh—had solemnly deposed that " these lands aforesaid belonged to the Primate, and that neither O Neill nor any other layman had any claim to them." O Neill then admitted that he had seized these lands " without right or covenant," at a time which is defined as " when he (Conn) was Lord and the said Primate was Primate." He now surrenders them back to the Church, " so that neither himself, his children nor his heirs should have any claim to them."

This agreement is of interest as showing the persistence with which each successive O Neill sought to extend his lordship in the neighbourhood of Armagh at the expense of the English Primates, whose position was weakened by their continued residence at Dromiskin or Termonfeghin. As far back as 1366 Primate Sweteman had found it necessary to threaten the O Neill of his day with excommunication, if he persisted in supporting those of his men who had invaded the Primate's lands of "Clondawyll" (*Cluain Dabhail*)—a territory which includes the parish of Eglish and part of the parish of Tynan.[2] Dowdall's register contains the text of a charter by which Henry O Neill guaranteed undisturbed possession of the tenements of " Maydown Clondawyll " to Primate Bole in the middle of the fifteenth century.[3]

[1] I am indebted to V. Rev. M. J. MacDermott, P.P., for the identification of these place names. The lands of Muintir Eachadha correspond with the lands of " the sept of Salomon Coffey " in the Inquisition of 1609 ; and the country of " the physician O Caiside " corresponds with " the sept of James O Casydy " : see above, p. 91.

[2] *Calendar of the Register of Primate Sweteman*, ed. H. J. Lawlor (in *Proc. R.I.A.*, 1911), no. 192.

[3] The text of this charter was copied into Dowdall's register (ff. 75-76), immediately before the text of the agreement of 1555.

Maydown is a townland in the parish of Eglish, not far from the border of the parish of Tynan. These three documents thus bear witness to a feud between the Primate and O Neill that was renewed intermittently for almost two centuries.

Dowdall's relations with some of his suffragans can be determined from a few entries in this section of his register. He had failed to please Bishop Staples of Meath in 1541, D.16. when he held a visitation of that diocese in Primate Cromer's name. Apart from the annual renting of the Dues of St. Patrick there is no further mention of Meath in this register. Two of the lost Christ Church deeds for 1547 show us a curious reversal of fortune.[1] In that year Bishop Staples of Meath was appointed by Edward VI to hear an appeal from the Primate's judgment.

On July 29, 1544, Dowdall revoked a commission which D.36-7. he had previously granted to Bishop Nugent of Kilmore. The prior of Lochoughter had complained to the Primate that he had been forcibly ejected from his priory by Thomas O Sheridan, priest of the diocese of Kilmore. The Primate commissioned Nugent to hear the case, but later " heard the truth " from Thomas and revoked the commission.

One entry for 1544 throws some light on the position of the Pope's bishop in Ardagh. Paul III had provided Patrick MacMahon to this see in 1541, but MacMahon had failed to dislodge the King's bishop, Richard O Farrell. I have already noted the commission which Primate Cromer issued on April 22, 1543, empowering his suffragans to D.27 v consecrate Richard as bishop of Ardagh. On May 15, 1544, Primate Dowdall collated Patrick MacMahon, whom he D.26. describes as his suffragan, to the vicarage of Aghaloo in Tyrone. A royal order of about this date provides that Patrick MacMahon is to be promoted to the next small bishopric that might fall vacant.[2] Meanwhile the Primate

[1] *Calendar of Christ Church Deeds*, nos. 438 ; 1210. The appeal was by John Fyane, *alias* Feth, vicar of Killary, whom Dowdall had deprived.

[2] *Letters and Papers* XX, Part 1, no. 475.

seems to have done what he could for the Pope's bishop of Ardagh by collating him to a small benefice in the diocese of Armagh *inter Hibernicos*.

D.34 v. On July 1, 1544, Cornelius O Cahan, bishop of Raphoe, is mentioned as having presided over the Synod held in St. Peter's, Drogheda, with Master Robert Luttrell. Bishop Thadeus, who presided with Master Robert Luttrell over
D.46 v. the synod of July 3, 1548 is almost certainly Bishop Thady Reynolds, the Pope's bishop of Kildare.[1] Like Patrick MacMahon of Ardagh, he had made his peace with the English government and was acting as suffragan to Archbishop Browne of Dublin.

D.40 v. A curious entry for April 4, 1544 or 1545,[2] deserves fuller comment. Heneas MacNichaill, a layman of Armagh, had been guilty of murder by strangling his own son. He had appealed for absolution to Dean Edmund MacCawell, who was then acting as *custos spiritualitatis* of the vacant see. This fixes the date of the incident to the summer or autumn of 1543. The dean, who was also prior of the Culdees of Armagh, was accustomed to Irish traditions of public penance and imposed an unusually severe burden of penitential pilgrimage as a condition of absolution. Heneas was sent to no less than fifteen famous Irish shrines. Some of the names mentioned in the list are not easily identified, but the pilgrim's penance took him from Armagh to Glendalough, from Glendalough to Ross, from Ross to the Skelligs, from the Skelligs to Aran of the Saints, from Aran to Crock Brendain in Kerry, from Kerry to Killaloe, from Killaloe to Croagh Patrick, from Croagh Patrick to Lough Derg, from Lough Derg to Inis Gorain at Gort, from Gort to Cornancreigh in the land of MacSwine, from Cornancreigh to Tyrebane in the land of O Donnell, from that northernmost point back again to Holy Cross and the Rock of Cashel in Tipperary, and thence back again north to Downpatrick,

[1] Robert Luttrell was archdeacon of Meath in 1560, when he refused to take the Oath of Supremacy (*Fiants Eliz.* 236). He died in prison *c.* 1578: D. Murphy, *Our Martyrs*, p. 106.

[2] The extant copy of the register gives the date as April 4, 1541. But the entry is certainly later than 1543.

Saul and Struell.[1] Heneas must have taken the best part of a year to complete this arduous pilgrimage. When his penance had been completed, the dean of Armagh was no longer *custos spiritualitatis*, and the pilgrim was sent to the Primate for absolution. Dowdall heard his tale, and inspected the pilgrim's proofs or certificates that he had visited all these shrines. He then (if I am correct in my interpretation of a difficult phrase) confirmed the fulfilment of the penance imposed by the dean and granted absolution to the pilgrim.[2]

If Dean MacCawell was hard on others, he was no less hard on himself. His obit has been entered in the extant Antiphonary of Armagh.[3] From it we learn that the dean, though suffering intolerable pains from his last illness, chanted the divine office in full on the day of his death (January 28, 1549); that before his death he had given to the poor all that was due to them according to the Church's law; and that, whilst chastising his own body, he had observed the duties of hospitality towards all.

There is one last entry which calls for comment in this section of Primate Dowdall's register. On June 20, 1545, Dowdall held a synod at St. Peter's, Drogheda, for the English clergy. Various decrees were passed by the clergy in this synod; but the most important was a decree ordering that in future the feast of St. Richard, archbishop of Armagh, should be celebrated every year in the diocese on the morrow of the feast of SS. John and Paul. The feast of the two Roman martyrs John and Paul is celebrated on June 26 according to the Roman calendar. The new feast was thus fixed for June 27.

D.44-5.

This decree of the Armagh synod has often been cited as an official canonisation of St. Richard of Dundalk. That

[1] Father John Ryan, S.J., suggests to me that this complicated itinerary may have been worked out to equal in length some famous European pilgrimage.

[2] The Latin text is: "Primas continuavit causam absolutionis." The verb *continuare* is used in medieval Latin in the sense of "confirm" or "approve."

[3] T.C.D. MS.B.I.I.; the obit is on the first page of the Calendar.

is not its true character. The cult of St. Richard had been maintained in Co. Louth for more than a century and a half—ever since the archbishop's bones had been brought back to Dundalk from Avignon, where he died in 1360. Walsingham's *Chronicon Angliae* has the following entry for the year 1377: "About this time God, wishing to declare the justice which Master FitzRaffe practised when he lived on earth . . . began to work many great miracles daily, by the merits of the said Richard, at his tomb in Dundalk in Ireland."[1] Walsingham was a Benedictine monk who did not like the friars, and Archbishop FitzRalph had been a great enemy of the friars during the last years of his stormy life. So the English chronicler adds maliciously: "and it is said that the friars were ill pleased at these miracles." None the less the cult became popular in the neighbourhood of Dundalk. During the Great Schism Urban VI appointed a commission to inquire into the life and miracles of Richard FitzRalph. His successor, Boniface IX, ordered Primate Colton of Armagh, together with the bishops of Meath and Limerick, to make inquiries as to the truth of the reported miracles.[2] Some witnesses were examined, and a report was sent to the Holy See. In January, 1399, Pope Boniface ordered Colton to make inquiries in England, with the help of the bishop of Bangor and the Augustinian abbot of Oseney beside Oxford.

Nothing more is heard of these official proceedings; but the local cult still continued. One of the Armagh registers once contained an entry for the year 1437, in which it is recorded that a certain John, chaplain in the deanery of Trim, was accused at Athboy of incontinence and confessed his sin. He was condemned to pay six shillings and six pence towards the repair of the windows of the Friars Minor at Drogheda, and to visit barefoot as a pilgrim the Holy Cross of Christ Church, Dublin, and the shrine of Saint

[1] *Chronicon Angliæ* (Rolls Series), p. 48.

[2] These details are in *Calendar of Papal Letters* V, p. 245.

Richard of Dundalk.[1] The chaplain refused to do this penance and was excommunicated. An old traditional rhyme still preserves the memory of such pilgrimages in Louth:

"Many a mile did I go, and many did I walk,
"But never saw I a holier man than Richard of Dundalk."

Dowdall's synod of 1545 was thus confirming a local cult, familiar to all who were present at the synod. The purpose of its decree was to provide for a public celebration of the feast, with nine lessons, on a fixed day each year. In the extant Antiphonary of Armagh the feast of "St. Richard Rowe, archbishop of Armagh" occurs on March 14 in the Calendar; and is no more than a "double feast," without nine lessons. The feast is thus older than Dowdall's synod of 1545. Had this synod been held in the fourteenth century, when the memory of the controversies connected with the name of "Armachanus" was still fresh, such an order must have been interpreted as an attack on the mendicant friars in Ireland. But the friars were no longer a menace to the Primate's peace of mind in 1545. It is very much more probable that George Dowdall was here seizing the opportunity of honouring an archbishop of Armagh who was not only one of his most famous predecessors in that office, but also a kinsman of the Dowdall family.

Dowdall's interest in the cult of Richard FitzRalph has, however, a deeper meaning than mere family pride or local patriotism. The archbishop of Armagh, whose authority is still cited in the Schools as "Armachanus," stands for a tradition which was being challenged in the sixteenth century. Henry VIII had never broken openly with the whole of that tradition, though FitzRalph held views as to the nature of the Pope's authority which would not have commended themselves to the Tudor despot in his later years. Henry died within a few months of this

[1] This entry is given by Dr. A. G. Little in his *Materials for the History of the Franciscan Province of Ireland* (Manchester, 1920), p. 188. It seems to have been copied by Fr. E. FitzMaurice from some older secondary source: no such entry is extant to-day in Fleming's register which is cited as the source.

Armagh synod. Under Edward VI the actively Protestant party in England had its way without further restraint; and the Protestant party in Dublin, though very much less numerous and less influential, were now free to push their programme of "Reform"—with all its characteristically violent hatred of the Mass and the Catholic priesthood.

One last document may be cited here for the light it throws on Primate Dowdall's policy in the last years of Henry VIII's reign. The provincial council of June 20, 1545, was followed by a formal visitation of the whole diocese of Armagh which took place in 1546. The Primate himself seems to have visited the cathedral city of Armagh as well as the diocese *inter Anglos*, and that section of the Irish territory which lay between Armagh and Dundalk. No record of this part of the visitation has been preserved; but the autograph report of two Irish prelates, Bishop Richard O Farrell of Ardagh and Canon Nicholas MacCraith of Clogher, survives as a loose paper document which has been bound between the two sections of the volume known as "Cromer's Register."[1] The two visitors make their report as commissaries of the Lord Primate; and their detailed account of their itinerary shows us that they covered a large portion of the two Irish deaneries of Orior and Tullaghog in a route that is plainly a survival of the traditional Irish circuit or *cuairt*. Beginning at the parish of Derrynoose, they went west to Tynan, where one of the two resident priests deposed that he had already been visited by the Primate himself during the official visitation of Armagh city. From Tynan the two commissaries crossed over the north-eastern corner of the diocese of Clogher, and resumed their visitation in the parish of Errigalkeerogue. Thence they passed to Aghaloo, Donaghmore, Drumglass,

[1] I found this paper stuck between the leaves of Cromer's register. No notice had been taken of it either by the scribe who made the modern transcript of this volume or by Father Murray in his summary calendar of Cromer's register. I hope to publish the full text of this visitation in the *Louth Archæological Journal*, with some of the entries in the Antiphonary of Armagh which belong to this period.

Donaghenry, Disertcrea, Derryloran, Lissan, Ardtrea, Ballyclog, Arboe, Clonoe, Clonfeacle, and Kilmore (Teythmor O Nellan).

In each parish the two visitors questioned the priests as to their duties of residence, recitation of the divine office, celebration of Mass and celibacy. They also examined the state of the church and the sacred vessels, and reported in detail as to what they found. In many of the parishes they reported that the priest, whether vicar or curate, was of good conduct (*solet celebrare et orare et non est concubinarius*). In others they reported that one of the priests was living with a concubine or that he had previously been living in concubinage, but had now put the woman away. The state of the church and its ornaments varied from parish to parish. Sometimes the parish church seems to have been in a ruinous condition, whilst the sacred vessels were in no fit state for the celebration of Mass. Elsewhere the report states that the fabric of the church was in good condition, and the vessels and ornaments suitable (*competencia*). Frequently the surviving paper text is so worn with age that it is impossible to be sure of more than the report's general drift. A general report at the end, which dealt with the existing rights of various erenaghs and other ecclesiastical tenants, is unfortunately so mutilated as to be almost entirely illegible.

Apart from its special interest for local history, this visitation of 1546, made within a few months of the death of Henry VIII, is most valuable for the light it throws on Primate Dowdall's policy as archbishop of Armagh and Primate of All Ireland. Throughout Henry's reign there is no doubt at all that Dowdall was consistently on the side of the King; and he had not hesitated in his choice between King and Pope in the critical years from 1535 to 1539. But nothing could be more misleading than to assume that, because Dowdall sided with the King in the first phase of England's quarrel with the Pope, his ultimate loyalty was to the Crown of England rather than to the Holy See. Dowdall's action during the brief reign of Edward VI is good proof to the contrary; and the Primate's deepest interests as an ecclesiastical ruler are revealed in the instructions which he gave to these two Irish commissaries, when he entrusted them with the duty of visiting his diocese *inter Hibernicos*. The regular celebration of the Mass and daily recitation of the divine office; the strict duty of celibacy, with the avoidance of even the appearance of scandal; the proper maintenance of the parish church, and of all the old customs necessary for recognition of the Mass as a centre of parochial life: these were the matters on which Dowdall concentrated his attention from the day of his consecration in 1543.

Five years after the date of this visitation, Primate Dowdall (who was then in open opposition to the King's government in Ireland) wrote to his cousin, Sir Thomas Cusack, who held office as chancellor in Dublin, that "he would never be bishop where the holy Mass was abolished."[1] The experience of those five years had taught him that the traditions of the Mass were endangered by the King's policy, which he had hitherto supported in the province of Armagh. Once that truth was brought home to him, he hesitated no longer. Feeling that he was now in a false position, he left Ireland and went into exile. A letter from George Browne in Dublin, dated August 6, 1551, shows us that Dowdall had left the country shortly before that date. Two months later the King's council in Dublin decided to punish him for his obduracy by transferring his primatial rights from Armagh to Dublin. The transfer was effected, so far as English law was concerned, by an order in council dated October 12, 1551.[2] Twelve months later Dowdall was adjudged to have forfeited his bishopric by his flight overseas; and Hugh Goodacre was nominated to the see, thus vacated, on October 28, 1552.[3]

[1] This phrase is cited from one of Dowdall's letters by Archbishop Browne of Dublin in his letter of August 4, 1551: Shirley, *Original Letters*, no. 23; Ronan, *Reformation in Dublin*, p. 366.

[2] Morrin I, p. 250 (no. 152); see also Edwards, pp. 135-40.

[3] Morrin I, p. 267 (no. 10).

Dowdall must have been in Flanders for some months when news reached him that his former rival, Robert Wauchop, was dead in Paris on his way to Ireland. There was now no papal archbishop to dispute his claims to the primatial see; and news from London must have assured him that Edward VI's reign was not likely to last much longer. The young boy-king died in the summer of 1553; and the accession of his half-sister Mary, for which English Catholics had been hoping and praying through many long years, was followed immediately by a general reconciliation with the Holy See. Dowdall, whose movements during these two years are most uncertain, may have gone from Flanders to Rome before the end of 1552. All that we know is that Cardinal Maffei recommended him for the vacant see of Armagh at a papal consistory which was held in the presence of Julius III on January 23, 1553. The Pope then provided the former schismatic archbishop of Armagh to Ireland's primatial see at the next consistory (March 1)—three months and more before the death of Edward VI.[1] Once Queen Mary had been able to assert her own rights to the English crown, Primate Dowdall could hope to return to Armagh secure in the favour of both Pope and Queen. He was recalled to England soon after Mary's accession, most probably in the autumn of 1553; and the Queen reinstated him in all his former primatial rights on March 12, 1554.[2]

The years of confusion were now over; and Primate Dowdall set himself to reorganise his diocese and province with the hope of a lasting Catholic restoration in England and Ireland. That hope was not to be fulfilled; but the first crisis was past. The next half century was to reveal Ireland's deepest loyalties, when subjected to the double strain of war and persecution.

[1] For the dates see Coleman, in his edition of Stuart's *Memorials of Armagh*, p. 155.

[2] Morrin I, p. 315 (no. 65); see also the Queen's earlier instructions, dated October 23, 1553: ibid. I, pp. 301-2.

ABBREVIATIONS

abp. archbishop. adn. archdeacon. bp. bishop. c. canon. d. diocese. v.g. vicar general.

INDEX

N

O

P

R

S

T